LAND

AND

LIBERTY

LAND

AND

LIBERTY

HUDSON VALLEY RIOTS

IN THE AGE OF

REVOLUTION

Thomas J. Humphrey

NORTHERN

ILLINOIS

UNIVERSITY

PRESS

DeKalb

Published by the Northern Illinois University Press, DeKalb, Illinois   60115

Manufactured in the United States using acid-free paper

All Rights Reserved

Design by Julia Fauci

Library of Congress Cataloging-in-Publication Data

Humphrey, Thomas J., 1965–

Land and liberty : Hudson Valley riots in the age of revolution / Thomas J. Humphrey.

   p.   cm.

Includes bibliographical references and index.

ISBN 0-87580-329-6 (hardcover : alk. paper)

1. Hudson River Valley (N.Y. and N.J.)—Politics and government—18th century.
2. Hudson River Valley (N.Y. and N.J.)—Ethnic relations. 3. Hudson River Valley
(N.Y. and N.J.)—Social conditions—18th century. 4. Hudson River Valley (N.Y. and
N.J.)—Economic conditions—18th century. 5. Riots—Hudson River Valley (N.Y. and
N.J.)—History—18th century. 6. Tenant farmers—Hudson River Valley (N.Y. and
N.J.)—Political activity—History—18th century. 7. Landlord and tenant—Hudson
River Valley (N.Y. and N.J.)—History—18th century. 8. Land tenure—Political
aspects—Hudson River Valley (N.Y. and N.J.)—History—18th century. 9. Power (Social
sciences)—Hudson River Valley (N.Y. and N.J.)—History—18th century. 10. United
States—History—Revolution, 1775–1783—Influence. I. Title.

F127.H8H95 2004

974.7'302—dc22

2004001435

To Laurie, for everything

CONTENTS

ACKNOWLEDGMENTS

•   It is my pleasure to thank those people who have helped me in so many ways, yet this is just a start. Some debts may never be fully repaid. This book started at Northern Illinois University, and I am thankful for the help I received there from, among others, Stephen Foster, J. Harvey Smith, George Spencer, and the late James Shirley. For most of my time in Chicago, I lived only minutes from the Newberry Library, where I met and was tutored by Alfred Young, who prodded me to take a broader outlook and encouraged me to put my work into an appropriate framework. Above all, I owe my greatest intellectual and professional debts to Simon Newman and Allan Kulikoff. They shared their own work with me and encouraged me to stretch my ideas to their limits. Simon and Allan urged me to rethink, to rewrite, and, when things looked bleakest, to continue. Because of that, I value their friendship most. Thanks also to Al Young, Staughton Lynd, Gary Nash, Jesse Lemish, and many others for clearing, and for continuing to clear, the path that I and others now follow.

While I was a fellow at the Philadelphia, now McNeil, Center for Early American Studies, an early draft of this book and I benefited from the insight of Roger Abrahams, Richard S. Dunn, Bruce Mann, Bill Pencak, and Mike Zuckerman. Christine Hucho and Judy Van Buskirk made my year there much more enjoyable. For research I imposed on archivists in libraries, courthouses, and clerk's offices throughout the Hudson Valley, Chicago, Philadelphia, and Boston. Notably, Steve Bielinski, at the Colonial Albany Project, allowed me to tap into his inexhaustible knowledge of the inhabitants of the city. And Megan Hahn only rolled her eyes a little when I asked for yet another box of "Miscellaneous" manuscripts at the New-York Historical Society.

When turning my dissertation into a book, John L. Brooke, Edward Countryman, and Paul Gilje kindly offered perceptive comments and keen insight. Cleveland State University also provided financial support for critical research. Along the path to this book, I made friends I continue to cherish. For all their friendship and good ideas, I want to thank Ed Baptist, Terry Bouton, Matt Dennis, Kon Dierks, Dallett Hemphill, Ruth Herndon, Brooke Hunter, Marjoleine Kars, Liz Lehfeldt, Bob Lockhart, Joyce Mastboom, Brendan McConville, Don Ramos, Marcus Rediker, Liam Riordan, James Tagg, Mark Tebeau, and Karim Tiro. Thanks to Jennifer Visocky O'Grady of Enspace Design for drawing the maps. Kevin Butterfield and Melody Herr have shepherded this manuscript along, cleared up stultifying prose, and made my manuscript far better than when they received it.

Over the past several years, a number of friends have happily contributed to this book by showing its author the outside world. From Glasgow to Bozeman to Hell, Michigan, and all parts in between, they have kept me focused on what is important. Thanks to Dean Bredenbeck, Annie Brosnan, Lynn Davey, Ben Dudley, Kevin Alten, Dave Pierson, and Ryan Hamilton. Susan Branson, Alison Games, Sally Gordon, Dan Gordon, Susan Klepp, Allan Kulikoff, Roderick McDonald, Mike McDonnell, Marina Moskowitz, Simon Newman, Leslie Patrick, and Billy G. Smith have all contributed to this book and made the author better in ways they can never imagine. I wish I could give back a fraction of what they've given me. Despite their best efforts, if errors remain, those errors are mine.

For me, as for tenants and and landlords in New York, success depends on family. I draw strength from living near my brothers and sisters and my mother. My sons, Owen and Ben, have never, and may never, read a word of what follows, but they love going to the pool and kicking a soccer ball. We are all so much the better for the diversions. Laurie Humphrey, to whom this is all dedicated, has done and endured the most. She has, I am sure, heard quite enough about landlords and tenants. Without her, I could not have done anything. For being able to stand with her, and for Owen and Ben, I am the lucky one.

LAND

AND

LIBERTY

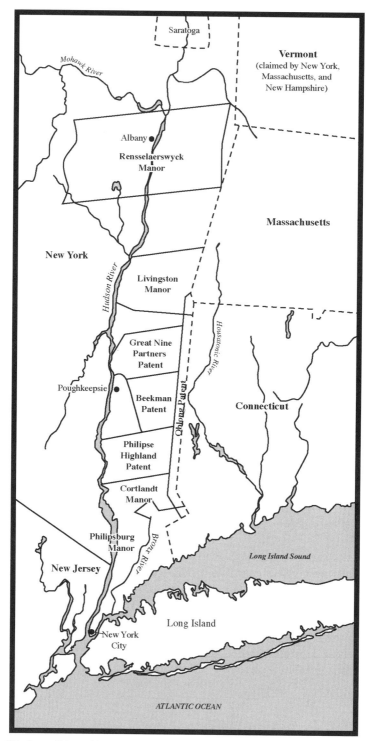

Hudson River Valley Manors, circa 1765

INTRODUCTION

- In 1765 and 1766, Irish immigrant William Prendergast led hundreds of insurgents in riots that challenged the distribution of land and power in colonial New York. The incredibly diverse group of rioters resorted to shocking violence either to drive out their opponents or to force them to join the cause. Although insurgents targeted landlords and manorialism, they most often squared off against officials and tenants loyal to the manor lord. In one sadly characteristic encounter in May 1766, Prendergast and approximately sixty of his followers marched to Robert Hughson's farm. Hughson had taken over the leasehold of an evicted insurgent, and Prendergast and his men went to make him either join the uprising or leave the land.

When the crowd reached the farmhouse, Prendergast took charge. He pounded on the door and ordered Robert Hughson out of the house to face the crowd. Hughson, however, was not at home; his wife was. What terror gripped her as she opened the door, knowing what stood on the other side, we can never know, but her appearance in the doorway flustered Prendergast and his men for only a moment. The leader of the rioters immediately demanded that her husband show himself and face the crowd. When she told the men that her husband was away, Prendergast shouldered his way into the doorframe and threatened to return and wreak havoc if she and her husband did not leave the farm immediately. But she knew she could not travel. She was close to delivering her baby and may have been in early labor when Prendergast confronted her. The Hughsons had no choice but to stay and risk another incident with Prendergast and his men.

While Hughson's wife was ultimately spared any further assaults, widespread rural rebellion over fundamental colonial power and social structures grew so disruptive that in July 1766 landlords and colonial officials called on the British army to suppress it. The troops quickly dispatched the rebels, capturing dozens, including William Prendergast, who had vowed to help the rioters restore "Justice" in their community but soon found himself in a colonial court standing trial for treason against the king. He defended himself against these charges with the help of his wife, Mehetibal Wing, a Quaker whom Prendergast had married in the early 1750s. Officials and landlords did not deal lightly with the leader of the rebels. After finding him guilty, the court delivered its sentence: Prendergast was to be hanged, drawn, quartered, beheaded, and burned so that his ashes could be scattered about the countryside. Stunned and utterly defeated, Prendergast fell onto the courtroom floor like a "slaughtered ox."[1]

Conflicts between landlords and tenants convulsed New York's Hudson Valley throughout the second half of the eighteenth century. By the 1740s, Dutch, English, and Scottish landed tycoons had gained firm control of their estates, had attained a virtual monopoly of property in the Hudson Valley, had made those estates profitable, and had secured power in the colony. While most tenants made do, and some even fared well, landlords grew fantastically rich. In the late colonial period, landlords sought to stabilize their incomes, and their wealth, by standardizing their legal and social relationships with tenants. In the process, they created and perpetuated a symbiotic but inherently unequal social and economic relationship with their tenants that resulted in the dramatic transferal of agricultural goods from tenants to landlords.

A society based on such inequality was rife with antagonism, and it exploded when landless Anglo-European squatters, tenants, and settlers from New York and New England, as well as Stockbridge and Wappinger Indians, began challenging the landlords' claims. The antagonists often settled their differences in New York courts, but landlords dominated these institutions and won nearly every case. After repeatedly failing to secure their aims legally and peacefully, landless squatters and tenants joined Stockbridge and Wappinger Indians to take land violently. In the late colonial period, landlords and colonial officials asked the British military for help to defeat the rioters, and the army marauded through the region, sending rioters, their families, and bystanders streaming into the woods for safety.

Insurgents next tried to acquire land by taking advantage of the chaos of the Revolutionary War. Early in the war, tenants in the southern Hudson Valley threatened to turn against Revolutionaries if the new state legislature did not sell off land it had confiscated from landlords-turned-Loyalists. To quiet mounting antagonisms, Revolutionaries gave in and sold confiscated Loyalist land in Westchester and Dutchess counties, enabling many tenants to become freeholders. Many of these new landowners voted for the first time during the Revolution. Social upheaval and dramatic political rebellion went hand in hand in the southern Hudson Valley. Thereafter, rioting waned considerably.

Discontented people in the northern Hudson Valley were not as successful. Rural insurgents timed their uprising to coincide with a rumored, imminent British invasion. Reports of the rebellion and the invasion swirled throughout the northern valley in the spring of 1777, putting everyone on edge. Ultimately, however, the dissidents fell short of turning the political revolution into a war to overthrow manorialism. The war changed the political climate and altered people's identities, but it did not turn tenants into freeholders. After the war, dissatisfied rural insurgents on Livingston Manor and Rensselaerswyck again took up their pens and weapons to transform their leaseholds into freeholds.

Situating land riots in relation to both colonial social structure and Revolutionary politics reveals new connections between them and leads to new conclusions about both. Previous examinations of the topic have been limited either chronologically or geographically, or have not examined links between land riots and the Revolution. This study explores land disputes and riots all over the Hudson Valley throughout the second half of the eighteenth century and exposes how the rioters shaped the Revolution and how the Revolution, in turn, influenced the rioters. Although the story of the uprisings—and of the relationship between landlords and tenants that spurred them—figures prominently, an analysis of class, households, markets, and farm production shows how and why inhabitants of the Hudson Valley resorted to violence to change their lives and their community from the early 1750s through the mid-1790s. Examining over half a century of these land disputes reveals that some insurgents opposed the political hierarchy and felt oppressed by their rulers both before and after the Revolutionary period. Historians have too often used the Revolution to explain such widespread discontent. Land disputes and the antagonism they generated, however, illustrate that at least one strand of opposition began before the Revolution and continued through it.[2]

In the second half of the eighteenth century, land rioting plagued most of the North American backcountry. Regulators in North Carolina assaulted landed elites in the late 1760s and early 1770s in hopes of getting a voice in government, while white yeomen pushed Virginia's elite closer to independence by threatening rebellion if they could not gain access to land west of the Appalachians. As in these southern communities, severe inequality in the Hudson Valley fomented debilitating instability. In Pennsylvania, Scots-Irish and German settlers, Connecticut squatters, Senecas, Delawares, and Iroquois all attacked each other in disputes over land in the northern Susquehanna River valley. Land rioting in neighboring New Jersey ground to an inconclusive end in the late colonial period more because the participants had exhausted themselves than because they had reached a solution. At about the same time, Ethan Allen led Yankees and Yorkers north to carve out a settlement in the Green Mountains, and New Englanders faced off in contests over land and power that hinted at deeper debates. These conflicts finally exploded in the 1780s in disputes over property, debt, and power. In all of these places, as in New York, colonial disputes over land and power became integral parts of the Revolution as the old combatants incorporated long-standing antagonisms into the Revolutionary War, making it as much a war for revolution as a war for independence.[3]

Although backcountry rebellions flared up throughout the colonies, New York's land riots were qualitatively different. Other backcountry settlers and rebels sought access to Indian land, removal of the 1763 "proclamation line" limiting white settlement, and self-government. In the Hudson Valley, insurgents sought to buy the land they already inhabited, and they rebelled against manor lords who owned it and refused to sell, making these land disputes primarily contests between landed tycoons and landless whites who aspired to be freeholders. Moreover, Indians in the Hudson Valley participated in the disputes in ways that they did not elsewhere, in ways that remain as yet unexplored. They encouraged white settlement of the region if it reaffirmed Indian ownership of the land and joined European insurgents to defeat landlords and to defend their claims to land.

Patterns of ownership also made land disputes in the Hudson Valley different than those in other colonies. Nowhere else in the colonies did great estates, huge tracts of land owned by single families, dominate the countryside the way they did in the Hudson Valley. In the seventeenth century, Dutch rulers hoped to inspire settlement of the Hudson Valley by giving enormous tracts of land to men who then encouraged tenants to settle and improve the wilderness. When the English took control of the colony, landlords who had obtained estates under the Dutch secured new titles. By the end of the century, a few families had obtained titles to enormous estates, ranging in size from eighty thousand to one million acres. They rightly figured that the Hudson Valley, still largely wilderness at the end of the seventeenth century, would rapidly become a major grain-producing region.

By 1710, a few landlords had amassed enormous estates that contained most of the farmable land in the valley. The Van Rensselaers had created their one-million-acre estate; the Livingstons owned 160,000 acres; the Philipses controlled approximately 200,000 acres; and the Van Cortlandts possessed roughly 82,000 acres. By the 1770s, landlords had expanded their holdings to approximately 2.5 million acres, and, although prospective farmers could buy land on the west side of the Hudson, the landlords' monopoly drove up land prices throughout the region. High prices benefited those speculators who sold their land, but landlords preferred to keep their valley estates even if they could sell at inflated rates. They sought the steady, long-term income of landlordism and hoped to fill their estates with tenants who would provide it. As a result, prospective freeholders who wanted to settle the Hudson Valley were often forced into tenancy, and on the eve of the Revolution more than half of all household heads in the Hudson Valley rented land. At midcentury, only parts of southeastern Pennsylvania, southern Maryland, and the northern neck of Virginia approached New York's level of tenancy. In most other regions in the late colonial period, freehold farm sizes declined, but most household heads owned some property. Moreover, New York landlords, like elites in other colonies, benefited from a legal and political tradition that put the power of the state behind them and against anyone who threatened the established social and political hierarchy.[4]

Over the course of the eighteenth century, European farmers turned the forests, hillsides, and cliffs of the Hudson Valley into grids of fields, fences, and roads characteristic of European farmland. The work was hard and was made even more difficult by unforgiving terrain and unpredictable weather. As travelers sailed north on the Hudson River from New York City to Tarrytown and Philipsburg Manor, the river opened to the Tappen Sea and then turned west to Haverstraw Bay. The land sloped away from the river to the east for a few miles and tended to get rockier near the Housatonic River and into Connecticut. Across the Hudson and west of Haverstraw, the land rose sharply enough to make travel arduous but not enough to prohibit farming. Farmers in this southern region enjoyed a 190-day growing season. A few miles further north, travelers entered the Highlands, which extended from the New England uplands. In this part of the valley, the land on both sides of the river rose and fell sharply. The terrain and altitude decreased the growing season by approximately ten to fifteen days per year.

As travelers passed Newburgh on the west banks and Poughkeepsie on the east, the land near the Hudson was still arable and loamy, but it rose to sharp cliffs and mountains away from the river in either direction. North of Poughkeepsie and past Hudson, toward Livingston Manor and Van Rensselaer Manor, the land opened to a narrow plain ten to twenty miles wide on either side of the river. Despite the rich soil near the water, some farmers worked soil heavy with clay while others labored to grow enough food in the sandy pine barren that spread west from Albany. Farmers in this region could usually count on a 160-day growing season. Away from that river plain, farmers in the rockier and hillier land of the Catskills to the west and the Taconic and Berkshire mountains to the east counted on slightly shorter seasons. North of Albany County, the valley was bound by a series of steep bluffs that continued to climb to the Green Mountains in the northeast and the Adirondack Mountains in the northwest. The steep and rocky land in both places forced farmers to work small patches of what level land they could find. This far north, the weather, land, and altitude reduced the growing season to 150 days in good years.[5]

The population that moved onto the varying terrain of the Hudson Valley was racially and ethnically diverse. Visitors could readily hear twenty different languages. Germans, Dutch, English, Welsh, Scots, Irish, Africans, African Americans, and Stockbridge and Wappinger Indians all lived in the region, scrambling to secure their place in a community that was becoming increasingly British and that favored whites, particularly landed whites, over others. During that process, New York society retained a distinctly European form at the same time its population developed all the diversity and divisions that characterized the rest of North America. Such diversity made the Hudson Valley unlike almost any place in eighteenth-century North America. Against this complicated and problematic background, New York residents played out their struggles over landownership, power relationships, and independence.

Several themes structure the story of land struggles that sometimes turned into riots. What constituted a riot? A riot, historian Paul Gilje defines, is several people "attempting to assert their will immediately through the use of force outside the normal bounds of law." Although force included outright violence and physical assault, a crowd that terrorized or intimidated people without physically assaulting them was also riotous. Who participated in riots and who was labeled a rioter often depended on perspective and on reporting. Whereas a landlord may have seen all insurgents as rioters, only a fraction of insurgents may have been arrested for, or charged with, rioting. Furthermore, crowds attracted or alienated participants as the riot proceeded, yet onlookers were not always rioters. Insurgents opposed landlords in various ways. They wrote petitions, refused to pay rent, squatted on land, and sued landlords for trespass. When they took up arms, assaulted a sheriff, or fought an official army or militia, insurgents became land rioters, and they attacked people and property with equal vigor.[6]

While the ethnic and racial diversity of the groups that united—on both sides—to fight over land is remarkable, the combatants' aspirations explain why rioters fought so hard and why landlords mustered all their resources to defeat them. Property was the basis for political and economic power in colonial and Revolutionary America, giving disputes over land wider implications and making the issue uniquely fraught in New York, where tenants had to take land from landlords in order to attain political independence and economic autonomy. Landlords, for their part, did not want to lose the wealth and power they and their ancestors had struggled to obtain. The region's elite had defined its identity in and through the manorial system. Men such as Philip Schuyler, Robert Livingston Jr., and Stephen Van Rensselaer thought their wealth, power, and status rightfully set them above other men. Their financial success legitimated their authority, and they used their political power to open doors to greater economic opportunity. Thus, land riots were more than simply conflicts for profit. They paved the way for farmers to obtain the political independence, economic autonomy, and status in their community that escaped tenants. Contests over land and power were, however, a zero-sum game: landlords lost what rioters gained.

The language these participants used to articulate their goals changed dramatically from the mid-eighteenth century through the Revolution. In the 1750s and 1760s, Stockbridge and Wappinger Indians declared that they were the original possessors of the land and that all titles should be derived from them. Some tenants on nearby Livingston Manor argued that landlords had illegitimately expanded their estates by taking land from these Indians, among others, and that manor lords did not rightfully own the land tenants inhabited. Insurgents simply declared that they owned the land in question. Others claimed the land by virtue of titles they received either from Indians or from another colonial authority, such as the Massachusetts General Court. Beginning in the 1730s, Massachusetts authorized several surveying parties to mark out towns in the eastern Hudson Valley in the hopes of winning their ongoing border dispute with New York; settlers in these towns rejected the counterclaims made by New York landlords. By the middle of the 1760s when William Prendergast led riots, participants incorporated all of these justifications to develop their own notions of property ownership based on occupancy, labor, and use. They infused their rhetoric with the simple credo that they had earned the right to own the land by living on it and by improving it.[7]

In the 1770s and 1780s, the fight for independence from Britain influenced land riots in the Hudson Valley as much as the riots stimulated revolution. Although rioters had made a great effort to get power in the courts and local communities when they fought for land in the late colonial period, political power and citizenship became entwined with property during and after the Revolution. While Revolutionary leaders in New York adopted a definition of citizenship that combined landownership with consistent and demonstrated loyalty to the Revolution, insurgents wedded their argument that their labor entitled them to own land with the Enlightenment notion that all men had the inherent right to pursue happiness. When Thomas Jefferson invoked that idea in the Declaration of Independence, he, like other enlightened men, knew that happiness and prosperity depended upon property ownership. Insurgents forced New York Revolutionaries to include their perspectives on citizenship and property ownership in the institutional cornerstones of the American Republic. Disputes over land after the Revolution incorporated these ideas and thus not only shaped the settlement of New York's emerging polity but also influenced the creation of the new nation.[8]

Almost all of the struggles and fighting took place between rebels on one side and tenants loyal to the landlords on the other. Both were landless. Rioters fought for land because they knew they could not be economically and politically independent unless they owned it. Tenants who fought for the landlords were often forced to attack rioters. Officials organized posses to execute warrants for the arrest of rioters, and tenants faced criminal charges and eviction if they refused to serve. Some were compelled to ride with the posses; other tenants joined in order to satisfy lease obligations and to pay down their debt. While these men may have faced rioters reluctantly, others opposed insurgents willingly. Landlords installed replacement tenants on the farms of evicted protestors, and these new tenants fought hard to keep their farms and to fulfill their obligations to the landlords. They also fought to save themselves from the rioters' attacks, for these replacement tenants became instant targets. Finally, some tenants likely fought for landlords because they thought they would win and, perhaps more importantly, because they thought that rioters stood no chance.

The struggle over land originated with the system of leases that fostered an unequal but symbiotic socioeconomic relationship between landlords and tenants. Landlords used leases to establish and operate a monopolistic land system in which they extracted wealth from their tenants through rental obligations and fees. Leases and the manorial economy in the late colonial period reveal how landlords grew wealthy by expropriating and then selling the agricultural goods tenants produced. Leases, however, entailed more than simply the economic relationship. Landlords turned the wealth they amassed from tenants into political power, and by the 1740s they sat at the top of New York's political and economic hierarchy. They legitimated their position, in part, by upholding a set of social rituals and practices designed to suggest the care of subordinates without actually providing it. While historians have called those practices paternalism, deference, or both, the activities were manifestations of the unequal economic relationship between landlords and tenants. Insurgents attacked that relationship.[9]

The riots that broke out in the 1750s and 1760s in the northern and southern sections of the Hudson Valley uncover the emerging plebeian ideals that threatened the distribution of wealth and power in colonial New York. Initially, some insurgents based their claims to land on the titles they received from authorities outside New York, from speculators, or from Indians. Others simply squatted on the land, and still others argued that they earned the land by improving it. By the end of the colonial period, however, rioters increasingly combined these notions of ownership, insisting that their labor and occupancy of the land entitled them to own it. This idea became the fundamental argument that land rioters used to challenge the manorial system that dominated the Hudson Valley.

As colonists moved toward independence, insurgents integrated Revolutionary rhetoric into their arguments for land, making land riots expressions of political discontent and forcing Revolutionaries to move in a more egalitarian direction. Most inhabitants of the countryside, however, resisted attempts by both the British and the Revolutionaries to induce them to join one side or the other. Tenants and other farmers wanted to own their land, and they wanted to reap the full harvest of their labor. These men and women based their support for one side or the other, or neither, on their perception of which side was more likely to satisfy their hunger for land. Land disputes continued in the post-Revolutionary period as the antagonists infused long-standing disputes with Revolutionary rhetoric to forge new definitions of citizenship, property ownership, and civic equality in the emerging nation.

Despite nearly fifty years of popular attacks on landed estates, landlordism survived in New York through the eighteenth century. But the language used to defend it and to attack it changed. Both sides invoked revolutionary rhetoric to justify their claims. By infusing their language with words and ideas drawn directly from the Revolution, insurgents gave their fight new meaning and made the Revolution more radical. Later, rioters built on these arguments when they dismantled the great estates in the 1840s. Over the course of the nineteenth century, however, Anti-Renters had enhanced the meaning of their riots by adding contemporary concerns about party politics, slavery, and capitalism. In 1839, Anti-Renters tellingly argued that each farmer was entitled to an "Independence Freehold, on which to labor for the support of his family." Thomas Ainge Devyr made that point again in 1845 in his newspaper, *The Anti-Renter:* "there never did—never could—exist a title save the possessory title of the Occupant who cultivates a fair-sized farm for the support of his family." William Prendergast would have agreed.[10]

Chapter One

LANDLORDS AND TENANTS

BEFORE AMERICAN INDEPENDENCE

• In 1758, Mary Philipse married Roger Morris with all the elaborate ritual their status required. Frederick Philipse, the bride's father, graciously invited his friends and his tenants to join in the celebration. When his friends arrived, usually by carriage, Philipse escorted them into his three-story Georgian mansion, where they had drinks before the wedding. For the ceremony, Philipse's black slaves and white servants ushered the landlord and his friends outside to sit under a red velvet canopy embossed in gold and bearing the family crest. Afterward, Philipse and his friends moved back inside the mansion where liveried servants and slaves brought them food on china and wine in crystal glasses. The celebrants danced with the bride and groom and wished them good luck with their marriage.

Tenants celebrated the event quite differently. Frederick Philipse did not greet them individually when they arrived on foot. He had not invited them inside his mansion, nor was he expected to do so. Instead, he waved to them as he walked to his seat under the canopy. During the service, tenants and their families sat outside the canopy that sheltered the Philipses and their friends and caught glimpses of the bride and groom. After the ceremony, tenant families dined while sitting on benches, tree stumps, or the ground. Later in the day, Mary Philipse and Roger Morris addressed the tenants from a second-story window, literally and figuratively looking down on them and signaling the time for them to go home. The Philipses' friends and relatives continued to celebrate inside the mansion for some time.[1]

Mary Philipse's wedding throws into stark relief the economic and political divisions that characterized the Hudson Valley in the eighteenth century. Landed elites such as those who ate inside the mansion and sat under the canopy dominated New York's political and economic landscape by creating and operating a monopoly over land and over the produce of their tenants. Landlords leased land to tenants and required leaseholders to pay rent and other fees and to use their mills and stores. In that way, they extracted goods and services from tenants, resulting in a disproportionate transfer of wealth from tenants to landlords. Landlords amassed that produce and sold it for hefty profits in the rapidly expanding Atlantic market. In New York, the landed elite was consolidated rather than factionalized, and intermarriage among the elites was one way of strengthening their position and of protecting their economic and political interests. Politically, landlords presumed that their tenants would defer to them; propertied men throughout the British colonies tied political power to economic wealth. They assumed they should rule, and their wealth ensured their ability to do so. By the 1740s, these landlords had successfully translated economic gain into political power and had secured their dominance in New York politics.

Tenants leased land largely because they had little choice. Landlords owned most of the arable land in the region, driving up prices of available land nearby and forcing people without much money into tenancy. Most migrants to the Hudson Valley arrived without enough money to pay inflated land prices. If these people wanted land to develop through their own labor, they had to rent it. When tenants affixed their signature or mark on a lease, they promised to pay rent on time and to remit fees for services. In return, tenants expected landlords to grant them some latitude when war, epidemics, crop blight, and inclement weather led to poor harvests and kept them from paying rent. Tenants also believed that landlords should keep the peace on the estate for everyone's benefit and trusted manor lords not to deal too harshly with destitute tenants. Leases, as a result, entangled tenants in mutual obligations and bound them to landlords in a reciprocal but unequal relationship.

Three characteristics define the landlord-tenant relationship of the colonial Hudson Valley. First, the language of leases illustrates what landlords and tenants expected from their association. As landlords standardized leases, the landlord-tenant relationship changed too. The relationship did not shift from a paternal and deferential one to an exploitative one. No landlord was either entirely exploitative or completely paternal at any one time. Instead, most landlords took what tenants delivered as rent and avoided pushing any individual tenant too hard if that tenant had paid some rent. Landlords knew that if they pressed tenants for rent, they risked antagonizing more tenants. Thus, they acted harshly when the situation seemed to call for it and treated tenants warmly when warranted. Landlords preferred satisfied tenants who paid rent often and who voted for them over unruly tenants who did neither. Nonetheless, income instability plagued them. To gain control of their income, and to optimize it, landlords standardized leases. While some made the switch earlier than others, by the late colonial period landlords throughout the Hudson Valley were moving toward a regularized lease system. A more systematized lease arrangement formalized the landlord-tenant relationship and allowed some landlords to turn tenants' produce into merchant capital.

Second, the ways in which tenants fulfilled these changing conditions demonstrates how the manorial economy worked. Tenants, in general, labored under the dual responsibilities of providing for their households and paying rent. Landlords, on the other hand, grew rich by accumulating and selling the goods that tenants delivered as rent and fees. Finally, landlords turned that wealth into political power, revealing some of the fundamental tensions in the landlord-tenant relationship.

Did the changing relationship mean that the manorial economy was inching toward capitalism? That question raises one of the key debates concerning the transition to capitalism in the countryside. The discussion covers a broad spectrum of behavior from market participation, the drive for profit, the use of capital, household production, and the desire for competency. What tenants or landlords thought of production, profit, and surplus remains the central, yet unanswerable, question in that debate. In an agrarian community, however, success hinged on possessing land and on profiting from agricultural production. These often lofty goals also depended on adequate labor, access to markets, and luck. Although landlords and tenants shared these goals, they defined and achieved them differently. Landlords ensured their income by restricting tenants' access to markets and by putting their own economic welfare ahead of their tenants' well-being. Tenants, on the other hand, refused to take food off their own tables to pay rent, and they often flouted the contracts they had signed in good faith. Insurgents went a step further. They sought competency—the ability to provide for their household and for the next generation—by attacking the stability, and competency, of their landlords. These sometimes conflicting goals shaped the world landlords and tenants inhabited.[2]

What becomes clear by studying the manorial economy is that landlords prospered by expropriating the goods tenants produced and then selling them in the Atlantic market. Landlords legitimated and kept their position by upholding a series of social, political, and economic rituals, often called paternalism and deference. These actions, however, were often momentary gestures made by men who had successfully turned their economic standing into traditional authority by creating and maintaining gross inequalities in access to and in use of markets and power. Landlords tried to apply a thin layer of paternalism and deference to veil what was, at root, the exploitative landlord-tenant relationship. In short, landlords derived fortunes by controlling the land and the goods their tenants produced.

THE LANGUAGE OF LEASES

In 1726, Henry Beekman (1688–1776) married Gertruyd Van Cortlandt—the daughter of Stephanus Van Cortlandt, the original proprietor of Cortlandt Manor. After the manor lord died in the 1730s, his heirs parceled up the estate and administered their respective parts. Beekman combined his own land with his wife's to increase his holdings to over one hundred thousand acres and began to lease the land to tenants. He issued leases written by a scribe who copied a form containing a general statement of what the landlord expected from his tenants. The scribe left blank spaces for specific information such as the tenant's name, the size of the leasehold, its location, and the rent. In 1737, Andrias Bergher signed such a lease for 237 unimproved acres. He leased the lot for three lives— his life and the lives of his sons Andrias and John—and agreed to pay £3 15s. per year for it. Because Bergher leased unimproved land, his lease contained a developmental period of four years during which he paid the nominal rent of 7s. per year. He started paying rent in full at the end of the developmental period.[3] Beekman required Bergher to bring his rent to a "Convenient Place in the Mannor as the said Henry Beekman or Gertruyd his wife shall app[oint]" that was within twelve miles of the leasehold every year on the "Feast Day of The annunciation Commonly Called Lady Day," in late March. Of the hundreds, and perhaps thousands, of leases issued and signed in the Hudson Valley before the Revolution, Bergher's is typical.[4]

Between the 1680s and the early 1730s, landlords like Henry Beekman had secured enormous estates throughout the Hudson Valley. The original proprietor of Livingston Manor, Robert Livingston (1654–1728), arrived in Albany, New York, in December 1674 or January 1675. In 1686, the royal governor of the colony, Thomas Dongan, issued an official royal grant of 160,000 acres to the Livingstons to encourage "Settlement" of the region. The English governor of New York also reaffirmed the patent that the Van Rensselaers had received in 1630 from the Dutch. By 1730, Rensselaer-swyck, including Claverack, contained one million acres. And in 1693, New York's royal governor issued a patent for land that Frederick Philipse (1627–1702) had accumulated during the late seventeenth century, creating Philipsburg. In the first decade of the eighteenth century, Philipse allegedly chopped down a tree that marked a corner of his land, rode for a day, and marked a new tree, increasing the size of his estate by several thousand acres. Whether the story is legend or truth, by 1730, the Philipses claimed close to two hundred thousand acres.[5]

Landlords had land, but obtaining a profitable income from it depended on securing tenants to improve it. To entice people to the land, manor lords offered developmental leases, like the one signed by Andrias Bergher. The Livingstons, for instance, owned thousands of unimproved and uninhabited acres that they dreamed of filling with tenants who would improve the land and then pay rent. At least twice in the late colonial period, in 1749 and again in 1764, the Livingstons publicly offered to lease land to people who could get to the Hudson Valley but who could not afford to buy land there. Tenants could live on the land rent-free while they improved it. The Livingstons knew that most poor people would choose tenancy over poverty and hunger, and they specifically targeted new immigrants who would presumably be grateful for the chance to take a long lease for farmland so they could provide for their households.[6]

Despite some onerous lease conditions, the combination of long leases and good land close to emerging markets drew cash-poor settlers to the Hudson Valley. Through good fortune Henry Beekman inherited land and tenants from Stephan Van Cortlandt; he also successfully lured new tenants to his estate. The Philipses likewise attracted new tenants. Only 309 people lived on the Philipses' land in 1712, but by 1760 approximately 1,200 tenants and their families farmed it. Over the ensuing sixteen-year period between 1760 and 1776, the number of tenant households on the Philipses' estate increased from 176 to 272. On the eve of the Revolution, Frederick Philipse III bragged that tenants had improved every inch of his family's land. The Livingstons' efforts to recruit new tenants also succeeded; the number of tenant households on Livingston Manor climbed from 50 in 1715 to approximately 460 by 1776, although unimproved land was still available. The Van Rensselaers saw fantastic growth; the number of tenant households on their land jumped from 82 in 1714 to nearly 300 in 1767, and approximately 1,150 tenant households dotted the manor in 1776. There was plenty of room for more on the one-million-acre estate.[7]

Most of these new tenants signed developmental leases that gave them cheap access to arable land. Even better, their leases allowed them to live rent-free while they made their farms productive. Making land fruitful was backbreaking work, and landlords left it to tenants. Tenants and their families cleared trees, uprooted stumps, removed stones, turned the soil, dug wells, and constructed fences and roads. They also built houses, barns, and other outbuildings, and, in some instances, they planted and maintained orchards. Tenants began paying rent and abiding by the other lease stipulations at the end of the developmental period, often between four and seven years. After that, most landlords required tenants to pay rent on time with a specific crop, usually winter wheat. As long as they did not encroach on other leaseholds, tenants could graze their pigs, sheep, and cows on and glean fuel from nearby unimproved land; as more people moved on to the estates, however, landlords restricted access to unimproved land. When tenants wanted to lease improved land, landlords simply scratched out or omitted any references to a developmental period and made tenants immediately liable for rent payments and fees.[8]

Leases for improved and unimproved land contained several provisions designed to give landlords control over the land and its products. When tenants sold the improvements they made to the leasehold—the barn, house, and orchards, for example—landlords insisted on taking from one-eighth to one-half of the sale. While some tenants sold the improvements to pay off rising debts to the landlord, others sold the immovable fruits of their labor so they could buy land elsewhere. Whatever their motives, the quarter-fee stipulation required tenants to pay part of the sale to their landlords. The Van Rensselaers, for instance, collected one-fourth of the value of the first sale of improvements and one-eighth of the value of all future sales. Other landlords followed a similar pattern.

Landlords also required tenants to pay a fee to reassign the lease when the primary lessee vacated the leasehold or died. Andrias Bergher's sons would have had to pay a small fee to Henry Beekman to take over the leasehold when their father died. Bergher also had to grind his grain and mill his lumber at facilities the Beekmans operated; Henry Beekman, like the Philipses, Livingstons, and Van Rensselaers, included these provisions in most of the leases he issued. These landlords also extended credit at their mills and stores to tenants so they could buy the supplies they needed while they improved their farms. While Bergher and other tenants may have found such services convenient, other tenants chafed at what they considered impositions and restrictions of their choices. Regardless, the fees for these services, in addition to rent payments, ensured that a majority of what tenants produced ended up in the landlords' storehouse.[9]

Individual landlords incorporated specific conditions into their general leases. The Livingstons required tenants such as Solomon Schutte, who signed a lease with them in 1748, to pay part of the salary of a "Protestant minister" and a "school master." The Van Rensselaers offered tenants leases that ostensibly lasted "for ever," but the leases included several limiting conditions. Although tenants on the manor could bequeath the improvements to an heir, they could not hand down the leasehold; the land ultimately returned to the Van Rensselaers. Tenants on the estate acted as surrogate landowners as long as they obeyed the conditions of their leases. If a tenant failed to live up to his end of the bargain, the Van Rensselaers reserved the right to take the leasehold back.[10]

The Van Rensselaers' leases were anomalies in most of the British colonies. At first glance, these leases appeared to grant the land to tenants "for ever," making them something more than mere leases. The agreements, however, did not transfer the land to tenants. Instead, while the leases granted the land to tenants essentially forever, the Van Rensselaers retained the legal, possessory rights of landlords, and they always kept the right to reenter a leasehold if the tenant violated the contract. The Van Rensselaers decided what constituted a violation of the lease. The condition that created these kinds of leases, called leases in fee, arose after 1290 when King Edward I accepted a law that brought an end to manors in England. But the law did not apply to territories that England conquered. New York was such a territory. As a result, the statute was not applied, and manors, and the lease in fee, thrived.[11]

The two items common to every lease, the size of the lot and the rent due, varied considerably. What really differed was the amount of woodland on the leasehold and not necessarily the amount of land in production. Given the tools, soil quality, and animals available, there was a limit on how much a farm family could cultivate in the eighteenth century. The most effective way for a farmer to increase production was to hire additional laborers, but few tenants had those kinds of resources. Estates in the southern part of the valley were generally less productive than those in the north; therefore, leaseholds tended to be larger. Over the course of the colonial period, the fertility of the land declined, forcing leaseholders to seek other production strategies. Many tenants shifted from wheat production to livestock and dairying. Pastoral farming was less land-intensive than arable farming. While it required more acreage, it could be successful on less productive land. Many farmers in New England had already made that shift, and more farmers in the Hudson Valley did so in the nineteenth century.[12] On Cortlandt Manor, three-quarters of the tenants rented between 150 and 299 acres, and the average leasehold was 237 acres. Approximately 90 percent of all tenants on nearby Philipsburg leased between 85 and 260 acres, 175 acres on average.

In the northern Hudson Valley, on Livingston Manor and Rensselaerswyck, tenants usually farmed smaller lots of somewhat better land than their southern counterparts. While tenants who leased land in the Pine Barren west of Albany had to lime their soil to make it productive, most tenants on these estates could grow winter wheat successfully through the end of the century. On Livingston Manor before the Revolution, approximately 90 percent of tenants rented between 60 and 160 acres, and the average leasehold contained 112 acres. On Rensselaerswyck, nearly 90 percent of tenants leased between 75 and 180 acres, with the average tenant leasing approximately 139 acres.[13]

Hudson Valley tenants leased farms that resembled in size the lots of farmers elsewhere. Tenants on the proprietary estates in Maryland, for example, leased approximately 150 acres. Colonial development tended to have more of an impact on farm size. Farms and leaseholds tended to be larger in developing regions than in long-settled places. In developing regions with smaller populations and more unimproved land, such as parts of the western Hudson Valley, Connecticut, and New Hampshire, farms were much larger than in the more settled and populated areas of New England. In Hannover, Ulster County, on the west side of the Hudson, farmers owned on average 128 acres in 1775. In Connecticut and New Hampshire, landowners typically lived on approximately seventy acres. In the settled regions of nearby Massachusetts and East New Jersey, however, average farm size had dwindled to between twenty and fifty acres by the late colonial period; these farms were so small that people there had to import food. Population increases and the resultant demand for land also pushed down farm sizes near Philadelphia, where the average farm size shrank from approximately 150 acres early in the century to just 100 acres on the eve of the Revolution. These comparisons suggest that freeholders and tenants shared some material conditions in the late colonial period, but their positions differed in one crucial respect: most of the farmers in New England, East Jersey, Maine, and New Hampshire owned the land they inhabited. They could will it to an heir, or to several heirs, and thus provide for their families in ways that tenants could not.[14]

Once tenants made their lots productive, they began paying rent. Rent branded farmers as tenants and separated them from freeholders. Like their counterparts elsewhere in the colonies, tenants in the Hudson Valley paid rent with whatever surplus goods or cash they had on hand regardless of what their leases said. By the 1750s, for instance, more and more tenants in the southern Hudson Valley began paying rent with cash, meat, or dairy products instead of winter wheat. Although most had paid rent with wheat for years, they had slowly shifted from wheat cultivation to raising livestock to optimize their land and to take advantage of the growing market in New York City. Obediah Ackerly, for example, raised wheat on his leasehold until 1774, when he and his wife began hauling barrels of butter and cheese to New York City to sell. Thereafter, he paid rent with cash.[15] Such a shift compelled some landlords to change their expectations. While Henry Beekman, Peter Warren, and Pierre Van Cortlandt had always demanded cash rent from their tenants in the southern region, the Philipses had required their tenants to pay rent with wheat. When tenants such as Ackerly began paying with cash, however, the Philipses began accepting, and then expecting, cash too.[16]

Landlords in the northern Hudson Valley demanded wheat from their tenants throughout the colonial period. The Livingstons required each tenant to pay approximately fifteen bushels of wheat per one hundred acres, making their rents the highest in the Hudson Valley. The Van Rensselaers, on the other hand, did not calculate rent rates so exactly at first. Early in the century, they required tenants pay 10 percent of their wheat production in rent, but they raised rates slightly in the 1760s. Thereafter, they determined that tenants should pay ten to twelve bushels of wheat per one hundred acres instead of the tithe. The tithe ensured that landlords would benefit from increased productivity, but it also meant that they suffered during poor harvests. Fixed figures per acre, on the other hand, stabilized landlords' incomes regardless of the harvest and encouraged tenants to increase productivity. The gain would belong entirely to them.[17]

Landlords calculated rent carefully because it provided the bulk of their income from tenants. They based their figures on what they considered to be the market value of the land, on the land's potential productivity, on the lot's proximity to markets and services, and on the general desirability of the region. Landlords charged higher rent for good land in well-populated regions near markets and services such as mills, and they usually asked for lower rent for less developed land in less densely populated areas. Rent valuations also changed with white settlement. Increased settlement would mean more services and greater safety for farmers; thus, the land would be worth more. In 1764, Robert R. Livingston thought £1 10s. a reasonable rent for one hundred acres of unimproved land in the still relatively unsettled Saratoga Patent, but he intended to increase the rate to £2 10s. if he could get enough tenants to settle the region.

Landlords' monopoly of land drove up land prices and inflated the values they assigned to it. In better-developed areas where tenancy predominated, notably along the coasts of Maryland, Virginia, and North Carolina, land prices had quadrupled in the eighteenth century. Landlords in these regions exercised a monopoly over land that drove up prices from approximately 8s. per acre to 22s. per acre. In less developed regions dominated by freeholders or where speculators proposed to sell land to yeoman farmers, such as the Delaware and Susquehanna River valleys and western Maryland and Virginia, unimproved land cost approximately half of what it did in the landlord-dominated Hudson Valley. Even within the Hudson Valley, the landlords' monopoly over land led them to value their own land too highly. In the 1770s, in Hannover, Ulster County, where freeholders predominated, land was valued at approximately £1 10s. to £3 per acre. The Livingstons and Philipses thought their land was worth at least that much. Robert R. Livingston valued unimproved land in Dutchess County at £1 to £2 per acre if sold, and valued improved land at three to four times that much. On the eve of the Revolution, Frederick Philipse valued the land on his estate at £5 to £7 per acre if improved, and £1 to £3 if unimproved.[18]

Despite inflated land prices, landlords did not intend to make their money by selling their Hudson Valley estates. They made their fortunes from rent, whether their tenants paid with agricultural produce or cash. Landlords who demanded wheat as rent saw their incomes increase when wheat prices rose and drop when prices fell. In general, landlords reaped greater profits after 1750 if they required tenants to pay rent with wheat, because wheat prices rose steadily as it became a valuable trade commodity in the emerging Atlantic market and demand for it skyrocketed. While some landlords amassed it from tenants who paid rent with it, those whose tenants paid rent with cash had to buy wheat if they wanted to trade it. In that way, wheat was more of an economic index than money. Landlords who asked for cash rent got rich too but not as fast as the others. Cash payments were stable, but if prices increased landlords saw their real income drop. Peter Warren asked for cash rent payments, but increasing wheat prices drove down the value of fixed cash payments and reduced the landlord's effective income. To compensate for rising wheat prices in the late colonial period, Warren increased his tenants' rent several times.[19]

Like Peter Warren, Frederick Philipse also raised his tenants' rent to offset fluctuating agricultural prices. Unlike Warren, Philipse went a step further by offering his tenants the chance to obtain printed leases. During the 1750s, the Philipses offered tenants verbal agreements. Anyone who wanted to farm land on the estate became tenants-at-will; they remained on the leasehold as long as the manor lord let them. Proprietors seldom turned out a tenant because they "did not like his face," and the Philipses only took the decisive step of evicting a tenant when that tenant threatened the peace on the manor. By the late 1750s and early 1760s, however, many tenants had been paying rent in cash, resulting in a slow downturn in the landlord's income. That Philipse had not raised the rent in years exacerbated that decline. He responded by taking the unpopular step of raising rents. To perhaps take some of the sting out of the hike, Philipse simultaneously offered tenants a concession: he gave them the chance to sign a more formal lease. A written lease, or a lease agreement entered into a copybook, gave at-will tenants more stability on the land by granting them a bit more protection from a capricious landlord. Both leases and copyholds regularized the customary verbal agreement without fundamentally changing the tenant's legal status or relationship to the land. In February 1760, for example, Philipse notified tenant James Hunter that he was raising the rent from £3 12s. to £6 4s. "If you incline to take a Lease for three lives," he wrote, "you may have one by applying to me."[20]

At least one tenant grumbled about the increase in rent. His new rent, £7 for a two-hundred-acre farm, was nearly double what the Philipses paid in quitrent to the crown for the perpetual lease on their entire two-hundred-thousand-acre estate. This unnamed tenant also worried that his landlord would take one-eighth to one-half of the sale price of his improvements to satisfy lease stipulations. The tenant knew, as others must have known, that the new arrangements offered them more security on the land without changing any of the Philipses' claims to it. But that security came at the price of higher rent, and the trade-off rankled at least this tenant.[21]

By moving toward a more formal lease arrangement, Philipse was hardly part of the vanguard. He was, in many respects, simply following other landlords as they moved toward a more standardized relationship with tenants. By the 1750s, Henry Beekman, the Livingstons, and the Van Rensselaers all issued standard leases. They paid to have leases written out, and in some cases printed, and all the leases contained general provisions such as quarter-fees, and the documents required tenants to pay all taxes and assessments levied on the leasehold. These form leases also contained blank spaces for specific information such as the size and place of the lot, name of the tenant, and rent. The Livingstons used printed leases by the late 1760s; after the Revolution, they simply scratched out references to a king or to Britain and inserted new references to independence and liberty. One political authority had been replaced by another, but the Livingstons wanted to keep the landlord-tenant relationship exactly the same.

The Van Rensselaers had issued standard handwritten leases and then used printed ones. Abraham Ten Broeck, the administrator of the Van Rensselaer estate, took the whole process a step further. He wrote out the general lease conditions at the top of the first page of a ledger and recorded the specifics of each leasehold and tenant in columns. Tenants received a copy of the lease, but Ten Broeck found it far easier to keep track of the manor's records in the ledger. He began entering tenants in the 1760s and entered more than two thousand tenants in the ensuing two decades.[22]

The move toward standard leases did more than help landlords stabilize their income. It formalized the relationship between landlords and tenants, clearly distinguishing propertied landlords from propertyless tenants. More than that, the intrinsic inequality of the relationship strongly illustrated that landlords stood above tenants economically and politically. Standard leases formalized the landlord-tenant relationship but did not change it. To earn income, landlords still depended on their ability to extract goods and services from tenants. Leaseholders relied on landlords for cheap access to arable land and for some understanding when circumstances inhibited production. That mutually dependent relationship was based on an unequal relationship to land that irrevocably divided manor lord from tenants. When landlord and tenant families met at celebrations such as Mary Philipse's wedding, the social and material differences leases characterized separated landlords from tenants. The difference between them was clear for all to see.

THE MANORIAL ECONOMY

How landlords and tenants fulfilled their agreement reveals how fluidly the manorial economy worked. John and Elizabeth Shaver, for instance, rented a farm on Livingston Manor from the 1750s through the 1780s. John Shaver moved to the manor to work in the Livingstons' iron furnaces in Ancram, in the southeastern part of the estate. He rented a plot there and paid £3 yearly rent. By the late 1750s, the Shavers had moved again. This time, they leased a nearly two-hundred-acre farm and had arranged to pay thirty bushels of wheat per year. John Shaver signed a standard Livingston Manor lease. The Shavers agreed to maintain the roads and fences that ran through or abutted the leasehold; to pay part of the salary of a Protestant minister; to plant and maintain an orchard of one hundred fruit trees; to remit a quarter of the sales of the improvements to the leasehold; to bring their lumber and grain to mills owned by the Livingstons; to sell and trade goods at the manor lord's stores; and to give the Livingstons the first chance to buy any surplus agricultural products the Shavers wished to sell.

The landlord provided the Shavers arable land, and he offered the new tenants credit at his stores while they turned wilderness into farmland. In return, he expected the Shavers to pay rent on time. But the Shavers rarely paid rent on time, and, when they bothered to pay at all, they rarely paid with wheat. Instead, the Shavers paid at least part of their rent by laboring for the Livingstons. From 1760 through 1769, John Shaver fixed rakes, built the Livingstons a cradle, and repaired the handle of a plow. Shaver also joined a posse organized by the Livingstons to quash land riots that erupted on the manor in the spring and summer of 1766. Elizabeth Shaver helped pay rent by sewing buttons, weaving cloth, making blankets and button molds, and spinning yarn and flax, which she then fashioned into stockings for the landlord and his family. Indeed, the Shavers delivered wheat as rent only once between 1769 and 1783; in 1775, they paid roughly half the rent due that year with wheat. At the end of the Revolutionary War in 1783, the Shavers reduced their now-substantial debt by hauling twenty loads of wooden rails, fifty-nine bushels of wheat, and eight hens to the manor house on rent day. They still owed 250 bushels of wheat valued at approximately £90.[23]

The Shavers' rent record reveals the essence of the landlord-tenant relationship in the late colonial period, illustrating how goods made their way from a tenant's land to the landlord's storehouse. It also shows the fluid nature of the manorial economy and the flexibility of its participants. Moreover, the Shavers' record exposes the mutually dependent but unequal character of the landlord-tenant relationship.

What the Shavers and other tenants delivered as rent offers a glimpse at agricultural production in the northern Hudson Valley. Like the Shavers, most tenants had agreed to pay rent with wheat. And, also like the Shavers, tenants often paid rent with something else. Tenants who paid rent with labor usually worked directly for the manor lord, making a far clearer demonstration of their subordinate status than mere payment would have. Tenants who paid rent with produce delivered a variety of goods. They grew oats, rye, and corn as well as wheat. Tenant households also kept chickens and likely had a vegetable garden with peas and potatoes near the house. Like the Shavers, tenants harvested the lumber on the leasehold. All of these goods made their way into the Livingstons' coffers. A Livingston Manor rent ledger covering the fifteen years from 1767 to 1782 reveals that approximately two-thirds of the 377 tenants listed paid rent with some combination of cash, credit, labor, wheat, oats, barley, rye, potatoes, hens, vegetables, and lumber. How much of these crops individual tenants produced remains unclear, but the Livingstons expected tenants to deliver approximately 15 percent of their wheat production in rent. If tenants on the manor abided by other lease stipulations, they also planted orchards. Tenants planted these various crops to minimize the risk of a bad harvest. They would not starve if they lost one crop of wheat or potatoes, but they could not stand to lose much more than that.[24]

Most tenants in the Hudson Valley, like most freeholders, lived uncomfortably close to the edge of subsistence. Agricultural production depended on weather conditions, seeds, tools, skill, and labor, as well as the quality of the soil. Farmers succeeded when they guessed right, their seed took, their tools held, the work went well, and the fickle weather cooperated. They suffered when any one of these conditions went wrong. While diversified production minimized the risk of starving, one or two poor crops pushed tenants further into debt. When pressed, most tenants chose to feed their families over paying rent. Landlords tolerated missed rent payments from otherwise peaceful and obedient tenants, and almost every tenant missed some rent payments. Most owed at least one year's rent, and many owed much more. For landlords, some rent collected regularly was better than no rent, so they let tenants carry debt from year to year. For tenants, that debt often became burdensome.

Although tenants might have used that debt to pressure landlords into changing their leases, landlords were unlikely to bargain with deeply indebted tenants. Landlords already charged what they considered low rent and were unlikely to go any lower. In the same way, landlords were unlikely to grant longer leases to indebted tenants. Landlords wanted to reduce risk, not saddle their heirs with more. Furthermore, most tenants in the northern Hudson Valley already had long leases and apparently stayed on their leaseholds for many years. Many of Henry Beekman's tenants had signed leases for three lives, and so did most of the tenants on Livingston Manor. Roughly 221 of the approximately 377 tenants listed in the Livingston Manor ledger stayed on their leasehold for at least a decade. Approximately 190 others were listed as tenants for the entire period, and most of these tenants had been tenants before 1767 or continued to be tenants after 1784. Their accounts, and their debts, were carried from one ledger to the next.

A similar story can be told for Rensselaerswyck. The bulk of the tenants on the manor in the colonial period had signed leases "for ever," and the trend continued during the Revolutionary period. The Van Rensselaers and their tenants apparently disagreed about what "for ever" meant, but roughly two-thirds of the tenants stayed on the land for approximately twenty years, and as many as half of the leaseholds may have remained with the heirs of the initial tenants. Moreover, the Van Rensselaers, like other landlords and creditors of the period, tended not to press debtors to repay unless the amount grew egregiously, and few landlords charged tenants interest on their debt.[25] Only Beverly Robinson charged his tenants interest on amounts owed him, and only Robinson aggressively pressured tenants to pay off their debts. Tenants were far more likely to remain peaceful, to pay rent, and to support a landlord who wielded his power prudently.[26]

More pragmatically, landlords rarely evicted even deeply indebted tenants. An eviction was a legal process initiated by landlords, and after a suit of ejectment was issued by a local court, the eviction was carried out by local officials. In many cases, a sheriff organized a posse from among the local population. This was not a request the men could refuse, and it meant that neighbors sometimes evicted neighbors, making evictions intimate and emotionally charged affairs that could turn violent. To avoid that upheaval, groups of rural people opposed evictions in various ways. Some closed roads to courts to stop justices from issuing eviction notices. Others attacked and closed the court buildings to reach the same result. Sometimes crowds assaulted local justices of the peace who were gathering evidence to be used against a tenant or farmer. Other groups of insurgents met posses at the farm of the person to be evicted and compelled the posse to turn around and go home. Finally, disgruntled tenants sometimes attacked a landlord or his agent for being so cruel as to throw a tenant family out of their home over money.[27]

However profit-driven landlords may have been, they also knew there were limits on how far they could go. Although the scope of their endeavors differed, landlords and peaceful tenants wanted the same thing. They sought to reap steady income from the land and to provide long-term stability for their families. Tenants fulfilled their role by paying rent as often as possible and by remaining peaceful. A landlord often had to play the part of a benevolent paternalist to continue to collect rent, to receive tenants' social and political deference, and, most importantly, to keep the peace. For landlords and tenants, tolerating some debt for the sake of peace was far better than collecting debts during the maelstrom of land riots provoked by unnecessary evictions.

When a landlord in the Hudson Valley decided to evict a tenant for debt, he usually did so because the tenant refused to pay the debt or to pay any rent at all. Landlords usually characterized that tenant not as an indebted tenant but as a rebellious malcontent. Such rebels threatened the welfare of everyone on the estate, landlords and tenants alike. Landlords also preferred to be seen as peacekeepers rather than as heartless men who could easily stomach throwing a family to the elements or who could wantonly crush another man's life and dreams. In 1752, for instance, Robert Livingston Jr. illustrated just that kind of economically motivated paternalism when he told the rebellious Josiah Loomis, who had refused to pay rent, that "Nothing but your poverty . . . is the Reason why I do not now Eject you." A few months later, however, Livingston tried to evict Loomis. By that time, Loomis had encouraged others to join him and to refute Livingston's land claims and authority, making him, in the landlord's eyes, an insufferable menace. Such a tenant needed to be evicted to preserve order, not because of debt.[28]

Sometimes, however, landlords evicted tenants specifically for debt. In 1784, in one of the few known cases of its kind after 1750, Philip Schuyler evicted Hannah Brewer over debt. Over the previous several years, Brewer had fallen hopelessly behind in her rent and finally indicated to Schuyler that she would be unable to pay the debt. Worse, she did not think she would ever be able to pay rent in the future. To recoup his losses and to ensure receiving some income in the future, Schuyler evicted Brewer, sold the improvements made to the leasehold, and pocketed the sale. She still owed him money, but he took what he could and forgot the rest.[29]

Although tenants regularly missed rent payments, landlords earned considerable income from rent (see table 1). In the late 1750s, Henry Beekman, for example, only collected about 70 percent of the rent his tenants owed. Still, he earned roughly £450 per year in rental income between 1750 and 1776. Beverly Robinson would have rejoiced at such high rates of return. Although he exacted a higher rent per acre than any other landlord in the valley, Robinson consequently collected a smaller proportion of what he was owed. By 1779, 146 of his 149 tenants owed at least one year's rent, and 55 percent owed at least two years' rent, totaling £7,191, plus an additional £1,338 in interest. Despite dismal returns, Robinson netted between £790 and £1,200 per year from the mid-1750s through 1776, his income growing ever larger toward the Revolution. Frederick Philipse earned between £2,200 and £2,700 per year in rent from 1760 through 1775. Like other manor lords in the valley, Philipse stipulated that tenants grind their grain at mills he owned and pay 10 percent of the milled grain in return for the service. Even after letting the tenant who operated the mill take a small cut, Philipse netted another £350 per year from the grist mills he owned on the manor, bringing his average yearly income to between £2,500 and £3,000.[30]

In any given year in the late colonial period, the Van Rensselaers usually collected between 50 to 70 percent of the rent their tenants owed. They received between 750 and 1,400 bushels of wheat per year, which

TABLE 1—Lease Conditions and Rental Income, 1750–1776

Manor	Number of Leases	Average Length of Leases	Average Lease Size	Average Rent Paid per Year	Est. Rent per 100 acres	App. Yearly Income from Tenants
Beekman's portion of Cortlandt Manor	158	3 Lives	237 acres	£4 10s.	£3 1s.	£450
Philipsburg Manor	274	At-Will/ 3 Lives	175 acres	£6 10s.	£3 17s.	£2,500 to £3,000
Beverly Robinson's portion of Philipsburg	146	At-Will/ 3 Lives	170 acres	£4 18s. to £7 10s	£6 8s.	£900 to £1,300
Livingston Manor	371	3 Lives/ 60 years	118 acres	£6 2s.	£4 18s.	£1,700
Rensselaerswyck	683	"for ever"	139 acres	£5 6s.	£3 10s.	£2,300

Sources: For Cortlandt Manor, see Kim, "The Manor of Cortlandt and Its Tenants," chapter 5; Kim, *Landlord and Tenant,* 154–56; and Rent Rolls for Beekman's Precinct for 1756, 1759, and 1779, in RRLP, roll 52. For Philipsburg, see Frederick Philipse's ALC, 12, vol. 19; "The Philipsburgh Manor Rent Roll of 1760," 102–4; and "Rent Roll of Frederick Philipse's Estate (Philipse Manor), 1776–1784," 74–78. For Beverly Robinson's activities, see ALC, 12, vol. 21. For Livingston Manor, see leases in LP, rolls 7 and 8; and Livingston Manor Rent Ledger, 1767–1784, NYHS. For Rensselaerswyck, see leases catalogued at NYSL; Rensselaerswyck Ledger A of Rents, 1768–1789; leases in Boxes 36, 84, and 86; and Abraham Ten Broeck's Lease Ledger, Box 84, all in VRMP.

equaled between £260 and £490, but they also collected a small mountain of other goods and services. Each tenant agreed to work one or two days per year on the manor to maintain fences and roads and to perform other odd jobs such as fixing tools or repairing the manor lord's house. Sometimes, tenants paid off part of their rent by laboring for the manor lord. All of this labor had value. On the eve of the Revolution, for instance, the Van Rensselaers received approximately one thousand total days of labor from tenants, worth roughly £1,200.[31] The Van Rensselaers also owned seven saw mills and three grist mills on their estate that tenants were required to use. Like the Philipses, the Van Rensselaers rented the mills to tenants. Robert Van Deusen paid a flat fee to run a grist mill and kept a small portion of the grain he ground for the tenants. He also agreed to mill one hundred bushels of wheat per year for the Van Rensselaers at no charge. From the mid-1760s through 1775, the Van Rensselaers earned an additional £1,000 to £1,200 annually from these mills even though some tenants invariably took their grain off the manor for milling. A conservative estimate of the rent and fees tenants paid and the labor they performed totals approximately £2,300 per year.[32]

The Livingstons fared a bit better than their neighbors. Like other landlords in the Hudson Valley, the Livingstons may not have wanted to publicize their specific income. But they tried to maximize their rent returns and certainly needed to keep meticulous records of who owed them what. Most of the Van Rensselaers' records were damaged in a fire in the early twentieth century, and the Philipses' manor records are scattered. The Livingstons' records, however, are centralized and fairly pristine. The rent ledger particularly allows for detailed discussion of individual tenants such as John and Elizabeth Shaver; it also offers the chance to make broader statements regarding tenants and rent payments. Rent records reveal that the Livingstons annually collected approximately 70 percent of the rent due over the twenty-five years before the American Revolution. In 1756, for instance, Robert R. Livingston collected 1,450 bushels of wheat, worth approximately £365, from his tenants on Clermont, the southern part of the manor; three years later, he collected 2,100 bushels of wheat worth roughly £735. In both years, he also took in another £100 worth of hogs, hens, and service from his tenants. Livingston crowed that it was not "improbable that I may be [the] absolute Richest Man" in all of New York. His sentiment was more fact than boast.[33]

From 1767 through 1775, tenants on Livingston Manor delivered an average of 3,443 bushels of wheat per year worth approximately £1,200 to the Livingstons. Together with other goods and services tenants paid as rent, the Livingstons earned approximately £1,700 per year in rent and labor. This represented the peak of their earnings in the eighteenth century. The Revolutionary War upset the manorial economy, and the Livingstons' income dropped precipitously after 1778. They spent the 1780s trying to bring their income back up to prewar levels. Despite the decline, the Livingstons earned incredible sums from their tenants, had grown rich, and were getting richer.[34]

Rent filled landlords' coffers, but tenants paid other fees that increased a landlord's income and epitomized a tenant's landless status. Landlords usually took 25 percent of the first sale of the improvements a tenant had made to a leasehold, or a quarter of the sale, and then one-eighth of all future sales. These quarter-sales fees, like rent, demonstrated to tenants that landlords ultimately controlled the land and reaped the biggest reward from it. Moreover, the stipulation gave landlords another way to control the estate by giving them the chance to reject a sale to a potentially disruptive person. The fees the Livingstons collected were typical of fees charged by other landlords. In 1763, John Robinson decided to sell the improvements he had made to his leasehold, and he asked an agent of Robert Livingston Jr. for permission to sell to Johan Barhart Koens for £90. Livingston reviewed Koens's reputation, approved the deal, and collected the £90 from Koens. The landlord took £30 of it to cover the quarter-sales fee and Robinson's outstanding debts and gave Robinson the rest. This procedure was normal.[35]

Although many tenants found these fees onerous, no landlord grew rich off them. Yet fees from their grist and saw mills and profit from their stores could amount to a tidy sum. The Livingstons, like other landlords, required tenants to pay to use the manor's mills and required tenants to shop at stores the manor lord owned. The Livingstons had built their first mills in 1699 and improved them to meet the demands of the growing tenant population. By 1765, Robert Livingston Jr. worried that the family was losing income because tenants were taking their goods to mills off the manor. To remedy that problem, he wanted to build new mills "as fast as [he] could." Like their neighbors, the Livingstons charged tenants 10 percent of whatever they milled for the service. Even if the Livingstons milled only half of the approximately 48,000 bushels of wheat tenants produced annually from 1767 to 1775, they still would have pulled in 2,400 bushels of wheat in fees, amounting to roughly £840 in additional income per year. In all, then, the Livingstons earned slightly more than the Van Rensselaers per year and averaged approximately £2,500 per year from rent and fees.[36]

The Livingstons also owned several stores on the manor and offered tenants credit to buy goods they needed to survive while they made their leaseholds productive. Some tenants no doubt ignored the requirement that they trade there, but others undoubtedly found the stores more convenient than burdensome. Most tenants probably traded at the stores when convenient and ventured off the manor when they thought the gains were worth the risk. The virtual monopoly led to abuse. In one well-documented case, the Livingstons tried to fleece their tenants by offering less-than-market value for wheat. In 1747, Philip Livingston ordered Peter DeWitt, who operated one of the stores on Livingston Manor, to offer tenants only 3s. per bushel of wheat when the market price was 3s. 3d. Tenants who had regularly traded at the store refused to sell, and Livingston retaliated by threatening to evict them. The tenants again refused, insisting that they would let their wheat rot rather than be cheated. Livingston gave in and bought the wheat at market price. The Livingstons, however, simply gave up one form of price gouging for another. In the 1750s, Charles DeWitt, at the time the manager of Livingston Manor, boasted that he sold earthenware to tenants for at least a 70 percent profit, and at a far higher price than tenants could have bought it off the manor.[37]

Once they amassed goods from their tenants, landlords turned agricultural produce into merchant capital by trading the goods in the transatlantic market. Again, the Livingstons offer a good example of landlords' extensive trade activities, and they provide an early illustration of the complexity and breadth of trade in a rapidly expanding Atlantic marketplace. By the 1730s, Philip Livingston began to realize the potential profit from the goods he collected from his tenants. To take full advantage of his position as landlord and merchant, he sent some of his sons to apprentice with his business partners in Europe, where they gained valuable mercantile experience while watching over the family's burgeoning endeavors. Robert Livingston Jr., for instance, learned to read and write French while facilitating the family's business there. By the late 1760s, when Robert Livingston Jr. was the manor lord, the Livingstons had built a vast enterprise that netted the family wealth, an international reputation, and political as well as economic power. Grain produced by tenants was the basis for that growth.

The Livingstons' trade activities in the late colonial period reveal how integral Hudson Valley grain and produce was to transatlantic trade. In 1766, the Livingstons collected grain from their tenants that they milled into flour. They shipped that flour, along with iron from their furnaces in Ancram, to Jamaica and Curacao. Agents working for and with the Livingstons traded flour for European textiles, Jamaican molasses, olive oil, and oysters. The Livingstons' ships then carried these goods back to New York City and Albany, where they were sold in local shops and, sometimes, to tenants. In 1767, Walter Livingston recounted a similar trade pattern. Ships carried the milled flour and lumber tenants paid as rent from Albany to New York City to Pensacola and, finally, to New Orleans, where merchants traded those goods for barrels of cod, mackerel, and gun powder in addition to crates of Spanish handkerchiefs, Bermuda potatoes, chocolate, capers, cotton, and sugar.[38]

By expanding their market endeavors into the Atlantic world, Hudson Valley landlords grew rich. They may not have been the wealthiest men in the British colonies, a contest likely won by Caribbean sugar planters, but they were as wealthy as any group of men on the mainland, and they were fantastically wealthier than their tenants. In 1779, Stephen Van Rensselaer's estate was valued at approximately £19,000, and John Van Rensselaer's portion of his family's land was valued at £10,000. The family's holdings thus totaled £29,000. The average tenant, on the other hand, leased realty valued at approximately £260. Far more starkly, the landlord's family owned roughly 110 times the value of the realty leased by an average tenant on Rensselaerswyck. Similarly, while the average tenant on Livingston Manor rented realty valued at £127, Robert Livingston Jr.'s real estate was assessed at £30,000, or 240 times greater. Frederick Philipse III valued his estate at roughly £40,000 in the late 1770s, while the leaseholds on his estate had a value of approximately £313. Even if Philipse overvalued his estate by as much as one-third to get more money out of British commissioners who awarded compensation for property Loyalists had forfeited during the American Revolution, his real estate was still worth approximately eighty-six times that of the average leasehold on his estate.[39]

Tenants could only dream of the wealth their landlords enjoyed, but if they lived on productive leaseholds they were not necessarily destitute. Still, if they could not aspire to riches, tenants could at least hope to live like their freehold neighbors. The average leasehold in the Hudson Valley in 1779 was valued at approximately £266. Average Cortlandt Manor and Philipsburg tenants inhabited leaseholds valued at £394 and £313 respectively. In comparison, tenants in the northern region leased less valuable lots. An average tenancy on Livingston Manor, for instance, was assessed at only £127, while the average leasehold on Rensselaerswyck was rated at £260. Despite these differences, leaseholds often resembled freeholds in the region in average acreage, assessed value, and agricultural rhythms and labor routines.[40] The average freeholder in the Hudson Valley owned land rated at approximately £228. Freeholders who lived in Hannover and Bedford, near Cortlandt Manor and Philipsburg, owned farms worth on average £201 and £408 respectively. In the neighboring regions of Livingston Manor, Kinderhook freeholders owned lots worth £194, and Halfmoon freeholders owned lots worth £144. Such a visible alternative to tenancy might well have spurred disgruntled tenants to fight for similar freeholds.

Although these figures illustrate that tenants and freeholders lived on similarly valued lots, they obscure the fundamental difference between landlords, freeholders, and tenants. To compare them without qualification or, worse, to conclude that tenants were small holders, is misleading. Landlords owned far more realty than freeholders and were far wealthier, but both owned property. Tenants simply did not. Freeholders could will their property to heirs and could sell the land to avoid instability and starvation. Thus, they always had one more asset to sell or will than tenants. That advantage, however thin, put freeholders further from the edge of poverty and despair and provided them with at least one measure of security that tenants did not have. Tenants could not reap the full value of the ground they cultivated because the land, and any improvements they made to it, inevitably returned to the landowner. Tenants made Hudson Valley land productive, but their status ensured that landlords reaped the wealth and profits of that labor.

Landlords exhibited their wealth by acquiring the physical trappings of their class. The Livingstons, for instance, began sending their children to Europe to receive aristocratic education and to develop their business activities. They and other landlords also erected mansions that dominated the physical landscape of the Hudson Valley. By the late colonial period, for instance, Frederick Philipse had made his house in Yonkers, where Mary Philipse married Roger Morris in 1756, a "showcase of English gentility." The mansion was decorated with oak balustrades, Dutch tiles, and engraved firebacks. Some accoutrements were human; the Philipses' thirty house slaves and servants lived in an attic with doors fitted with leather washers on the hinges so slaves and servants could open and close them without waking those who slept below. Philip Schuyler, a wealthy Albany merchant who married into the Van Rensselaer family in the 1760s, modeled his house, The Pastures, after James Logan's Georgian mansion, Stenton, outside of Philadelphia. Schuyler's mansion, like George Washington's Mount Vernon, looked out across a meadow that stretched to his personal dock on the Hudson River. His house servants and slaves lived in an outbuilding near the kitchen behind the house. In the 1760s, the Van Rensselaers began constructing a mansion that dwarfed these others. It contained four primary rooms on the first floor with two patio-style rooms on either side of a main hall that was dominated by a massive, curved mahogany staircase. Bedrooms and sitting rooms were upstairs. The Van Rensselaers filled the house with accessories and decorations such as Dutch tiles, carved bookcases, and expensive rugs. Although the building was still under construction in the late 1760s, no visitor who traveled to Albany from the north could miss it.[41]

Tenants' houses tended to be neither luxurious nor ramshackle and resembled the houses of freeholders in and around the Hudson Valley. Most tenants lived in utilitarian houses that reflected their status as accurately as mansions exhibited landlords' wealth. Tenants dotted the Hudson Valley with houses they built from materials found on their farms and in styles that reflected their generally limited means and their various cultural origins. Coenradt Lasher, a German who became a tenant on Livingston Manor in the 1750s, re-created a familiar form in New York when he constructed his standard German stone house. Jacob Camer, a Dutch tenant on Rensselaerswyck, built a wood-beam house with the steep gable roof typical of houses built by tenants and farmers of Dutch ancestry. Irish, Scottish, Welsh, and English farmers who moved from New England into the Hudson Valley often built clapboard houses around a simple frame construction.[42]

Perhaps more than anything else, these modest houses physically illustrated the culturally diverse Hudson Valley population. John Van Gelden, who threatened to kill Robert Livingston Jr. during land disputes in the 1750s, bore a Dutch name but was half Dutch and half Stockbridge Indian, and his children were racially mixed. Michael Hallenbeck was Dutch or German. But in the 1750s, he cast his lot with a New England migrant, Josiah Loomis; in the late 1750s and 1760s, Hallenbeck and Loomis allied with Joseph and Robert Paine, New Englanders who had settled on Livingston Manor before the 1750s. William Prendergast, who figured prominently in land riots in Dutchess County in the 1760s, had emigrated from Ireland and married Mehetibal Wing, a Quaker whose family moved to New York from Rhode Island. Of the roughly 2,038 tenants identified in various records from the 1740s through 1779, approximately 54 percent (1,100) bore either Dutch or Germanic surnames. Roughly 44 percent (897) had English, Welsh, Scottish, or Irish surnames. The rest, 2 percent (41), had surnames that could not be identified easily. Ascribing ethnicity by surname is unscientific. It ignores married women's origins, men's maternal ancestry, and couples of different origins invariably married. The practice is fraught with difficulties and provides at best a general description of the community's inhabitants. The records, however, do not indicate either the country of origin or the race of the tenant. Changes in name spelling or further investigation would probably change these percentages, but the general conclusions regarding the diversity of New York's tenant population would stay the same: The tenant population in the Hudson Valley in the late colonial period was remarkably ethnically diverse.[43]

Tenants, as a group, lived only a bad harvest or two away from poverty. They struggled to produce enough for the household, to pay rent, and to avoid falling deeper in debt to their landlords. Tenants, however, were unlikely to take food off their own tables to put it on their landlord's table as rent. Landlords worried about poor production too but more because it affected tenants' ability to pay rent. While a season or two of bad weather and poor harvests could devastate tenants, landlords could survive as long as tenants delivered something as rent. They could not, however, endure year after year of poor rent returns. To avoid that, landlords pressed tenants who fell too far into debt. That kind of pressure did not usually result in a windfall for landlords. They could hardly sue if tenants were destitute, and few landlords were willing to antagonize the whole group by evicting one or two impoverished tenants. Thus, landlords took a different tack in the late colonial period. They sought to stabilize their returns and to optimize (and even maximize) gain by standardizing their economic relationship with their tenants. They created and maintained an increasingly hierarchical economic and social system that continually widened the chasm between landlords and tenants. Despite their constant worries, by the end of the colonial period landlords were harvesting the returns from a manorial economy, shifting wealth in the form of agricultural goods, money, and labor from landless tenants to prosperous landlords.

POLITICS IN COLONIAL NEW YORK

Despite their economic advantages, Hudson Valley landlords did not gain political control quickly, or keep it easily. Landlords strengthened their position in the late seventeenth century when Stephanus Van Cortlandt, Frederick Philipse, Robert Livingston, and Kiliaen Van Rensselaer together confronted men from Queens, Suffolk, Long Island, and Westchester counties who opposed the Stuart monarchy and supported Jacob Leisler. By the 1690s, Cortlandt, Philipse, Livingston, and Van Rensselaer had carved out estates in the Hudson Valley and the English governor had reaffirmed their patents, making the dispute as much a contest between urban opponents and landed Hudson Valley gentry as it was a fight over important cultural and political differences. But the split reflected competing economic and political interests within New York and arose out of long-standing bitterness between the two groups. Many of the men who supported Leisler were also New York City merchants who had unsuccessfully sought the landed trappings of the Hudson Valley gentry. Landlords had no intention of giving up their monopoly of arable land. After Leisler lost, politics in New York remained a domain fought over by the landed and merchant elite of the colony well into the eighteenth century.[44]

In such a contentious political setting, Hudson Valley landlords had to scramble to maintain their positions. While each landed family had secured its political base in the countryside, they fought fierce battles among themselves for control of the few seats in the assembly that swung the legislature one way or the other. They also quarreled with the confrontational merchant elite that was emerging in New York City and Albany, they squabbled with competing colonial authorities, and they fended off attacks from sometime allies such as Cadwallader Colden, New York's lieutenant governor in the late colonial period. Finally, landlords faced nearly continual threats to their estates, the root of their power, from rebellious tenants, squatters, Indians, and settlers from New York and other colonies. How landlords kept their firm grip on power in colonial New York reflects their political acuity, as well as the fluid nature of New York politics.

Landlords managed to stay atop the hierarchy by adopting aspects of their opponents' agenda. Nonetheless, this learning took time, and they sometimes learned their lessons through hard setbacks. In the 1730s, for example, John Thomas and Frederick Philipse squared off in an election over an assembly seat. Philipse won the election easily but publicly admonished Thomas for daring to topple a mighty landlord from power. Thomas was not entirely subdued and won the seat seven years later, and he kept it only because the Philipses joined him later to defeat a common enemy. By the late colonial period, landlords in the northern Hudson Valley were no less powerful. The Livingstons, for instance, were locked in a political death struggle with the DeLanceys, a faction of elite merchants in New York City, for colonial control, but they could still easily sway local elections. In 1761, the enormously influential Robert Livingston Jr. announced his support for first one candidate and then another in an election in Albany County. The election ultimately turned on Livingston's support, and his man won handily.[45]

In New York as in the rest of the colonies, property was the basis of political entitlement. Voters routinely chose between candidates who represented warring factions of the colonial elite and regularly elected socially superior men to offices that the voters would never hold. By 1750, New York voting laws stated generally that adult white men who possessed at least £40 of realty could vote and enfranchised all freemen in the colony's two biggest cities, Albany and New York City. These voters could also sit on petit juries, but men had to possess at least £60 of realty to serve on grand juries and to run for office. Such men might have stood for office, but they rarely contested the elite's political hegemony successfully, and few tenants dared to openly challenge their landlord's authority. While approximately 50 percent of New York's adult white male population could vote in the late colonial period, the laws denied the vote to some tenants, poor men, sons living at home, and slaves. Tenants who had life leases, or leases for a series of lives, as well as those on Rensselaerswyck who leased land "for ever," were able to vote. Thus, almost all but the poorest of tenants on Cortlandt Manor, Livingston Manor, and Rensselaerswyck were enfranchised, and men who stood for election in these districts cultivated the tenants' support. Voting laws, however, particularly stung leaseholders on Philipsburg, where most tenants leased their land at the will of the lord and, as a result, did not satisfy property requirements for voting.[46]

The voting process inhibited the electorate. Qualified voters cast their ballots in front of the candidates, and agents of the landlords dutifully wrote down how tenants voted. Tenants worried about offending their landlord if they voted for the wrong candidate. Some members of the elite observed that this method of voting clearly favored landlords, and they periodically proposed the use of secret ballots. But who favored secret ballots often depended on who had won the previous elections. Secret ballots appealed to voters, so men on the outside advocated them in the hope of winning over voters; however, men in power usually thwarted attempts to change voting procedures. The Livingstons "were opposed" to secret ballots when they had power, but they changed their stance after they fell out of power in 1768. On the outside of politics for the first time in decades, the Livingstons argued that rulers could not influence voters who cast secret ballots. They were right, but they had benefited from just that kind of coercion for nearly seventy years.[47]

The political order these landlords dominated was characterized by three critical elements. First, politics in the colony were remarkably fluid. Edward Countryman correctly points out that the very flexible and changing nature of New York politics encouraged assemblymen such as Robert R. Livingston and others to develop and then refine their political agility. It was the only way they could keep their seats. Second, the electoral system ensured that politics in New York, as in other colonies, would be dominated by wealthy men. Finally, New York politics accurately reflected the colony's strict social hierarchy, which was greatly influenced by the landlord-tenant relationship that structured the manorial economy.[48]

How successfully did landlords dominate colonial politics? The Philipses might not have had a guaranteed seat in the assembly, like the Livingstons and Van Rensselaers, but they treated their estate as a pocket borough, and with good reason. John Thomas stayed in political power only after he joined Frederick Philipse to defeat their common foe, Lewis Morris Jr., in a 1750 election. Philipse and Thomas so dominated the election that Morris quit before everyone had voted. Voters knew that Morris was beaten long before he knew. Of the approximately 600 people eligible to vote in Westchester County that year, only 289 bothered to cast their ballots at all. The others already knew that Philipse would win. In the late 1750s and early 1760s, sheriff elections in Albany County turned entirely on Robert Livingston Jr.'s support. These specific elections show landlords flexing their muscle, but nothing illustrates how landlords completely dominated politics like the political run enjoyed by the Livingstons and Van Rensselaers in the colonial eighteenth century. In every election between 1700 and 1766, tenants on Rensselaerswyck and Livingston Manor elected their manor lord or his agent as the manor's representative to the colonial assembly.[49]

J. R. Pole found similar voting patterns in colonial Virginia. Pole argued that voters in Virginia usually deferred to the political wisdom and experience of their social superiors and elected wealthy men to office. In his analysis of politics within the context of landlords and tenants, Sung Bok Kim invoked that theme by arguing that voters in the Hudson Valley, and particularly voters on the four prominent manors, accepted the landlords' "leadership as natural." Maybe they did, but voters in the Hudson Valley rarely had the chance to choose anyone not affiliated with the colony's economic elite. Voting laws dictated that only men from the landowning elite could stand as candidates for election. From the tenants' perspective, it hardly mattered who stood for election or who won. Then, as today, wealthy candidates turned riches into political influence and power. In that system, deference was the political manifestation of economic relationships and social hierarchy. Thus, in the Hudson Valley in the colonial period, landlords and their agents were not simply the "natural" candidates for a colonial political office: They were the only men for the job.[50]

By the late 1740s, the manorial society was firmly in place in the Hudson Valley, and landlords dominated New York politics. Although some tenants prospered, others strained against the limits landlords imposed on them. Tenants were expected to conduct much of their business—such as grinding grain and selling surplus goods—with the manor lord and faced retaliation if they went elsewhere. Worse, they could not sell the land they labored on, and they could not will it to heirs. Some tenants recognized their limited political power and realized that they could not hope to reform the system. Landlords, on the other hand, began to enjoy handsome profits from their investments. They had increased the number of tenants on their estates, along with their income from rents and fees. They had successfully entrenched themselves at the top of New York's colonial government, and the increasingly standardized manorial economy ensured the transfer of wealth from tenants to landlords. At the very moment they began to enjoy the fruits of decades of effort, landlords found their estates assailed from nearly every angle. Discontented tenants, rebellious squatters, cantankerous neighboring landowners, and disgruntled Indians, all of whom lived on land claimed by manor lords, questioned the validity of the landlords' claims. This challenge had become impossible to ignore by the time Roger Morris and Mary Philipse said their vows in 1758; few Hudson Valley landlords would spend as festive or as peaceful a day for the next fifty years.

Chapter Two

PROPERTY AND POWER

IN THE NORTHERN VALLEY

• In February 1755, William Rees, a tenant on Claverack, the southern portion of Rensselaerswyck, looked up from his work in horror to see his landlord, John Van Rensselaer, leading a posse up the rutted path to his house. By that time, land disputes and violence plagued the manor, and Van Rensselaer decided to quash the violence by seizing Rees, one of the insurgents' leaders. In 1753, Rees, a Welshman who had been a tenant on the lower part of Rensselaerswyck for several years, had joined a band of insurgents headed by Robert Noble. During the next two years, Rees had grown into an insufferable leader, as insurgents began staking freehold claims to land also claimed by the Van Rensselaers and the Livingstons. Some insisted that they had bought it from Stockbridge Indians, and others petitioned other colonies for titles to it. Still others simply claimed it. Some of these insurgents pressured tenants to side against the landlord and threatened to attack otherwise peaceful tenants if they refused to join. Rees was one such insurgent.

By the winter of 1755, after trying to settle these disputes without resorting to violence, John Van Rensselaer decided he had endured enough and decided to take Rees into custody. A witness testified that the posse of loyal tenants, "abandoned Irishmen and Negroes," rushed Rees while he worked in the fields. Rees saw the crowd, fled into his house, snatched up his gun, and "snaped" off several shots at his enemies.[1] The posse "broke into the House" to get its man but found Rees squirming his way through a hole in the roof. Once outside, Rees dropped to the ground and ran, but Matthew Furlong, a member of the posse, shot him in the back and killed him. When colonial officials investigated the shooting, Van Rensselaer endorsed such lethal force, insisting that the rioters "all swear they will be Kill'd or kill before they are taken."[2] Although Van Rensselaer had not confronted Rees with the intent of killing him, the landlord hoped that the killing would end insurgency in the region. He was wrong. For the next twenty-three years, disgruntled rural people sought land, fueling uncertainties concerning manorial and colonial borders and disrupting the peace of the area.

Colonial border disputes sparked some of the discontent. Throughout the colonial eighteenth century, officials from New York and Massachusetts disagreed over their common borders. New Yorkers maintained that

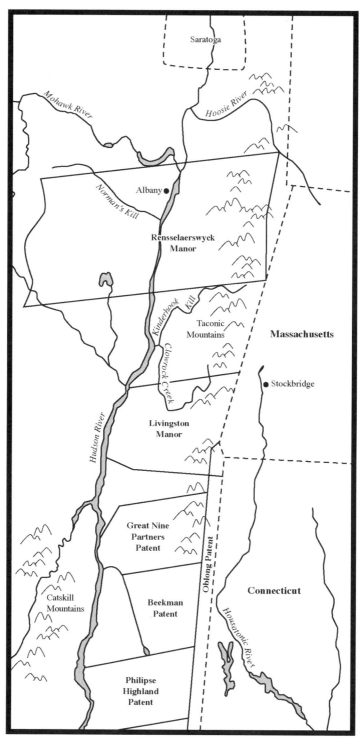

Great Estates of the Northern Hudson Valley, circa 1765

the Connecticut River divided the two colonies, but New Englanders put the border at the Hudson River and gave nearly anyone a Massachusetts title to land in the disputed territory between the Hudson River and the Berkshire Mountains. New Yorkers awarded grants to the same land, making the countryside a patchwork of overlapping land claims. These uncertainties led landlords, tenants, squatters, and Indians to dispute and then fight over their claims to the land.

At first blush, these disputes pitted Yorkers versus Yankees, but that interpretation glosses over myriad internal complexities. In fact, disparate groups of Indians, tenants, and squatters from both regions stood together in the conflicts over land that shook the social and political foundation of the Hudson Valley in the two decades before the American Revolution. Although New Yorkers and New Englanders naturally defended their claims from external attacks, they also fought among themselves over who had the best claim. New York landlords argued that New York claims bested those from Massachusetts and that their claims trumped any from inside or outside the colony. Disgruntled people from both regions cared far more about getting a title to the land than they did about which colony granted it or governed them. Massachusetts's assemblymen were more likely to grant these insurgents a title than were New Yorkers, but not if it meant giving away another New Englander's land. Insurgents tried different strategies for the same reason they diversified crops, to ensure their odds of success. Some insurgents declared simply that they owned the land; others asserted that they had lived and worked on the land long enough to own it. To the north, New York landlords, Connecticut settlers headed by Ethan Allen, and New York squatters and former tenants all claimed land between the Connecticut River and the Green Mountains. To the south, in Westchester and Dutchess counties, tenants rebelled when landlords attempted to redesign their leases.

Characterizing the strife as a Yankee versus Yorker conflict falls short of appropriately describing the role Indians played in contests over land. Stockbridge Indians defied attempts by the Livingstons and Van Rensselaers to expand their estates at the Indians' expense by noting that they maintained an ancestral claim to their traditional land. Early in the eighteenth century, some Stockbridge Indians had moved away from the region, but others had never left. Some had recently moved back in the 1740s, and these groups insisted that they kept up their claims to land. Still other Stockbridge Indians had moved back into the region and joined William Rees and other tenants in protests against landlords and landlordism. In the south Hudson Valley, Indians also aligned with insurgents to get land. Wappinger Indians and their Anglo-European tenants found themselves displaced in the mid-1750s when Roger Morris, Beverly Robinson, and Philip Philipse took the Wappingers' land after the men of the tribe left to fight the French in the Seven Years' War. Although Wappinger Indians had remained on the land for most of the colonial period, they faced increasing pressure from landlords to give up their land. Both groups of Indians also believed landlords had reinterpreted deeds written in misleading language to fraudulently expand the titles they had obtained from the native inhabitants of the region.

In the late colonial period, insurgents honed both their strategies for claiming land and their methods of rioting. The riots were more than simply attempts to grab land. Rural insurgency challenged New York's traditional political hierarchy, making land riots one of many movements that surfaced in the Hudson Valley in the late colonial period that questioned the authority of current rulers. This particular challenge, however, remained distinct from the Revolutionary movement of the 1770s and 1780s, and it survived into the post-Revolutionary period. By tracing this strain of egalitarianism from before the early stages of the imperial crisis through the Revolutionary period, we may see how it influenced and moved separately from that brand of egalitarianism usually associated with the imperial crisis after 1763.

The riots on Rensselaerswyck and Livingston Manor led by Josiah Loomis and Robert Noble, the revolt spearheaded by Ethan Allen in the Green Mountains, and the uprising led by William Prendergast differed in details. But they shared a common cause. Through these conflicts over land and power, plebeian New Yorkers developed new views of landownership, labor, and independence that fundamentally challenged the legitimacy of landlordism and attacked the ruling hierarchy. The process began in the 1740s and 1750s and reached a critical juncture in the mid-1760s, when rioters, landlords, British soldiers, and colonial officials from Massachusetts and New York squared off in open battle for land and authority. By the end of the colonial period, the two sides had fought to a dissatisfying standoff. Landlords and New York officials successfully reasserted their authority over the land and the community, but insurgents remained on the land.

Landlords' authority, however, was tenuous, and the threat of renewed fighting lingered. Wappinger and Stockbridge Indians strove to legitimate their claim to land in New York courts by facilitating white yeoman settlement of the land. They had plenty of takers. Insurgent New York tenants and squatters from New York and New England streamed onto the land. They continued to flout New York's authority and to cast their loyalties with Massachusetts, whose leaders appeared willing to give freeholds to the insurgents so they could expand their boundaries at New York's expense. Regardless of their ethnicity or cultural origins, these disgruntled people cast their political loyalties with whichever colony gave them title. Stockbridge and Wappinger Indians, New York tenants and squatters, and New England squatters often lived near each other and were bound together in fights against landlords and New York officials. Some individuals belonged to more than one specific group, moving freely between them. These multiple social actors coalesced to oppose landlords and landlordism, but their separate identities and histories remain important to how the conflicts proceeded. The debates changed after 1776, when each side infused its arguments with Revolutionary rhetoric, but their goals remained the same. They each wanted to own the land.

Titles have always provided the best proof of landownership. Disputes often arose because landlords and many insurgents held some kind of overlapping claims. In some cases, two, three, or four groups of people held titles to roughly the same plot of ground. While landlords had authorized titles from New York officials, insurgents countered with titles obtained from various sources including Indians, rival colonial officials, or both. Sorting out these titles could be incredibly confusing, and every decision invariably dissatisfied someone. New York courts skirted these debates by refusing to acknowledge deeds granted by any colony other than New York. That strategy simplified the contests while ensuring landlords' and officials' colonial agenda. Insurgents next tried asserting that they were entitled to own the land because they lived on it and improved it. Landlords countered by redefining the relationship between use and ownership. To supplement their titles, landlords argued that they had lived on the land and had been making it available to tenants for decades.

These debates threw into stark relief contrasting visions of a property system that underpinned the society and defined relationships of class and community. Landlords wanted to own land, preferably tens of thousands of acres, and they wanted to lease it to tenants who would improve it and pay rent. While they forced that vision on Europeans who wanted to farm land in the Hudson Valley, landlords also imposed their particular model for land use on Indians, who practiced what Daniel K. Richter described as a "sort of upside-down capitalism, in which the aim was, not to accumulate goods, but to be in a position to provide them to others." Although Richter was describing Indians before they became enmeshed in trade with Europeans, the description remains relevant for the eighteenth century. Wappinger and Stockbridge Indians continued to try to establish their title to the land within the British system while they retained a distinct group identity. By obtaining titles to land from either New York or Massachusetts, Stockbridge and Wappinger Indians owned private property in a European sense by the middle of the eighteenth century, but the Indians retained their traditional ideas of land use. As a result, their ownership of unoccupied, unimproved land depended on using the land and on offering others a way to make a living on it. They fulfilled that ideal by leasing it to white settlers.[3]

Land rioters articulated yet another position. Prospective yeomen did not have enough capital to buy land, so they settled for tenancy. Most hoped to accumulate enough money to buy land, but as that dream sometimes faded some invariably began chafing at their subordinate status and at their inability to will land to heirs. These dissatisfied tenants and squatters sought to create a community of freeholders who had earned their land by the sweat of their brow. To build that community, they had to destroy landlordism and tenancy. Land disputes contained dramatic political implications—a point that was hardly lost to either side. Insurgents threatened to upend New York's land-based political hierarchy. New freeholders would rule the community they inhabited and would not brook being ruled by landlords.

That new community had to be forged out of conflict, and culturally diverse groups of people took up arms to do it. Dutch, Germans, Scots-Irish, Welsh, English, and Indians fought side by side to destroy landlordism and to obtain freeholds. Their shared goals enabled them to set aside the differences that might have divided them, and they did whatever they could to win. Landlords were as willing as their opponents to use whatever means necessary to crush the rebellions that threatened their estates. To defeat their enemies, landlords even put arms into the hands of their subordinates, wage laborers, and Africans who were either wage laborers or tenants. Each side spurred the other to act more decisively, and, by the mid-1760s, both sides had exhausted almost all available options. As a result, landlords and insurgents resorted to dramatic, and even horrific, violence. Neither side, however, achieved its goals, setting the stage for future antagonism and more violence.

PROPERTY AND JURISDICTION

In May 1739, New York's lieutenant governor, George Clark, pleaded with the Board of Trade to settle the boundary between Massachusetts and New York. He feared any further delays would incite the rivals to violence. Settlers urged on by Massachusetts officials had already marked out some townships within sixteen miles of the Hudson River, settling land that was, Clark asserted, part of New York and owned by the Van Rensselaers. Some of these New Englanders established communities with local Stockbridge and Housatonic Indians. Settlers all hoped that if they could settle towns in the region in the name of Massachusetts, the Board of Trade would make it part of the colony. The Board of Trade, however, preferred to let colonial officials settle the matter and turned the problem back to the colonists. Unfortunately, neither New York nor Massachusetts would give up any territory, so the boundary issue remained unresolved for decades and Clark's unease deepened.[4]

When he wrote in 1739, Clark was complaining of only the most recent attempts by rulers of Massachusetts to take land from New York. Massachusetts's leaders had spent the previous two decades trying to extend Massachusetts at New York's expense. Earlier in the 1730s, they had encouraged Protestant ministers to convert Indians who lived between the Hudson and Housatonic rivers and to settle towns with them. While the ministers hoped to save the Indians' souls, leading men from Massachusetts wanted to gain the converted Indians' support for New England settlements in the territory that abutted the eastern boundaries of Livingston Manor and Claverack. In 1736, three years before Clark complained of New England squatters in the region, the government in Boston had granted a six-square-mile tract for a mission township in Barrington for the converted Housatonic Indians. The town included farmland for the Indians and enough land for New England ministers and their families. By the fall of 1737, New Englanders had started building a schoolhouse and a meetinghouse for the converted there. At much the same time, other New England ministers, notably Ephraim Williams and Jonathan Edwards, formed a partnership to buy approximately four thousand additional acres of land in the same region. These men did not intend to settle the land themselves or to keep it for the converted Indians to use. Instead, they planned on selling it to land-hungry New England farmers who, by the time Clark wrote to the Lords of Trade in 1739, had moved onto the land and had claimed it for Massachusetts.[5]

Once the pathways to that land had opened, Indians and Anglo-Europeans flocked there. In the early 1740s, several Stockbridge Indian families moved into the region around Great Barrington, and others moved into New Canaan. Both towns sat in the disputed territory between the Hudson and Housatonic rivers. Some Stockbridge Indians moved onto the land to escape mounting pressure from New York landlords to give up their ancestral land, but others merely sought land they could farm. Landlords such as the Livingstons and Van Rensselaers increasingly asserted that their claims superseded those of local River Indians, and the New York government supported them. Stockbridge Indians had been pushed off their land and had no other legitimate alternative. They were likely hoping to gain unquestioned ownership of the land by getting a Massachusetts seal on their titles. Having failed to convince New Yorkers that they owned the land, they pressed their case in imperial courts, hoping to receive a fair settlement. Other Stockbridge Indians were recently converted Christians looking for a place to live in a religiously based community where they might practice their faith. Some bore Dutch first names, suggesting that they had been baptized by Dutch ministers; others had become Congregationalists who settled in praying towns organized by Massachusetts. These were only a few strategies of many that Indians in predominantly European communities used to secure land and a stable future for themselves and their families.

White settlers moved into the region, too, and provoked local and intercolonial antagonism. By the early 1750s, at least three other groups of New Englanders surveyed land near the Taconic Mountains. In 1751, one group settled near the Taconic Mountains on land the Livingstons had claimed. Robert Livingston Jr. wanted to eject them and furiously, but futilely, hoped his peers in the Massachusetts assembly would settle the problem they started. His hope was misplaced. In fact, the manor lord fumed when the members of the General Court questioned his "quiet

Possession and undoubted Rights" to the land. While he thought his social peers would, and should, recognize his claim, they made quite plain that they wanted to expand their colony at his expense.[6]

Disgruntled New York tenants and squatters took advantage of these disputes to further their own quest for land. Some took their cues from New England settlers and claimed the land outright. Others sought grants from the Massachusetts assembly, which happily seized another opportunity to undermine New Yorkers' claims to the disputed territory. In 1751, for instance, Josiah Loomis of Livingston Manor told his landlord that he now owned the land he had leased for the previous twelve years. Loomis lived near the Taconic Mountains close to the spot Massachusetts squatters had surveyed for a town. Already facing external threats to his estate, Livingston refused to countenance any attacks from within it. To nip this insurrection in the bud, Livingston ordered Loomis, whom he regarded as the "promoter & first inventor of giving me some Trouble with Regard to my Lands," not to "put any tool in the Ground again." Within a few months Loomis had started encouraging his neighbors to oppose Livingston as well, making him too dangerous to tolerate. Livingston evicted him and installed Robert and Johannes Van Deusen on the leasehold.

Not one to give up easily, Loomis brought a suit of trespass and eviction in a New York court against the Van Deusens. Livingston knew his chances in court were excellent, so he pushed the case forward. On safer ground, Livingston argued that his title had been granted to his family by a New York governor and that the members of the community had acknowledged that he had owned it for decades. Many of them had, after all, signed leases with the landlord. One seventy-five-year-old tenant, for instance, testified that he always thought the Livingstons owned the land and that it had always been part of New York. The landlord demonstrated both authorial and communal recognition of his claim. Loomis, on the other hand, based his case on the title he had received from the Massachusetts General Assembly.[7]

Loomis's case illustrates several of the crucial elements of the land disputes that characterized the northern Hudson Valley for the remainder of the colonial period. The colonial government in Boston facilitated and supported new Christian Indian settlements in the disputed region and encouraged white settlers to move into these towns. New York landlords pressured converted and local Stockbridge Indians to give up their land. The Indians joined with tenants and squatters from New York and New England to oppose manorialism and to bolster their claims. Together, they seized what appeared to be a likely opportunity to get the land on which they lived and labored. They saw no other way to achieve their goal of landownership. Josiah Loomis's case signals one moment when these distinct threads of opposition came together. What had started as a dispute between landlord and tenant grew into a more serious conflict that incorporated boundary disputes, debates over Indian and squatter settlements, and the complaints of insurgent tenants. Despite the widespread support he enjoyed among his neighbors, Loomis lost in court.

For Loomis, the setback was temporary. He refused to give up, and he tried to persuade other tenants to join him in his uprising. By early 1753, Joseph Paine and Michael Hallenbeck, both longtime tenants on Livingston Manor, had joined Loomis, and they sent a new petition to the Massachusetts legislature for titles to their leaseholds. Again, the legislature complied. A short time later, John Van Gelden and his son joined Loomis. The Van Geldens were half-Dutch, half-Stockbridge Indians who had leased land from the Livingstons. In doing so, the Van Geldens, like other Stockbridge Indians, followed an alternative strategy to survive in the increasingly European world of the Hudson Valley. Indians faced unique challenges not necessarily faced by other insurgents and utilized various strategies to keep their land. They encouraged white settlement, took part in it, and sought a crown grant to their traditional land all to validate their own claims. Crown titles for Indians' indigenous claims, however, could backfire. While Indians thought the crown's grant legitimated their native claims, whites turned it against them, arguing that Indians who obtained or sought crown titles were thereafter submitting to the king's authority. Taken together, these different paths show how, as Richard White points out, "diverse peoples adjust[ed] their differences through what amount[ed] to a process of creative, and often expedient, misunderstandings."[8]

Unlike the peaceful paths some people followed, events involving the Van Geldens took a violent turn. In response to the Van Geldens' petition, the Massachusetts General Court characterized Livingston's claims as "extraordinary" and encouraged the insurgents to "go on in troubling" him. So, when Livingston then told the Van Geldens to leave the manor, the elder Van Gelden threatened to burn down Livingston's house and to kill the manor lord. While the threat shook him badly, Livingston countered by again ordering the Van Geldens, and the rebellious Joseph Paine, to move off the manor immediately. They all refused. Paine, however, decided to punish the Livingstons by girdling over one thousand trees near his farm, killing them. When Livingston confronted him about this, Paine told his manor lord to "Kiss his A-s."[9]

Landlords showed that they could be as vicious as insurgents. In a petition to a sympathetic Massachusetts assembly, several insurgents complained bitterly of their ill treatment at the hands of New York landlords and their agents. In one case in late July 1753, Jopheth Hunt, Jacob Spoor, and Catrina Hallenbeck gathered in front of Michel Hallenbeck's farmhouse as a company of men advanced on them with swords and pistols. Spoor confronted the men in the road and asked them what they were doing. One of the men hit Spoor over the head with the broad side of a sword and threatened to cut off his ears. The landlord's men then confronted and harassed Hunt and Catrina Hallenbeck too.[10]

When outright threats and unsanctioned violence failed to quiet discontent, landlords called on officials to compel order. In early 1755, Livingston sent the sheriff of Albany County, Abraham Yates, to arrest the rebels. Yates initially captured one of the rioters, but was quickly surrounded by others who ordered the release of their brother. The sheriff complied, hoping that the insurgents would let him go his way, but the rioters seized him, carted him to Sheffield, Massachusetts, and tossed him in jail. Yates gained his freedom by signing a bond for £150 for his "Appearance at their Next Court," when he would face charges for attacking the insurgents. Yates presumably ignored the bond and went on his way. Later that month, he finally captured Josiah Loomis. By February 1755, insurgency had spread to nearby Rensselaerswyck when a group of squatters from East Haddam, Connecticut, moved onto Claverack, the lower part of the estate on the east side of the Hudson. Like Livingston, John Van Rensselaer wanted to douse this spark of discontent by arresting well-known rebel William Rees. But the killing of Rees failed to slow the activities of the squatters on the land. By the end of 1755, these squatters were parceling out lots in the town they had named Spencertown.[11]

Despite their efforts, Livingston and Van Rensselaer faced growing dissidence. At much the same time the people of Spencertown were distributing land, Robert Noble was promising disgruntled tenants that if they joined him they could get their land for "Nothing." Among others, Andries Rees, Jonathon Darby, Andries Brussie, Christopher Brussie, Hendrick Brussie, Benjamin Franklin, and his son, Benjamin Franklin Jr., all joined Noble's group to get freeholds. A short time later, Noble joined a surveying party from Massachusetts that negotiated to buy a six-mile tract of land in the region from Peter Pophquunnaupeet and John Paphuckawok, representing the Stockbridge Indians. By transferring their claim to the settlers, these Stockbridge Indians acknowledged the settlers' rightful ownership of the land. Again, the Stockbridge sided with white New York and New England insurgents to form a veritable coalition against the Van Rensselaers and Livingstons. They overcame regional, ethnic, and racial differences to challenge landlordism and to get land. Overall, seventy-four men, including Robert Noble, Josiah Loomis, men from Spencertown, and Stockbridge Indians signed the deed. As he had before, Livingston sent Yates to derail the rebels' activities. Yates was more successful this time. He apprehended the elder Van Gelden, who had shot a tenant who had served on a posse sent out to arrest the insurgents. When John Van Gelden learned of his father's arrest, he rode off to invite other Stockbridge Indians to help him break his father out of jail. If they declined, he threatened to go straight to the "Mohawks and require assistance from them."[12]

After two years of nearly constant fighting, mounting antagonisms, and the threat of Indian wars on his estate, Livingston's patience ran out. In June 1757, he ordered Yates to assemble yet another posse to arrest a "number of Men" who had "unlawfully and riotously assembled together with Arms" at Jonathon Darby's house on the manor. The manor lord accused the men of entering "into a Combination with some people of the Massachusetts Bay in order to dispossess" him of his land. Many of these men, like Darby, were New York tenants, but they threw their loyalty to Massachusetts because that colony guaranteed them freeholds. Yates gathered a posse of tenants and laborers from Livingston's iron furnaces. These men had to serve in the posse; they faced criminal charges if they refused. Yates and the posse made their way to Darby's farm and began shooting as soon as they saw the insurgents. The rebels ran inside, grabbed what guns they had, and returned fire. The posse forced the rioters out of the house, chased several down in the nearby woods, shackled them, and took them to jail.[13]

However successful Yates had been, the manor lord was convinced that he needed British troops to finish the job. Livingston worried that rioting would begin anew, and he grew especially nervous after learning that colonial officials had released most of the captured insurgents because the courts would not meet for several months. One rioter, Benjamin Franklin Sr., had died of small pox while in jail, and Livingston hoped more would suffer the same fate. The manor lord, however, continued to plead with the British army to help him, but officials retorted frankly that Livingston had to fend for himself. The army was busy fighting a war with France.[14]

Livingston's hard tactics worked for a short time as insurgents returned to less violent means to get land. The Stockbridge Indians particularly renewed their quest to own land concurrently claimed by the Livingstons and Van Rensselaers. How they proceeded illustrates that the Stockbridge Indians played an integral role in land disputes in the colonial period. Generally, historians have described Indians as either antagonists to white settlers or as participants in some kind of negotiated but tenuous agreement with whites to coexist on land that they both used. The Stockbridge, however, followed a different path to keep their land and to live with whites. In the 1750s and 1760s, they sought to secure their claims to most of their traditional land by encouraging whites to settle some of it. Such a move indicates that they wanted to work with insurgents to dismantle the great estates. In 1761, two Stockbridge Indians, John PoskNehonnohwok and David Nannaunookkunuck, contended that their group's land included parts of Livingston Manor and Rensselaerswyck. Nannaunookkunuck was the son of Benjamin Kokhkewenaunaunt, the head sachem in the 1740s, who had moved with other Mahican families to Stockbridge. These men insisted that the land was theirs by virtue of an aboriginal claim that they had legitimated with a grant from the crown's representative. In this case, the Stockbridge obtained a title from the Massachusetts General Court. The Van Rensselaers countered with a deed from New York's royal governor that entitled them to a strip of land two miles north and south of Albany that ran sixteen miles east and west on each side of the Hudson River. This English deed restated the boundaries set out in the deed the Van Rensselaers had obtained from the Dutch in the seventeenth century.

Although three Mahicans had allegedly agreed to sell some of their traditional land early in the eighteenth century, PoskNehonnohwok and Nannaunookkunuck contended that white colonists had never paid for it. Thus, the Indians retained possession of the land.

Not surprisingly, disgruntled white settlers in the region supported the Stockbridge Indians. Jacob Vosburgh, an insurgent tenant on Rensselaerswyck, swore that he "never heard that said Lands was owned by the Rensselaers untill last Fall." Another, Jonathon Reed, noted that "one Yookum an Indian of Stockbridge . . . spoke of two Several Tribes of Indians as possessors and owners of the Lands lying on [the] Haussatonnock River." Reed thought the Stockbridge owned the land, not the Van Rensselaers. Of course, their desire to buy land biased their testimony. Both men could have bought land from the Stockbridge if they won the case. The New York court that heard the case, however, decided that the landlords' claims bested those of Indians; the Van Rensselaers owned the land.[15]

The Stockbridge quickly found themselves squeezed on both sides. At about the same time they suffered defeat in New York courts, they learned that Massachusetts intended to settle nine new townships in the disputed territory. King Ben, sachem of the Stockbridge, asked Sir William Johnson to explain the move, but the British liaison to the Iroquois Confederacy declined. Instead of addressing their complaints, Johnson suggested that they send representatives to Boston to argue their side. Jacob Cheeksaunken and Johannes Mtohksin traveled to the General Court to ask the legislators to pay off old debts with the Indians and to negotiate a new price for the land in question. The legislators had initially offered the Stockbridge approximately £1,700 for the land but then reneged on the deal. The Stockbridge Indians were not discouraging Massachusetts settlers from moving to the territory. They simply wanted to be paid a fair price for the land. Such an admission, however, illustrates their declining status and power. The Stockbridge sought what they thought they could attain. In this case, they knew that they could no longer impede white settlement if they wanted to stay on the land, so they had been reduced to scrabbling to get what they could. The two sides agreed on a price in late 1762 and cut a deal, and the Stockbridge saw their already diminished power and land holdings dwindle even more.[16]

The Van Rensselaers, like the Stockbridge, also soon felt pressed on two sides. While they were fending off Indian claims to their estate, Solomon Beby and forty-three others petitioned the New York government for a grant that included part of Claverack, which was operated by John Van Rensselaer. Claverack's boundaries had been debated hotly for decades. One border was marked at an Indian place called Wawanaquasick, a heap of stones, but Beby claimed the marker was closer to the Hudson River than did the Van Rensselaers, implying that the Van Rensselaers had moved the stones to expand their estate. The head of the Kinderhook Creek apparently marked another corner of the estate, but Van Rensselaer either forgot or refused to mark the estate there even though he and his family had been promising to do so for years. Taken together, these imprecise boundaries left one entire side of the estate hopelessly unclear. The Van Rensselaers were not entirely to blame for the problem. They hardly relished the ambiguities and had tried to fix the problems several times. Henry Van Rensselaer, for instance, had tried unsuccessfully to clear them up in 1717 by obtaining a confirmation of his family's preexisting patents. In 1761, Beby demanded that the Van Rensselaers produce these documents, or what documents they thought might help, to etch out the proper boundaries of Claverack.

Beby, like the Stockbridge Indians, enjoyed support from surprising circles. While insurgents hoped Beby would win so he could sell them some of the land in question, New York's attorney general, John Tabor Kempe, pushed the case forward because he thought the Van Rensselaers could not rightfully claim all the land. In language reminiscent of the insurgents, Kempe argued that the Van Rensselaers had done nothing to improve the land; they had not "settled any Persons" on it; and vast stretches of it lay in "Wast for any settlers." Whoever won, Kempe reasoned, would be more likely to bring people into New York and to settle that land. Lieutenant Governor Cadwallader Colden also supported Beby. Colden worried that landed men like the heads of the Van Rensselaer and Livingston families had seized control of New York's government and that they would never relinquish either their political power or wealth without a fight. Colden's political concerns, however, were tied to personal gain. If the Van Rensselaers lost the land, he had hoped to buy some of it.[17]

Newly appointed governor Robert Monckton presided over the council that heard the case in October 1762. Rather than issue a formal decision, Monckton and the council simply dismissed Beby's petition. The council also stipulated that John Van Rensselaer mark a more permanent boundary on Claverack's eastern border. This new line depended on the resolution of ongoing New York–Massachusetts boundary disputes, which officials failed to resolve for years. Thus, doubts about Claverack's boundaries persisted for over a decade. In 1773, John Van Rensselaer tried to resolve the issue once and for all. He gave up approximately sixty-six thousand acres to prevent any future complaints against him. As a reward for giving up that part of his estate, Van Rensselaer received a firm patent to the rest of Claverack. The decision left insurgents dissatisfied. They wanted Van Rensselaer to relinquish all his land. Thus, despite years of legal wrangling and Van Rensselaer's concessions, insurgents continued to question who rightfully owned the land and to assert their claims to it.[18]

The Livingstons faced a different attack on their claims, and it came from closer to home. While Monckton was deciding against Beby, Abraham Yates broke his alliance with landlords in the northern Hudson Valley. Like more famous Revolutionaries such as Thomas Jefferson and George Washington, Abraham Yates Jr. was born in the colonial world and died in the new country he played a prominent role in creating. Yates was the ninth child of a modest Albany family, and, although apprenticed to a cobbler for a short time in his youth, he aspired to public office.[19] By the early 1750s, he had found patronage among the Livingstons, he served as sheriff for Albany County, and he acted as the Livingstons' blunt agent to defeat rebellion on the manor. Although he held his position because the Livingstons supported him, Yates insisted on being his own man, selecting his deputy and sometimes acting without direct orders from his benefactors. When the Livingstons withdrew their support, Yates lost his post as sheriff. After floundering for a year, he tried for a seat in the colonial assembly. Livingston initially sided with Yates, but the manor lord changed his mind. Perhaps he had learned of Yates's sudden interest in the legitimacy of the Van Rensselaers' deeds. Whatever the reason, Yates lost the election.[20]

With time on his hands, Yates wrote a brief essay on the original grants to Rensselaerswyck. He noticed several discrepancies between the wording of the Indian deed for the estate and the language of the patent that the Van Rensselaers received from the Dutch government and the grant English officials affirmed in 1685. Yates concluded that the two "Documents could not have been more Differently Worded if they had intended two Different Places of Land." Although Yates specifically criticized the Van Rensselaers' deed here, he was also implicitly questioning the deeds of all landlords, including his former benefactor. Later, Yates addressed the Livingstons more specifically, accusing them of wriggling "themselves in and elbow[ing] their antagonists out of their property and jurisdiction" by taking land from Dutch settlers who had bought it from Indians.[21]

Yates circulated his charges privately. Samuel Jones, who became a Loyalist and then a friend and confidant of both Governor George Clinton and Alexander Hamilton, read a copy and strongly disagreed with Yates. The Dutch colonists, Jones countered, had settled the land under the "Protection of the States General" of Holland, and they had either conquered Indians, making Dutch acquisitions the spoils of war, or had bought the land from them. Moreover, Jones continued, the land became part and parcel of the empire when England defeated the Dutch in battle in the 1660s. New York was a conquered territory, allowing Jones to dismiss the titles of Dutch settlers and enabling the Van Rensselaers to resuscitate a medieval lease practice. More pragmatically, Jones wondered why anyone worried about these issues at all. He considered Yates's proposal a mere exercise. Jones knew that New York "Courts will not now go into an Examination whether the People of Albany were wrongful dispossessed of their Lands or divested of their Privileges by the West India Company." The British government was not going to return land to Indians under any circumstances, nor was it ever going to transfer title to the descendants of Dutch settlers.[22]

John Lydius of Albany hoped for a better, but as unlikely, conclusion to his dispute with New York landlords. He claimed approximately one million acres of the New Hampshire Grants, but Robert Livingston Jr. held a grant from New York for 2.1 million acres in the same region. Governors of Massachusetts had also granted land there to settlers from their colony, assigning all but 180,000 acres of the land in question. In some instances, three people competed for the same plot, creating a patchwork of overlapping claims that all carried some kind of authoritative approval. The situation was so difficult that officials worried lawless bandits would take matters into their own hands. Their fears soon blossomed horribly when competitors began driving off opponents before officials could announce a decision.[23] Still, few of these bandits would be able to muster the power that backed Lydius or Livingston, who were most likely to win title. Both men wanted to make money from the land. While Lydius hoped to divide it for sale to prospective farmers, Livingston wanted to rent it to tenants.[24]

To push the case to trial as quickly as possible, New York officials charged Lydius with trespass in 1763. Before a New York court, Lydius attested that he held the original deed to the land from the Mohawks and that the government of Massachusetts had validated his claim. But, as Attorney General John Tabor Kempe pointed out, Lydius was hardly a man to be trusted. His reputation with Indians and whites was notorious. Indeed, some Indians widely regarded Lydius as a "Devil" who got Indians drunk and swindled them out of their land.[25] For the New York court the case was simple. The court declared the crown to be the original possessor of all colonial land, even land claimed by indigenous people, and ruled that only deeds that originated from the crown or its representatives could be legitimate. Lydius failed that test and therefore lost the case.[26]

Like Beby and the Stockbridge Indians, Lydius found wide support among various groups of insurgents, business partners, and people outside the ruling, landed elite. Thomas Young had been, or became, all three when he championed Lydius's fight outside the court. Young, who later became an outspoken critic of Parliament during the imperial crisis and helped draft the radical Pennsylvania Constitution of 1776, had invested in some of Lydius's speculative ventures and, thus, had a financial interest in the case as well. In his support of Lydius, Young invoked the increasingly popular plebeian ideals that tied farmers to the land and that linked political power and independence to a vision of landownership composed in equal parts of title, labor, and occupancy. He insisted, "it is a maxim in law, that the possessor's title is ever good till paramounted by a better." According to Young, Lydius owned the land legally because he had bought it from the Indians and the Massachusetts government had validated the deal in the name of the crown. When New York landlords countered that the king had made all Indians British subjects in 1736, making Indians' land the crown's domain, Young warned that if they ripped "*Indian* Titles to pieces" they may as well "tear the country to pieces." He knew, as did landlords and colonial officials, that most property owners based their claims on deeds derived from Indians. Young also chastised landlords, including Livingston, for relying on the "industry" of others to improve the land and make it more valuable. That tactic kept farmers from providing for their households and restricted their political autonomy. Like Yates before him, and Jefferson after him, Young knew that political independence and power depended on landownership, declaring that farmers had as much right as anyone to the "*Household* Gods of Englishmen," liberty and property. In the end, Young's reasoning carried little weight.[27]

PULLING DOWN HOUSES AND DESTROYING GRAIN

After this new round of legal and civil defeats, insurgents felt they were running out of options. In 1765 and 1766, they again took up arms to protect what they considered to be their property. In that respect, land rebels closely resembled contemporaneous Stamp Act protestors who published reams of opinions on the loss of their liberty and property, assaulted rumored stamp tax collectors, or both. Other protestors turned that political dispute into a critique of the increasing social and economic disparities that wracked the colonies. Rebels in cities throughout the colonies were taking up pens and weapons in political and social protest. For rioters in the countryside, however, the issue worth fighting for, and dying for, was land.[28]

Violence erupted in late 1765 and continued through June 1766 as Robert Noble led groups of insurgents as they tried to convince otherwise neutral tenants to join them. This was no easy decision for a tenant in the middle. If a tenant was daring, or just foolhardy, he might risk what he had to get what he desired. A tenant who sided with insurgents risked being persecuted by the landlords or being attacked by the British army and imprisoned. He faced possible eviction and the loss of the years of labor he and his family had spent improving the land. A leasehold was no freehold, but it was better than no land at all. Insurgents rarely gave tenants in the middle much time to decide. Bands of angry, yelling, and usually armed rioters filled undecided tenants' doorways and demanded answers immediately. If a tenant joined the rioters, he put his life and his family's welfare at risk. Hesitant tenants appeared antagonistic. And if a tenant remained loyal to the manor lord, the situation could turn ugly. In one instance, Peter Witbeck refused to join their cause. The rioters warned Witbeck that if he stayed on his leasehold any longer they would "pull down his House and destroy his Grain."[29]

Rioters revisited old enemies too. Robert Van Deusen had taken over Josiah Loomis's leasehold in the 1750s and faced angry rioters shortly afterward. Nearly ten years later, rioters targeted him again. They broke into his house, pulled him out by the hair, beat him, threw his family out, and then destroyed his house and all of his family's belongings. Sometimes, rioters confronted landlords directly. At one point, emboldened by recent success, rioters marched to Robert Livingston Jr.'s house and warned him that if he refused to meet their demands, they would demolish his house and kill him. Unlike Van Deusen, Livingston had plenty of support when he looked at the rioters from across the threshold of his house. He was afraid but not in imminent danger, so he ignored them.[30]

According to the rioters, they had refrained from violence for as long as they could. Joseph Van Gelden and Ebenezer Smith later stated that they were content to live peacefully on their farms, but they could find no peace. The Livingstons and New York officials badgered them so much that the "Numerous familys of small children" were "unable to Support themselves." "Their families," Van Gelden continued, were "in Danger of Perishing for want of Necessary Subsistence." Similarly, William Kellogg admitted that the rioters had been pushed into doing "some things which we ought to be sorry for." Kellogg, for one, had reached his limits. "It is true," he wrote, "That oppression will make a wise man mad."[31]

After watching his loyal tenants and friends such as the Livingstons endure these attacks for months, John Van Rensselaer of Claverack organized a posse to arrest Noble and to drive the rest of the rioters from the region. Van Rensselaer and Robert Livingston Jr. would have preferred that the British army defeat the rioters, but army officials refused to get involved until some blood was shed. So the manor lords sent out the posse. While they hoped that their posse would defeat the rioters, they also knew that if it failed, the skirmish would compel the army to restore the king's order. On 26 June 1766, Van Rensselaers and Livingstons headed a posse of approximately 130 men and marched to Robert Noble's house. Late in the afternoon, the posse confronted Noble and thirty others at a blockade the insurgents had built across the road. After Noble and Van Rensselaer exchanged heated words, Albany County sheriff Harmanus Schuyler pushed the top rail off the blockade and began to climb over. When Schuyler swung a leg over the fence, the rioters attacked him with clubs. He signaled for the posse to retaliate; his men fired into the rioters and drove them back to Noble's house. The rioters then picked up their muskets and shot back. The shooting lasted for the better part of an hour and left at least three rioters and one member of the posse dead and several others wounded: Noble was shot in the back; the sheriff's hat and wig were shot off; Robert Van Rensselaer's horse was killed underneath him; Henry Van Rensselaer was shot in the arm. The firing stopped when the posse broke for the woods. Walter Livingston tried to gather the posse for another attack, but the men refused and sulked home.[32]

With blood on his hands, on 27 June 1766, John Van Rensselaer asked for military help to quash the rebellion. Van Rensselaer complained that during recent uprisings the rioters had threatened order and good government. But his pleas rang of irony because he and several pro-landlord men—notably Robert Livingston Jr., Dirck Ten Broeck, Abraham Ten Broeck, Thomas Hun, and Walter Livingston—had all recently protested Parliament's attempts to usurp their liberties during the Stamp Act crisis. Some of these men had joined the crowd that had attacked Henry Van

Schaack, the rumored distributor of stamped paper, in Albany earlier that year. Army Captain John Montresor cynically noted that these Sons of Liberty were "of opinion no [one] is entitle[d] to Riot but themselves." The landlords saw no such irony. They were protecting their estates, and thus ultimately colonial order, from all comers.[33]

One month after the skirmish at Noble's farm, Jeremiah Van Rensselaer and Sheriff Harmanus Schuyler accompanied 250 British regulars on a rout of the rioters. While colonial officials and landlords sought to capture and prosecute the leaders of the riots, British troops harassed rural people regardless of their alliances. The troops stole livestock and hauled away all the valuables they could carry, terrifying nearly everyone they met and generating only fear and animosity in their wake. The troops then decimated Nobletown and Spencertown, sending the nearly two hundred families fleeing into the woods. By the first of August, British troops had arrested thirty-two rioters and had driven away the rest.[34]

British troops quashed the riots, but the disagreements that provoked insurgency in the first place remained unresolved. Colonial borders remained unclear, and as a result the boundaries of the estates were left largely undefined. Landlords mistakenly thought the disputes were over even though they still faced a Massachusetts government bent on taking their land. And Indians, squatters, and disgruntled tenants still haunted the hills and valleys of Rensselaerswyck and Livingston Manor. From the rioters' point of view, landlords had only kept their land by flexing muscle, but they had failed to invalidate the insurgents' claims. In fact, that landlords had to resort to such force weakened their arguments. Insurgents continued to believe that they were entitled to own the land because they lived and worked on it. Many people had died in the previous thirteen years, but little had changed: Insurgents still hungered for land in a world dominated by landlords.

The Livingstons quickly paid a price for such a show of force. In a crucial election in 1768, tenants voiced their discontent with their status, their landlords, and the recent use of British troops to quash the country rebellion. The Livingstons had long counted on the votes of their tenants to keep their assembly seats, and they had been incredibly successful for the first sixty-six years of the eighteenth century. They had won the seats every time. By the 1760s, the Livingstons faced stiff competition from the DeLanceys, a group of New York City merchants with some land claims in the valley. These two sides fought hard for the few seats because the seats could easily swing New York's assembly one way or the other. While the Livingstons depended on tenants' votes to keep one much needed seat, who else could tenants support? Any tenant who voted against his manor lord or agent could expect some kind of reaction from the Livingstons. Instead of voting and putting themselves at risk, in 1768 tenants simply stayed home, thereby undermining their landlord's power without confronting him. The DeLanceys' candidate won. Peter Livingston noted that

Justice Robert Livingston had lost his seat despite all the influence that "power could give him." Livingston lost again the next year, and he traced his loss directly to his tenants who refused to vote.[35]

Discontented tenants in the region reveled in Livingston's political defeat. William Moore, a twelve-year-old boy whose family lived in the area, acknowledged it in a poem. The poem reflected the sentiments of a discontented, landless rural populace that felt pressured by landlords to bow to their power. The poem reads:

> One night in my slumbers, I saw in a dream
> Judge Livingston's party contriving a scheme
> To set up great papers and give some great bounty
> For to be an assemblyman in Dutchess County.
> But Leonard [Van Kleek] and Derrick [Brinkerhoff] are both chosen men,
> The Livingstons won't get a vote to their ten,
> So pull down your papers, talk no more of bounty,
> You can't be assemblymen in Dutchess County.
> > Your printed relation
> > Wants confirmation
> Tho' signed by Judge Thomas' Hand
> > Your Writings are discreet
> > But in them there's deceit
> Not a vote would you get if it wasn't for your land.

As the poem suggests, insurgents refused to defer to the Livingstons any longer. Instead, they supported Dirck Brinkerhoff, a well-known rioter. It is, in fact, likely that Brinkerhoff received support from the DeLanceys because he was a rioter. While Brinkerhoff certainly benefited from the DeLanceys' support, voters knew that the former rioter would represent them in the assembly and that he would oppose landlords. These elections, and the land riots, combined to produce a growing strain of discontent for current rulers among the region's rural population that was separate from the anti-parliamentary sentiment expressed by Stamp Act protestors. These insurgents wanted to own the land they occupied and improved and to rule themselves. The king may have ignored them, and the army may have burned their houses, but rural insurgents spewed their venom at the landed rulers of New York.[36]

Although neither side resorted to such extreme violence during the next several years, dissidents refused to give up the dream of owning land. Again, Stockbridge Indians took a lead role. Soon after the rout of Nobletown and Spencertown, several Stockbridge Indians traveled to London with Daniel Nimham, a sachem of the Wappinger Indians from the southern Hudson Valley. Together, they intended to ask the king to review their dispute with New York landlords. In 1766, they met with the Earl of Shelbourne to discuss colonial and manorial boundaries. The earl, however, deferred any concrete decision on the matter until he spoke with the king. He promised to bring the matter to the king shortly and sent Nimham and his group back to New York with the promise that his answer would be right behind them. Shelbourne's response arrived months later and gravely disappointed the Indians. Like the king, Shelbourne thought that the matter was a local one and should be handled by New York's governor. The governor, Henry Moore, was no ally of the landlords, but he had no intentions of giving the land back to the Indians. When the Stockbridge learned that Moore sided with the landlords, they "began committing Disorders" around Livingston Manor and Claverack for a "second time." As they had before, groups of disgruntled squatters, tenants, and Indians attacked tenants loyal to the manor lords, beating some and turning others "out of Possession of their Houses."[37]

The violence did not reach the fever pitch of 1765 and 1766, but in the early 1770s, insurgents who lived on and near Livingston Manor and Rensselaerswyck again beseeched New York officials for title to the land on which they lived and labored. In one instance, petitioners complained that "Some Evil minded persons" were going to get a patent to the land they lived on and force them to live "under bondage" of tenancy. In another petition submitted in November 1772, the insurgents encapsulated their struggle for land and combined several of the themes expressed during the nearly twenty years of discontent. The petitioners accused the Van Rensselaers of stealing several hundred thousand acres from Indians by falsely interpreting and expanding their patent to Rensselaerswyck. According to the petitioners, the manor lord's claims could not "be more preposterous." Worse, the Van Rensselaers had left the land "Vacant and altogether Destitute of Inhabitants" for decades. The settlers and squatters, on the other hand, had made "great Improvements" to the land and made it valuable. "The Labour they Bestowed in Improving the lands," the petitioners continued, "will Recommend your Petitioners To Your Clemency and Favourable Considerations as in Some Measure Intitled to a Patent of Said Lands." This petition, however, met with the same response as the previous ones; it was rejected.[38]

THE GREEN MOUNTAINEERS

In February 1763, while Solomon Beby sued the Van Rensselaers, Lieutenant Governor Colden complained that a man who appeared to be "no better than a Pedlar" was selling land to thirty new townships north of New York in the New Hampshire Grants and near the Green Mountains. Disputes arose because John Lydius and plenty of New Yorkers, including Colden, claimed some of that same land. Colden had hoped to sell his land when land prices rose. What galled him was not simply that the "Pedlar" sold someone else's land but that he sold it at scandalously low prices, attracting dozens of settlers. Colden accused the "Pedlar" of selling land at low prices to subvert the crown's interests, making him a threat to both profit and political order.[39]

Colden's "Pedlar" was only a forerunner to a wave of migrants who set-tled the Green Mountain territory and New Hampshire. By early 1765, surveyors had mapped out more than 130 towns in the region, each on the New England model: six miles square with a town common in the center and the rest divided into 100- and 150-acre lots. People flocked to the towns from eastern New York and from western Connecticut and Massachusetts, seeing them as an alternative to the landlord-dominated Hudson Valley and as a real chance either to escape tenancy or to avoid it altogether. These settlers refuted the titles of New York landlords, who pre-ferred to make them tenants, and aligned themselves politically with whatever colonial power recognized their own titles; they favored Massa-chusetts's authority over New York's. In the fall of 1765, New York landowners tried to shoulder the settlers aside by declaring their New England titles invalid and by distributing eviction notices. In response, settlers in Pownal, Bennington, Shaftsbury, Arlington, Sunderland, Man-chester, and Danby appointed Samuel Robinson of Bennington and Jere-miah French of Manchester to represent them in these various suits.[40]

The cases made their way to New York courts, where most settlers shared the fate of James Breckenridge. By the late 1760s, Breckenridge had moved to the region and had staked out a farm. New Hampshire officials granted him a title for it. In 1769, George Clark and Peter DeLancey from New York tried to force Breckenridge off the land by suing him for tres-pass. They took the suit to a New York court, which, not surprisingly, de-clared Breckenridge's title null and concluded that all titles granted by colonial officials outside of New York were invalid. When Breckenridge was ordered off the land, he defied the court's decision and stayed. Other settlers whose claims were rejected by New York courts followed Brecken-ridge's lead and remained on their land too. Like Breckenridge, they re-jected any New York claims to the land and challenged anyone who had one. But if cases ended up in New York courts, the insurgents stood little chance of success. Like their Hudson Valley counterparts, Breckenridge and his followers soon resorted to violence to settle the dispute. John Wal-warth, for example, moved into the region to claim his land by virtue of his New York deed. The Bennington settlers would have none of it. In May 1771, Breckenridge and several of his neighbors confronted Walwarth and ordered him to move. When he refused, the crowd "dragged him from his land, beat and whipped him."[41]

Similar patterns played out after a small but staunch group of New Yorkers and New Englanders settled the region west of the Green Moun-tains around Bennington. They too had received titles from Massachu-setts, and they too rejected New York titles and New York's authority over them. They rapidly became thorns in the sides of New York landlords who also claimed the land. The settlers had moved to the northern reaches of the Hudson Valley to get freeholds and to rule themselves. They equated political participation and freedom with owning land.[42]

In the early 1770s, New York landlords and New York colonial officials no longer differentiated between the insurgents in the New Hampshire region led by Breckenridge and those called the Green Mountaineers. The officials decided to take more decisive measures against both. In the late spring of 1772, a New York sheriff led a posse to take control of the courthouse in what New Yorkers called Cumberland County, which was just west of the Green Mountains, but armed Green Mountaineers drove the posse back.[43] In June 1772, New York governor William Tryon prepared to lead British troops into the region to throw the insurgents off the land. The Green Mountaineers decried Tryon's methods as "illegal and unconstitutional" for violating the "laws, restrictions, regulations, and œconomy, both of God, and man." Worse, according to the Bennington people, the British troops used excessive force, firing on and "wounding innocent women and children" to drive squatters off the land. To avoid what seemed to be imminent and horrifying violence, the two sides brokered a deal in which they agreed that while the Bennington people could keep the land they lived on, New York landlords would get the rest.[44]

That accord crumbled almost immediately. In late 1772, a Bennington dissident outlined a distinct communalist vision of landownership and government that depended on the settlers' ownership of the land and on New York giving up all claims to the region. New Yorkers with interests in the region felt they had offered and given enough; they were loath to give in any further. The two sides went back and forth over the issue for the next three years and moved no closer to a settlement. Instead, both sides moved closer to extremes, where only a total victory was acceptable. By 1775, New Yorkers had abandoned all pretexts and resorted to prosecuting the Bennington people for debts. New Yorkers vowed to evict anyone who could not or would not pay, and they set up a court in Westminster just west of the Connecticut River to facilitate evictions. The Bennington people thought they were being prosecuted unfairly, and they urged the justice, Thomas Chandler, to delay the proceedings until after the next harvest. Chandler agreed, but more powerful New Yorkers insisted that he hear debt cases immediately. Whether the inhabitants planned on leaving or on paying off their debts remained uncertain, but when Chandler tried to open the court in early March, he found the entrance blocked by approximately eighty men armed with clubs and guns. He offered little resistance, and the rioters took over the courthouse.

The following day, Sheriff William Patterson of New York and a group of men attacked the rebels and took back the courthouse. Several rioters were wounded, and at least one died during the fighting. On 14 March, three hundred to four hundred rioters forced their way back into the courthouse, ordered the release of their neighbors, and put Patterson and his men in jail. The rebels then organized an inquest that found Patterson and others guilty of the murder of a rioter. After what he called the "Westminster Massacre," Ethan Allen built on this organized resistance to establish a new political entity that denounced the authority of New York and governed the Green Mountain territory. Like their riotous brethren on Rensselaerswyck and Livingston Manor, these insurgents directed their anger at New York landlords instead of British officials or British soldiers. They refused to be ruled any longer by anyone but themselves. Still, the question of who owned the land and who should rule the inhabitants remained unresolved through the Revolutionary War. Although the fight for land and for the allegiance of the men led by Ethan Allen shaped British and Revolutionary strategy, the Green Mountaineers' dream of becoming a separate political entity went unfulfilled until after the war.[45]

WHO WERE NOTORIOUS RIOTERS?

In 1757, colonial officials delivered an arrest warrant for Jonathon Darby at his farm. Dozens of insurgents were waiting and refused to give him up, sparking a violent clash. Less than a decade later, Sheriff Harmanus Schuyler claimed to have an arrest warrant that named Robert Noble in June 1766 when the sheriff and the landlords' posse broke down the fence that barred the road to the rioter's farm. One month after that, the British army captured thirty-two rioters when they destroyed Spencertown and Nobletown, but they sent nearly two hundred other families, almost six hundred people, scampering for safety in the nearby woods.

The landlords' tendency to prosecute only the leaders of the riots such as Darby and Noble makes it difficult to determine how many people rioted in the 1750s and 1760s. That trend pushed inhabitants toward either end of a far more complicated spectrum of choices. People who fought on one side or the other represent but two choices rural people made. Some people opposed landlordism but, for their own reasons, chose not to take up arms against landlords or colonial officials. Others supported landlords, officials, and order, but decided not to take up arms against their neighbors, family, and friends. The landlords' decision to prosecute only some members of the crowd clouds some of these differences of degrees among leaders, activists, and followers and supporters.

Landlords and colonial officials wanted to restore peace and order to the community without inciting future antagonisms and violence. Although hundreds of people participated in the riots, colonial records that name rioters list 146 people who became well known enough that a landlord or colonial official tagged them as notorious rioters. The group was quite diverse. Approximately half of the surnames of these rioters were of non-English origin. It included men of known origin, such as Michael Hallenbeck, a German tenant, and the Van Geldens, who were half-Dutch, half-Stockbridge Indians. The Riises, who were Welsh, were longtime tenants in the Hudson Valley; the Scottish McArthurs were most likely New England squatters who possibly became tenants after the Revolution.[46] While Jonathon Darby, Robert Noble, Levi Stockwell, John McArthur,

Josiah Loomis, Joseph Paine, John Van Gelden, and a handful of others stand out as the most notorious leaders of these riots, they led heterogeneous groups of people in crowds numbering, at the peak of the rioting, close to 250. John Montresor, a captain in the British army stationed in New York City and no friend of either landlords or rioters, noted that roughly 250 people rioted against the Livingstons and the Van Rensselaers in June and July 1766. That number may appear insignificant, but landlords such as Robert Livingston Jr. and John Van Rensselaer trembled in horror and indignation as roughly one-fifth to one-quarter of the population of these manors took up arms against them. As culturally diverse as the crowds were, rioting was a family affair. Families of Van Geldens, Clarks, and Bagleys all rioted for land. Indeed, 66 of the 146 known rioters, 45 percent, came from 22 families, and these families tended to live near each other near the eastern boundaries of Livingston Manor, Claverack, and Rensselaerswyck.[47]

The same records that reveal the rioters' names, however, make it difficult to determine how or if women participated in the riots. When Michael Hallenbeck defied Robert Livingston Jr.'s order to leave his farm, his wife and daughter remained in the farmhouse to maintain the family's claim to the land. He apparently figured that the manor lord was less likely to throw women out of their homes. But Livingston consistently ordered agents and sheriffs to evict everyone associated with rioters, including women and children. Although perhaps callous, Livingston was only protecting his land and his loyal tenants. On the other side of the dispute, Robert Van Deusen's wife had as much to fear from the crowd as her husband. She and their children were beaten by rioters who demanded that the family move off the farm. In June 1766, Lucy Spencer, Mary Johnson, and Mary Millard were all in or near Robert Noble's farmhouse when the landlord's posse opened fire on it. One month later, they, their husbands, and their children all fled for their lives from the approaching British army.[48]

One might conclude that women did not participate in the uprisings because they were not prosecuted for rioting. But women were more than bystanders. They did more than simply endure attacks by posses, rioters, and the British army. Hallenbeck's wife and daughter, for instance, stayed on the farm and confronted the landlord's agents when they came around looking for notorious rioters. Other women did not stand by when British soldiers raided their homes or killed their husbands, fathers, sons, or brothers. They participated in the disputes, incurring the anger of the landlords and soldiers. A more likely conclusion is that, although officials were unwilling to prosecute women, women took part in the disputes in various ways.

The diversity of the crowds demonstrates that the land riots on Livingston Manor and Rensselaerswyck in the late colonial period were more than just attempts by Yankee land grabbers and the Massachusetts General Court to take land from the Yorker inhabitants of the northern Hudson Valley. New Englanders were rapidly moving into the Hudson Valley in the last thirty years of the colonial period, to be sure, but they joined an already diverse rural population. By the time Robert Livingston Jr. tried to evict tenant Michael Hallenbeck in 1752, the rural Hudson Valley had become a complicated place inhabited by Stockbridge and Wappinger Indians, English, Scots, Welsh, Irish, and German settlers. Nor were the rioters merely squatters spurred to act by rival colonial powers. Of the 146 known rioters, 60, or 42 percent, were tenants on either Livingston Manor or Rensselaerswyck Manor (including Claverack) when they rioted.[49]

Tenant rioters joined squatters and Indians who put their lives and livelihoods at risk for the common goal of landownership when they attempted to replace landlordism with communities of freeholders. They did so either to escape or to avoid tenancy and to gain greater autonomy over what they produced. Property ownership, however, transcended mere economic concerns. Land rioters wanted to create a community of freeholders that they would govern. Power and status in their community, and in their households, depended on their relationship to the land on which they lived and labored. Their landlord opponents strove to preserve the manorial economy they and their families spent their lives creating. At the end of the colonial period, neither rioters nor landlords had defeated their opponents or had obtained their goals, setting the stage for land disputes and rioting during the Revolutionary period.

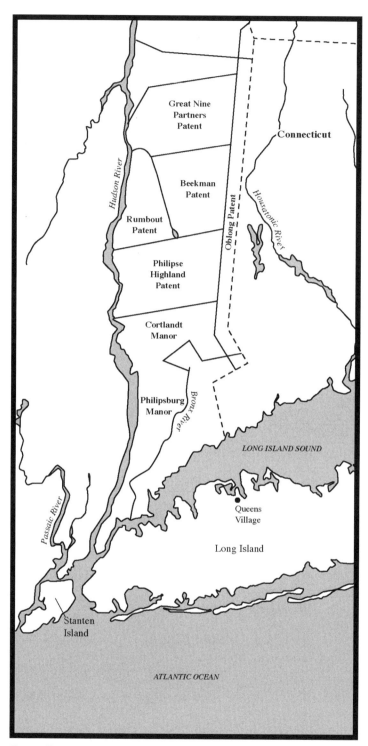

Great Estates of the Southern Hudson Valley, circa 1765

Chapter Three

DISCONTENT

IN THE SOUTHERN VALLEY

• In November 1765, disgruntled tenants gathered at Samuel Towner's tavern near Pawling, New York, to voice their disgust with the changes to their leases proposed by Beverly Robinson, Philip Philipse, and Roger Morris. William Prendergast, an Irish immigrant, stepped out of the crowd to lead the insurgents. On that cold November afternoon, he stood on the porch of the tavern and vowed to restore order to the community, to fight for "Justice," and to "relieve the oppressed." Between November and August 1766, Prendergast and the insurgents raided tenants who took over leaseholds of evicted insurgents and assailed anyone who collected evidence against the rioters. Although some loyal tenants came from outside the community, others had lived on the estate for years and incurred the ire of rioters by turning on their neighbors. Rioters usually tried to convince their neighbors to join them and harassed and assaulted the ones who refused. Insurgents also attacked colonial officials and threatened to burn New York City to the ground. By July of that year, the Philipses and colonial officials called on the British military to stop the rebellion. Later that month, British troops clashed with Prendergast and the rebels at King's Bridge near New York City and then chased the rebels back into the countryside, where the army made short work of the rioters. By August, the rebellion was effectively over, and Prendergast had surrendered. Within a few days, Prendergast was again fighting for his life, this time in a New York court, defending himself against charges of capital treason. Again, he lost.[1]

The riots in the southern Hudson Valley followed the same pattern as disputes in the northern region. Insurgents initially submitted petitions to get land. When that tactic failed, they turned to courts for justice, but there too insurgents were defeated. After failing to influence officials with petitions and after losing in court, insurgents began to argue that their labor and occupancy entitled them to own land. When these peaceful methods were again unsuccessful, insurgents ferociously attacked colonial officials, tenants loyal to the landlord, and property. Most of this fighting took place between rebel tenants and squatters on one side and the landless men and women who supported landlords—who again stood behind the scenes—on the other. Although these people shared common goals—the chance to provide food and shelter for their households and for the next generation, long-term stability on the land, and peace in their community—the cultural, political, and religious traditions they drew on influenced their choices. Fighting on one side or the other, however, represents only the extreme choices people made. Some rural people supported the insurgency but refused to participate in the riots. Others supported landlords but rejected shorter leases and refused to move onto farms of evicted rioters. Still others tried to stay out of the fracas entirely. Once landlords and colonial officials realized they and their landless supporters fell short of routing the rioters, they called on the British army to quash the riots, which it did. Although the insurgents were severely beaten, they refused to leave permanently, and those who left returned to the land within a few years.

Land disputes in the southern Hudson Valley differed from those in the north in two significant ways. First, contests over land in the southern valley were more exclusively New York affairs. Insurgent tenants, squatters, and Indians who lived on or near Livingston Manor and Rensselaerswyck were able to appeal to colonial officials outside of New York in their struggle for land. Disgruntled people in the south could not pit colonial forces against another. Second, Indians played a far more significant role in land disputes in the southern Hudson Valley. In fact, land disputes in the region erupted when Anglo-European landlords tried to take the Wappingers' land. The Philipses claimed land that the Wappingers had lived on for generations and had leased to Anglo-European tenants. Leasing land to white settlers helped the Wappingers maintain their claim of ownership, especially because they offered settlers very long leases. In the end, however, the results were the same. Landlords won, and Indians, tenants, and squatters lost. Yet the problems that sparked the rioting remained unresolved, setting the stage for future discontent.

THE WAPPINGERS AND THE PHILIPSES

Rural unrest in the southern part of the Hudson Valley broke out over disputes between the Philipses on one side and Wappinger Indians, tenants, and squatters on the other. By the mid-seventeenth century, the Philipses claimed approximately fifteen thousand acres in the southern Hudson Valley. In the 1690s, Adolph Philipse allegedly expanded his family's estate when he bought land from Jan Seabrandt and Lambert Dorlandt. Shortly afterward, he petitioned the governor for permission to expand his estate to the Connecticut border. In 1697, Governor Benjamin Fletcher granted Philipse a patent that included all this land to create an estate that contained approximately 205,000 acres. Even with this new patent, however, Philipse suspected that he might have a fragile claim to the land. So, in 1702, he arranged to buy some of it from Indians who may or may not have had the authority to sell it. When Adolph Philipse died in 1750, his nephew Frederick Philipse inherited the land. The new manor lord combined Adolph Philipse's acres, the Highland Patent, with his 156,000-acre estate, Philipsburg, in Westchester County. Frederick Philipse died one year later, and he willed his estate to his sons, Frederick and Philip, and his three daughters, Mary, Susannah, and Margaret (who died intestate). Frederick III inherited Philipsburg and became lord of the manor, while Philip, Mary, and Susannah received the Highland Patent. Beverly Robinson and Roger Morris married into the family, and each became administrator of his wife's portion of the estate.

By the mid-eighteenth century, the Wappinger Indians had lived on the land in question for generations. Early Dutch settlers described the Wappingers as "ordinary [in] stature, strong and broad shouldered," "light and nimble of foot, subtle in disposition," and "of few words." The Indians the Dutch encountered were divided as nations, and "differ[ed] even in language." Dutch traders in the region wanted to reap the harvest of pelts, and peaceful Indians and good relations facilitated that goal. In August 1645, the Dutch brokered a peace with the Wappingers and asked the Mohawks to oversee the proceedings. The peace thus bound all three and made each watch out for the other. It was, however, a tenuous agreement. In 1650, the Dutch feared that the English intended to attack Wappinger Indians and take their land. The alternative fear was that the English would turn the Wappingers against the Dutch. Either English victory would have given them the chance to divide New Netherland and to take control of the northern Hudson River valley. By the 1660s, the English made clear their desire to take New Netherland, and they began negotiating with the Wappingers for help to defeat the Dutch. The Wappingers offered to help if they could keep their traditional land under the new English regime. As the English secured power and as the Dutch receded, Wappingers looked for other European allies to force better terms from the English. But, by the end of the seventeenth century, the Dutch and the French had withdrawn enough that the Wappingers had to deal directly and almost exclusively with the English, a situation that dramatically changed the Indians' negotiating position for the remainder of the colonial period.[2]

The Wappinger Indians, like other native inhabitants of the region, believed that use of the land equaled ownership of it. To use the land and to preserve their claim to it, Wappingers leased it to Anglo-Europeans. Like Stockbridge Indians in the northern valley, Wappingers aided and even encouraged white settlement of the area as long as the white settlers stayed away from Indians' claims and avoided inhibiting their use of the land. Fostering white settlement also legitimated the Wappingers' claims in the prevailing English legal system and gave the Indians another way to reaffirm their aboriginal claims.

As in the northern Hudson Valley, landlords in the southern region posed a greater threat to Indian claims than did yeoman farmers or tenants.

In 1756, Morris, Robinson, and Philipse asserted that they owned the Wappingers' land by virtue of the deed Adolph Philipse had obtained from Dorlandt and Seabrandt. Philipse, Morris, and Robinson claimed what appeared, at least to them, to be empty land. At the very beginning of the Seven Years' War, many Wappinger men had joined the British to fight against the French, while the remainder of the Wappingers moved to stay with the Stockbridge Indians in the northern Hudson Valley. Thus, Philipse, Morris, and Robinson claimed the land during the relatively short period when no Wappingers were living on it. Once Philipse, Morris, and Robinson made their claim to the land, they began notifying the white inhabitants, some of whom had signed long leases with the Wappingers, that they either had to leave the land or had to sign new leases with the Philipses.[3]

In November 1763, thirteen disgruntled tenants petitioned the king for their land and for relief from the Philipses. They argued that the Philipses had so far "Discouraged people from Building Houses &c. and planting Orchards" on it, inhibiting the farmers' ability to seek the "tranquility and Liberty which properly Belongs" to them. The following year, twenty-four new signers joined the original thirteen in another appeal to the king. They charged that Robinson, Morris, and the Philipses had "disinherited and thrown [them] out of possession" of their farms, to which they held a "good and warrantable title by Lease Deed." This time, they singled out Robinson particularly for flatly refusing to acknowledge that any tenants held perpetual or life leases to the land. Robinson allegedly overlooked that many of the petitioners had already "Lived on it for 30 years: past and had manured and cultivated" it. If labor and occupancy on the land entitled them to own it, insurgents contended that landlords had not really lived on much of it and had never worked any of it themselves. Thus, petitioners held the best claim to the land.[4]

These claims and counterclaims inspired New York attorney general John Tabor Kempe to investigate the Wappingers' claims. His conclusions were bad news for the Wappingers. According to Kempe, Daniel Nimham, a leader of the tribe, asserted that the Wappingers held the land by virtue of a grant owned by a relative of Nimham's mother. Nimham's father had apparently sold some of the land in question, but the bulk of it had been reserved "for the Indians." Kempe, however, put more stock in what was familiar. He favored European, and particularly British, descriptions and titles over Indian deeds. The Indian names of the places confused him, leading him to surmise that the description of the land "now claimed by Daniel Nimham seems not to agree with the Description" of the land and titles under investigation. In 1765, a council headed by Lieutenant Governor Cadwallader Colden drew on Kempe's interpretation when it reviewed and rejected the Wappingers' petition for the land.[5]

While the council reviewed the Wappingers' claims, in 1764 and 1765, Beverly Robinson and Sheriff James Livingston began forcing people living on the land to sign new one- to three-year leases and evicted any tenant who refused. While Robinson certainly wanted to get rid of anyone who opposed him, suits of eviction served other purposes as well. Landlords such as Robinson used eviction to negate future claims to the property anyone might make by right of adverse possession, a situation in which a squatter might claim positive title after twenty-one years of occupancy if the owner failed to acknowledge the squatter's presence. To avoid these kinds of disputes, landlords needed to exercise a claim to the territory. Suits of eviction easily satisfied that obligation. Filing a suit did not necessarily mean that the landlord wanted the squatter off the land. On the contrary, landlords often pressed squatters to become tenants, and many squatters signed leases rather than give up the land they had already improved. The law as practiced in colonial New York favored continuous possession of property as an argument of right title. Robinson issued eviction notices to scare insurgents off the land, to be sure, but he also used them to compel squatters to become tenants and to stake out his claim to contested territory.[6]

Squatters and tenants of the Wappingers who chose to sign leases with Robinson found their security on the land greatly undermined. Many of them had already signed long leases with the Wappingers, some for 999 years, but Robinson demanded that they sign new leases that lasted one to three years and required tenants to pay rent with cash. These new lease conditions resembled the onerous Scottish-style leases landlords in New Jersey demanded tenants sign in the 1740s and 1750s. Tenants in New Jersey, like tenants everywhere, preferred long leases and preferred to pay rent with agricultural produce. Long leases gave tenants some security on the land, and cash was hard to come by in the countryside. Those who signed short leases could not plan for the future; the landlord might refuse to renew their leases. They also felt more pressure to pay rent after a bad harvest even if it meant that the household had to make do with less. Robinson put his profits ahead of the welfare of his tenants and imposed these leases on the people who lived on the Wappingers' land. Then he demanded that his own tenants sign them. Many tenants in both places simply refused. Robinson responded by evicting them to make room for tenants who would sign short leases. When the current occupants refused to move and resisted being evicted, Robinson and the local sheriff, who delivered eviction notices, sometimes burned them out.[7]

Disgruntled rural people balked at Robinson's oppressive and coercive lease restructuring. At first blush, these rebels fought for longer leases, not to rid themselves of landlords. In short order, however, they made their fight a struggle against landlordism and the Philipses. They fought for their claims and those of the Wappingers and opposed the claims of the Philipses and Robinson. In the fall of 1765, as they met at Samuel Towner's tavern to organize their protests, the rioters selected William Prendergast, Isaac Perry, Elisha Cole, and nine others to lead them in raids to "turn out all the People who had taken the short leases" and to replace them with rebels. Together, these men and their followers unleashed rebellion in the southern Hudson Valley.[8]

POOR MEN WERE ALWAYS OPPRESSED BY THE RICH

By the early eighteenth century, the Prendergasts had resided in Ireland for nearly seven hundred years. In 1170, Maurice de Prendergast traveled to Ireland to oversee English endeavors there, and he received land in the counties of Tipperary, Waterford, Wicklow, and Wexford for his services. The family grew into its role as gentry over the ensuing four hundred years but had apparently grown too distant from England for Henry VIII's taste. He charged them with threatening to take over Ireland and rendered the family nearly impotent by having several Prendergasts beheaded. The family, however, survived. Sir Thomas Prendergast (d. 1709) was a Roman Catholic and a Jacobite who suffered at the hands of Oliver Cromwell during the Protectorate and later supported William and Mary, for which he was rewarded with a barony in 1699. He was commissioned as a brigadier general and died at the Battle of Malplaquet. Sir Thomas's first son, Colonel Thomas Prendergast, Lord Gort (1698–1760), was a Protestant convert who was often called "Noisy Tom" for his anticlerical views. "Noisy Tom" and his wife, Mary (or Eunice), had four children—James, Richard, Jeffrey, and William.

William Prendergast was born in Watertown in County Kilkenny in 1727 and worked as a ship carpenter until the early 1750s when he immigrated to New York. Kilkenny became a focal point for anti-landlord rioting by groups such as the Whiteboys in the 1750s and 1760s, and Prendergast likely carried knowledge of them with him to New York. In 1755, only a few years after he landed in Dutchess County, Prendergast, a Protestant, married Mehetibal Wing. Wing was a Quaker who lived with her family in Quaker Hill, New York, near Pawling. She and her sister, Abigail, were the daughters of Jediah and Elizabeth Wing, and both had been born in Rhode Island.[9] Prendergast and Mehetibal Wing leased approximately 120 acres from the Philipses in the Highland Patent and paid £4 12s. in rent. They lived near Abigail Wing, who had married Nathan Hiller, also a Quaker from Rhode Island. Mehetibal had her first child when she was eighteen, in 1756, and the couple had five children by 1765 when William Prendergast announced at Towner's Tavern that insurgents wanted to "require Landlords" to give them "leases for three lives," and to pay the low "Rents which had been formerly fixed." Essentially, insurgents wanted to do away with landlords, to hold their land in fee simple, and to pay a quitrent for it. Elites sometimes paid a quitrent to the crown for their estates rather than provide military service for the king.[10]

It seems unlikely that the descendant of an aristocratic, titled Irish family would lead an uprising against landed men. In fact, gentlemen or lords sometimes led lower-class rebellions. The wellborn and well-connected Nathaniel Bacon led an uprising of lower-sort farmers in Virginia in 1676, and the Duke of Monmouth led, as Christopher Hill said, "the heirs of the radical revolutionaries of the Interregnum" in south Wales in 1685. While Prendergast was born to the breed, he lacked the title and land. He came to New York to acquire land. Unlike other European aristocrats, Irish lords passed their titles only to their oldest sons or, rarely, to inheriting daughters. Like Bacon, however, Prendergast had no intentions of leveling society. He had seen the deleterious affects of landlordism in the countryside of his homeland, and he hoped to escape that kind of oppression in New York. Thus, Prendergast and his fellow insurgents simply wished to escape the control of landed men in New York by owning the land they inhabited so they could govern themselves. To do that, Prendergast knew that insurgents had arrived at a critical moment: they had to act, and "the great Men such as the Atty Gen: & the Lawyers, should be pulled down."[11]

Rioters started attacking New York's landed hierarchy almost immediately by assaulting the most vulnerable representations of a landlord's authority. After the meeting at Towner's Tavern, on 21 November 1765, Samuel Munro Jr., whose father had helped the Stockbridge and Wappinger Indians in other disputes with European landlords, led about forty men to James Covey Jr.'s house. Covey had taken over the leasehold of an evicted insurgent. When Covey refused to open the door, the rioters broke in, grabbed Covey and his wife, and threw them out of the house. The rioters told the couple to leave and never to return. A short time later, Ebenezer Weed and Felix Holdridge were thrown out of their houses and farms and warned not to return. For the rest of the day, Munro Jr. and approximately two hundred others roamed the countryside, assaulting tenants and their families who had taken short leases. After driving out tenants such as Covey, Weed, and Holdridge, the rioters usually gave the farm back to the evicted tenants.[12]

In late spring 1766, colonial authorities tried to stop the attacks and managed to capture a few of the rioters. They took their prisoners to jail in New York City. When William Prendergast learned of the arrests, he proposed that the rioters free the prisoners "by Force" if necessary. He led approximately two hundred men to the edge of the city and threatened to burn it down unless the rioters were released. Such a threat could hardly be dismissed. A fire could completely destroy an eighteenth-century town, and on several occasions slaves and other disgruntled people spread rumors threatening to burn New York City. Prendergast also demanded that the rioters receive leases forever and that all stipulations other than rent be eliminated. Six representatives went into the city to negotiate the rioters' release, but Governor Henry Moore refused to meet them. Some of the leading men in the city supported the governor, but they were affiliated directly with the landlords being attacked. Prendergast also asked for help from the New York City Sons of Liberty, but some of the landlords and their agents, such as John Van Cortlandt, John Morin Scott, and Peter R. Livingston, were also prominent Sons of Liberty. Although the urban and rural insurgencies took place at the same time and involved similar assaults on public officials for attempting to undermine people's ability to provide for their households, the Sons of Liberty of New York City refused to help land rioters. Political opposition apparently did not equate to social upheaval for these Sons of Liberty. The governor then issued warrants for the arrest of the leaders of the rural crowds, and he requested that officials in Westchester and Dutchess counties organize a militia to restore order once and for all. The rioters set a few small fires around the city and fled.[13]

Beverly Robinson and the Philipses refused to be intimidated and took matters into their own hands. In May 1766, they sent out their agents to stop the insurrection. That month, five men approached Jonathon Hobby and his wife as they worked in the field. Jonathon Hobby recognized his opponents in the distance and ran to hide in the woods. The landlords' men instead attacked Hannah Hobby, who was pregnant, and ordered her to "go fetch her husband or Death should be at her Portion." They told her that officials or British troops would take her husband dead or alive. She refused to take them to her husband, fearing that they might kill him on the spot. The men pushed her to the ground and shoved her back down while they continued to question and berate her. She finally ran away when one of the men pointed a pistol at her and cocked it. Although the distance of time somewhat dulls the intensity of Hannah Hobby's terror when these men stood over her with clubs and guns at the ready, the beating was so vicious that three days later she miscarried her baby. A short time later, these same men similarly attacked John and Mary Gonong on their farm. They woke the couple in the middle of the night by pounding on the door and demanding that someone open it. Mary Gonong put the men off while her husband climbed out a window, but the men broke in and chased John Gonong out of the house, caught him, and beat him. They ordered the Gonongs to leave the leasehold within a few days, or they would return and burn the house down with them in it.[14]

Rioting in the southern Hudson Valley was not only a man's affair. Women such as Hannah Hobby and Mary Gonong worked alongside their husbands and cared for their leaseholds when their husbands, brothers, or fathers were away; they defended their stake in the land as vigorously as any man in the household. They confronted posses and rioters, and they stood up to those who wanted to throw them off the land. Rural residents often acted against anyone who violated community standards of behavior. Although colonial officials rarely named women as rioters, probably because they were reluctant to arrest them and throw them in jail, women offered their husbands advice, stood with them in court, pleaded with officials to free their male relatives, and signed petitions against New York landlords. They opposed landlordism and sought to own the land they had inhabited and had improved because these women, like the men they stood next to, strove to provide for their households.[15] Together, men and women in the countryside stood up to riotous tenants or to oppressive landlords and their agents to preserve the order and stability of their households. Tenant husbands and wives worked side by side in close harmony to make their households productive and to defend what they both regarded as family property. Most tenant households sat too close to the edge of subsistence to do otherwise. The success of their households depended on that coordinated effort.[16]

Relationships within tenant households in the Hudson Valley also depended on religion and cultural origins. Quakers stood out because of the greater equality and independence of women in the households. Wives acted independently from their husbands, giving women like Wing a genuine political identity in their communities. The law, however, inhibited women from participating in more formal political processes to the same extent as men. Women could not, for instance, vote or serve on petit juries. Many male heads of tenant households could do both, but their participation in politics was constrained too. If Quaker women stood out, so did German women for performing fieldwork often regarded as man's work by middling English settlers. Hannah Hobby's story, however, suggests that women on subsistence farms periodically worked in the fields regardless of ethnicity. Finally, Dutch law had determined that Dutch women had far greater control over property than their English counterparts. While tenants of Dutch heritage lived within a British legal system, they may not have followed the British pattern of gender relations. Tenant households acted as families even though officials treated the individuals within them differently.[17]

About one week after the attacks on the Hobbys and the Gonongs, William Prendergast led approximately sixty rioters to Robert Hughson's house either to evict Hughson or to compel him to join the rioters. Hughson, who had taken a short lease and lived in the house of an evicted rioter, was not home, but his wife was. When she refused to open the door, Prendergast pushed it open. He told her that if she and her husband did not leave the house immediately, the rioters would burn it down with them inside. Hughson and his wife rightly feared the rioters, who had already demonstrated their willingness to use violence. Hughson's wife was close to delivering their baby; she could not travel. Robert Hughson complained of the attack to his father, George Hughson, who retold the story to Dutchess County justice of the peace Samuel Peters. Peters obtained writs for the arrest and eviction of the rioters, but a crowd of rioters chased and caught Peters and George Hughson while they were attempting to deliver the writs. After securing their prisoners, the rioters carried them to Towner's Tavern to convince the men to destroy the writs and to compel them to swear an oath not to collect more evidence against the rioters. Both men refused. That night, 26 May, the rioters "railed" and beat both men outside the tavern for several hours, turning their protest against landlords into public, ritualized punishment.[18]

Violence dominated ritualized punishment, and that violence took many forms. In some cases, crowds punished their victims by making them ride a rail, which probably resembled rails used by crowds in Europe, consisting of either a rough-hewn log or of two wooden planks nailed together to form a trough. The victim was usually placed on the pointed side of the wooden "V." The rail may have also resembled the wooden horse used in Massachusetts to punish soldiers during the French and Indian War. The rural rioters, for their part, made Peters and Hughson ride rails on at least two occasions, on the night they were captured and again the next day on the way to a country courtroom. They may have been placed backwards on the rail, as some victims were, to enhance the humiliation. The victims also endured other kinds of violence. Many were beaten, whipped, dragged, or dunked in water. Peters and Hughson faced all of these assaults. Whatever form violence took, it had to be inflicted in front of, and administered by, the aggrieved members of the community.[19]

The rioters' attack on Peters and Hughson demonstrates how colonial New Yorkers invoked the European tradition of ritualized punishment to reprimand neighbors who violated the community's codes of behavior. Members of a community sometimes punished violators if the authorities had failed to do so or had taken the wrong side in a local dispute. Members of these crowds thought they had the right to replace local authorities and to mete out justice if necessary. In late February 1758, for instance, a crowd in Rye, New York, attacked bigamist Hezekiah Holdridge, rode him around town on a rail, beat him, and burned his hair. Holdridge had abandoned his wife and children in Rye and had then married another woman on Long Island. While Holdridge was attacked for sexual misconduct, land rioters attacked Peters and Hughson for putting their neighbors at risk and for serving men who had undermined the tenants' ability to provide for their households. Worse, from the rioters' perspective, Peters and Hughson had left rural people to a tenuous fate so rich men might get richer. For these transgressions, they needed to be punished.[20]

The day after the rioters attacked Peters and Hughson, they carried their victims on a rail to a nearby field to stand trial for crimes they committed against the rural community and specifically against the rioters. Once Hughson and Peters stood inside a makeshift dock in the meadow, twelve men gathered to decide the fates of the prisoners. Approximately two hundred rioters gathered around the courtroom, shouldering each other aside for a better look. Prendergast strode into the fenced-off court, brandished a cutlass, and warned Peters and Hughson what would happen to them if they refused to comply with the rioters' demands. He declared that the crowd would take them to "the first convenient Place of mud and water, and there duck them as long as we think proper, and from thence we would take them to a White Oak Tree, and there whip them as long as we think proper, and thence take them out of the county and there kick their Asses as long as we think fit." Prendergast then demanded that Peters and Hughson renounce the evidence they had gathered against the rioters and that they swear not to give evidence against the rioters in the future. Peters, for his part, remarked that Prendergast had an "Odd way of treating Men." Prendergast responded by yelling back, *"if the King was there he would serve him so for Kings had been bro't to by Mobs before now."* Hughson asserted that he would not be bound by an "oath not [to] take the Mobmen." Such an oath acted against the King's wishes and was therefore treason. Prendergast again invoked the power of crowds when he said to Hughson that "Mobs had overcome Kings before and why should not they overcome" them. In the face of this cutlass-wielding rioter, Peters and Hughson succumbed and swore their oaths. The rioters, however, refused to be denied their chance to inflict their brand of punishment on men who had so openly threatened their welfare. They grabbed Peters, dragged him through the mud and beat him, stopping only when he promised not to "take advantage of them for keeping him Custody." The rioters also beat Hughson before releasing him.[21]

William Prendergast infused the assault on Hughson and Peters with more volatile references to English and Irish history. Prendergast may have been alluding only to a stout tree against which the rioters might whip their antagonists, but his references to a "White Oak Tree" suggest other potentially rebellious meanings. In the 1760s, ship carpenters in Philadelphia called themselves "White Oaks" and marched in parades under the insignia of the white oak, often affixing a sprig of the tree to their coats or hats as a way to identify themselves with their craft and with their fellow ship carpenters. During the Stamp Act crisis, Philadelphia White Oaks protected Benjamin Franklin's house from rioters because he had organized laborers in the city into military organizations in the 1740s and 1750s.[22]

The White Oaks in the colonies were loosely arranged as an Irish organization and were related to anti-authoritarian groups such as the Whiteboys of Ireland and the Hearts of Oak in Ulster. Arthur Young described the Whiteboys as rural rioters from Kilkenny who reached the height of their popularity and power from the late 1750s through the 1770s. But anti-landlordism had characterized the Irish countryside for decades in the eighteenth century. The Whiteboys, like the Hearts of Oak, rebelled against the growing trend toward absentee landlordism and the increasing power of English landlords over Irish tenants. Young denounced the Whiteboys as threats to private property and British order and condemned them as "levellers." The execution of five Whiteboys in Watertown, Kilkenny, in 1762 invoked the folk belief that simple men historically had been oppressed by wealthy men. The Whiteboys asserted that they were the only ones "true to Sive and her children." They represented just one of the many rebellious groups that poor Irish farmers joined for protection against demanding English landlords.[23] That Prendergast knew of the Whiteboys, the White Oaks, and the Hearts of Oak is more than probable. He grew up in Kilkenny, where the Whiteboys enjoyed particular popularity, and he labored as a ship carpenter in Watertown, Ireland, before migrating to New York.[24]

In the same breath that Prendergast alluded to Whiteboys and Irish rural rebels, he invoked the shared memory of the English Civil War, and specifically that of the execution of Charles I in 1649. Some figures from the period of the English Civil War, such as the regicides and Oliver Cromwell, resurfaced as important figures for eighteenth-century Americans. While colonists differed in their opinions of the men responsible for the execution of Charles I, they disagreed hotly over their interpretations of Cromwell. Some denigrated Cromwell as the father of standing armies, and others rekindled in their folklore far more favorable images of him.[25]

When Prendergast proclaimed that "Mobs had overcome Kings before," he drew on the crowd's persistent memories of the English Civil War and the regicides. In doing so, he combined these folk traditions to remind his listeners of the power of crowds. Further, he created a rhetorical strategy that announced the seriousness of the rioters' endeavors by using historical allusions he knew needed no explanation. One member of the crowd that day probably understood Prendergast's references as well as anyone. Samuel Munro Jr., who had helped the Wappingers in their legal battles with the Philipses and had participated in the assault and trial of Peters and Hughson in May 1766, was the descendant of William Munro, a Scotsman who was captured by Cromwell at the Battle of Worcester and who was deported with other prisoners to Boston, where many were sold as indentured servants.[26]

Antagonists of the rioters played a similar game by summoning up images that reminded people of the implicit dangers of radical and revolutionary excesses. During the English Civil War, some English radicals called themselves "True Levellers" because they called for the abolition of base tenures and for the redistribution of land. After Cromwell seized power, he quickly forced them underground. Gerard Winstanley, the best known spokesman for the group, noted that as long as landlords controlled tenants in England, "or for one to give hire and for another to work for hire; this is to dishonour the work of creation."[27] As Alfred F. Young rightly notes, landlords and colonial officials in New York, like elite colonists elsewhere, used "a number of derogatory terms such as 'democratical,' or 'popular,' or 'leveller'" to disgrace rioters who wanted to redistribute land and, subsequently, political power.[28] Justice Robert R. Livingston knew that rural rebels wanted to take apart his family's estate and give the land to the people who lived on it. He pleaded with other landlords not to make any concessions to the rioters. If they did, he warned, landlords "must give up everything." In 1766, John Montresor remarked with some concern that "Levelling esteemed to be of service . . . having taken place already on the lands belonging to Mr Courtlandt at Westchester and in the Highlands" of the Philipse Highland Patent. He, for one, named William Prendergast as the chief of the "Country Levellers."[29]

Beverly Robinson and the Philipses refused to endure the insurgency of these "Country Levellers" any longer. In July 1766, they, like the Van Rensselaers and the Livingstons, appealed to the British army to defeat the rioters. Shortly thereafter, British troops encountered and skirmished with a small band of rioters near a bridge in Patterson, New York. Two British soldiers were wounded, and one later died, but the army routed the poorly armed rioters. The army trounced them so completely that the wives of the remaining rioters appealed to their husbands to see the situation for what it was. They knew they had been beaten, and they wanted to end the conflict with as little bloodshed as possible. These women persuaded many rioters to surrender and to plead for the governor's mercy. In fact, so many rioters surrendered that they swelled the local jails to overflowing, and officials had to move them to a nearby church. Prendergast did not surrender, but he was captured a short time later. In late July, Prendergast was taken under heavy guard to Poughkeepsie to stand "Tryal for Misdemeanours laid to his Charge." His arrest and removal excited many rural people throughout the eastern part of the southern Hudson Valley, and approximately 150 people threatened another general insurrection if he was not released. They positioned themselves near Quaker Hill, New York, and vowed to fight to the last man, but the British troops easily sent them on their way and regained control of the countryside.[30]

Once in irons, Prendergast never stood a chance. New York landlords ruled courts as completely as they dominated politics. Robert R. Livingston, who sat on the bench of the specially convened court of oyer and terminer that heard the case, was the cousin of the lord of Livingston Manor, and he operated part of his family's estate in Dutchess County where insurgents rioted. William Smith Jr. had married into the Livingston family. Although he worried that his "wife's connections with the Landlords rendered it improper that [he] should be one of the Judges," he stayed on the bench after the governor pressured him to do so. Another member of the court, John Morin Scott, was simultaneously representing the Philipses in their ongoing struggle with the Wappinger Indians over the very land for which Prendergast rioted. Further, Scott was a leading member of the Sons of Liberty in New York City, which had refused to help the land rioters when they marched on the city in the spring. Edward Countryman correctly points out that the urban Sons of Liberty "operated in response to different problems and within different traditions" than did rural rioters.[31] Regardless, Scott's legal and personal interests tainted his judicial objectivity. Prendergast recognized the hypocrisy immediately and ruefully noted that "if opposition to Government was deemed Rebellion, no member of that Court were entitled to set upon his Tryal." Prendergast saw no allies in the jury box either. Tenants, for their part, could only sit on petit and grand juries if they satisfied colonial realty holdings, and few in the region met the requirements to sit on the grand jury that heard Prendergast's case.[32]

In his opening remarks, New York attorney general John Tabor Kempe explained that Prendergast was on trial for the capital offense of treason against the king for leading men into conflict against the British army. Moreover, Kempe accused Prendergast of inciting a widespread conspiracy against the crown. Prendergast had, after all, "associated with disaffected persons in other Counties." Additionally, Prendergast had illegally freed jailed rioters, assumed "regal power," disturbed "the peace of the province," and levied "war [against] the King."[33]

Prendergast defended himself with help from his wife, Mehetibal Wing, and she became a focal point in the trial. Her behavior "attracted the Notice of the Audience," and she "never failed to make every Remark that might tend to extenuate the Offence, and put [his] Conduct in the most favourable Point of View." Her attention to the details of the prosecution's case, her ability to refute it, her pleasing appearance, her solicitous manner, and her "affectionate Assiduity fill'd every Observer with a tender Concern." Her skill, in fact, prompted one of the King's attorneys to "make a Motion to move her out of Court, lest she might too much influence the Jury," but the justices denied the request. Despite Wing's powerful presence in court, Kempe easily proved his case. Prendergast had become a well-known folk hero in the countryside, and few doubted his leading role in the uprising. The testimony lasted three days, the jury returned a guilty verdict one day later, and the justices rendered their sentence twenty-four hours after that.[34]

The court gave Prendergast what it described as the "usual severe sentence for Treason." He was to be taken back "whence he came and from thence shall be drawn on a Hurdle to the Place of Execution, and then shall be hanged by the Neck, and then shall be cut down alive, and his Entrails and Privy members shall be cut from his Body, and shall be burned in his sight, and his Head shall be cut off." The court further ordered that Prendergast's mutilated body be quartered and disposed of at the "King's Pleasure." When he heard how the court proposed to execute him, Prendergast "fell like a slaughtered ox," uttering a cry that melted to tears "even those least susceptival of Compassion." However shocking the punishment, it was seldom actually administered in that form. The threat of the punishment was intended to deter future rioting but was far too brutal to be carried out in any but the most extreme circumstances without fear of inciting more riots. As a result, the justices fulfilled their ritual role as authorities in the community and recommended that the king mercifully review the prisoner's fate.[35]

When Mehetibal Wing heard the sentence, she ran out of the courtroom and allegedly borrowed her sister's prettiest dress and dashed seventy miles on horseback to New York City to appeal to the governor for the life of her condemned husband. Governor Moore agreed to her plea and ordered Prendergast's execution be delayed so the king could review the case. In the meantime, Sheriff James Livingston, who was charged with conducting the execution, proceeded with his plans, but he could not find anyone willing to help with the deed. By leading the riots, Prendergast had become enormously popular with the people in the countryside, and rebels who rioted after he was arrested did so in his name. During the trial, other rioters attempted to break him out of jail, but Prendergast convinced them that his escape would only incite more attacks on the rioters and their families. Men who might otherwise have helped with the execution refused the job this time because they feared reprisals from neighbors who backed Prendergast. In fact, Prendergast was so popular that even though the sheriff offered double and then triple the ordinary pay for executioners and promised to preserve their anonymity, no one stepped forward. In December 1766, King George III confirmed the ritual of the trial by granting Prendergast an official pardon. Prendergast returned to his farm in the Philipse Highland Patent, which he gained in fee simple in 1771. How he obtained the land, unfortunately, remains unclear.[36]

Prendergast's trial, his popularity, and the widespread uneasiness of the rural populace presented landlords and colonial officials with a dilemma. They needed to restore order without inciting more violence. First, they prosecuted only the leaders of the riots. Of the hundreds of rioters arrested, only sixty were ultimately tried for crimes related to the riots, and only Prendergast was charged with capital treason. Officials and landlords then exercised their power shrewdly during the trial. They initially reaffirmed their ultimate power over the community by sentencing Prendergast to suffer a horrible death they knew they could never peacefully carry out. By recommending that the king pardon him, however, they demonstrated the ultimate power of sparing the life of an enemy. While an outright pardon seems overly generous, landlords and royal officials may have shown mercy out of fear of making Prendergast a martyr for rioters in the future. His execution may well have inspired more violence, not less.[37]

The sheer size and diversity of the crowds may have intimidated landlords and officials. At the height of the rioting in the spring and summer of 1766, William Prendergast led a group of rioters that was as diverse as the group that rioted in the northern Hudson Valley. Prendergast was an Irish immigrant who married a Quaker. Wing's sister's husband, who joined Prendergast in the riots, was a New Englander. The Munros, who also stood against the Philipses, were Scotsmen, and they were joined by men of English origins such as James Secord, Elisha Cole, and Isaac Perry, and by the Dutch Micab Vail and Jacobus Gonsoles (alternately spelled Gunsalez). Together, these Quakers, Scots, Scots-Irish, and Dutch all joined in the rioting. These known rioters led hundreds of unnamed others in a widespread attempt to rid the community of landlordism. Roughly sixty rioters, for instance, ordered the Hughsons to leave their farm in May

1766. When Perry, Cole, and Prendergast harassed Samuel Peters and Robert Hughson a short time later, they were urged on by two hundred fellow rioters. The courts, however, had no desire to prosecute them all and quickly dismissed most of the rioters with promises of their future good behavior. They only prosecuted the most notorious rioters.[38]

Landlords and rioters fought over land and power, but their ideas of property and governance differed tremendously. Rioters knew that the political and economic system in New York was oppressive and that elites used the political system to keep or to render tenants landless. Landed elites in New York used their political power to control economic wealth, and they used their economic wealth to attain greater political control. When they attacked the owners and validity of great estates in the Hudson Valley, insurgents were also trying to wrest away some political and social power and to establish a more permanent hold on land in their community. The rioters particularly described their community in stark and uncompromising language. Prendergast noticed that it was hard that his followers were "not allowed to have *any property*." By the time he led rioters in 1765 and 1766, they could only get property by bringing down landlords. Only then could they eradicate tenancy once and for all. Moss Kent noticed that the rioters often had "equitable title" to land, but that these claims "could not be defended in a Course of Law because they were poor." "Poor men," Kent complained, summing up the problem succinctly, "were always oppressed by the rich."[39]

CLAIMING THE LAND OF THEIR ANCESTORS

While the rebellion of 1765–66 raged throughout the countryside around them, the Wappinger Indians renewed their legal disputes over land with the Philipses. By the summer of 1765, the Indians, and specifically Daniel Nimham, knew they would not get a fair analysis of the dispute from New York authorities, so they traveled to England to ask the king's council to review the problem. In their plea for help, Nimham combined the Wappingers' claims to land with those of the Stockbridge Indians. The Philipses claimed the Wappingers' land in the southern Hudson Valley, while the Livingstons and the Van Rensselaers claimed some of the Stockbridges' land in the northern part of the valley. The king, however, had referred both disputes to New York governor Henry Moore. He and his council—Daniel Horsmandon, William Smith Jr., John Watts, Oliver DeLancey, Charles Apthorp, and Joseph Reed—heard arguments from both sides. Roger Morris usually sat on the council, but he vacated his seat during the hearing because the case concerned land he administered. The dispute again focused on who had the best claim to the land. The Philipses were represented by John Morin Scott and James Duane, who argued that Adolph Philipse bought the land in question from Seabrandt and Lambert.[40]

Two men opposed the Philipses' team of lawyers. As sachem, Daniel Nimham represented the Wappingers' interests. Samuel Munro Sr. joined him. Munro was from Connecticut and had leased land from the Wappingers, but the Philipses had thrown him off the land shortly after the Wappingers moved at the beginning of the French and Indian War. Munro thought his deal with the Wappingers was legitimate, and he refused to take a new lease from the Philipses, so they evicted him. Nimham and three other Wappingers awarded Munro power of attorney so he could act for them. When the case began, the Wappinger Indian and white settler faced the landlord together. Although Nimham represented the Wappingers and Munro stood for the squatters and tenants, they shared a common interest and goal that transcended their ethnic and racial differences. They wanted land.[41]

To defend the Wappingers' claims, Nimham combined Indian and European perceptions of what entitled people to possess property. He declared that the Wappingers "Claimed the Lands in Controversy under their Ancestors, in whom was the native Right." The deed on which the Philipses based their claim only named a few members of the tribe, but, Nimham continued, one or two Indians could not sell the tribe's land. Nimham expanded his argument, asserting that the Wappingers had supervised the land for decades. As a result, the Wappingers deserved to own the land because they had lived on it for generations, because they had cared for it, and because they had allowed others to improve it long before the Philipses claimed it. Several witnesses reiterated Nimham's points. Peter Anjuvine, who had rioted against the Philipses, testified that the "said Patented Lands had become in a Considerable Measure Setled, before the Indians" left the land to fight with the British in 1756. "The Tenants who there Setled," Anjuvine continued, "either paid their annual acknowledgements to said Indians for the Use of their Farms, or in some more general way, made their agreements with them therefor." Moreover, the Philipses had proved reluctant to give permission to others to improve the land, suggesting that the Philipses knew they did not own it. Last, and here Anjuvine and Nimham hoped to finally undermine the Philipses' case, Adolph Philipse had apparently confided to one of his tenants that he "never purchased that Land of the Indians."[42]

While Nimham argued that crown titles legitimated the Wappingers' aboriginal claims, the Philipses' attorneys insisted that crown titles meant the Wappingers had given up their ancestral claims. The Wappingers had sold the land, had not improved it, and had left the region because they knew they did not own the land. On the first point, Beverly Robinson produced the deed dated 1702 that Adolph Philipse had apparently manufactured to validate his claims. During the proceedings, Robinson pulled the deed from his breast pocket and read it aloud; Munro looked at the deed briefly before Robinson secreted it away. It was never entered into evidence, and Robinson did not let anyone else look at it. On the second and third points, John Morin Scott and James Duane noted that the Wappingers gave up the land when they sold it, the deed was proof of the sale, and the Wappingers had abandoned the land "to the Crown of Great Britain" in the late 1750s. They overlooked the fact that the Wappingers were off fighting for the British.[43] Lieutenant Governor Cadwallader Colden specifically investigated the ambiguities of the 1702 deed by asking an older member of the Wappingers if he knew the names of the Indians listed on it. The man recognized the names but added that the men did not have the authority to sell land that belonged to the whole tribe. Another Wappinger concurred, testifying that Adolph Philipse understood that the whole tribe needed to agree to sell the land. Thus, even if the deed was real, the Philipses had brokered an illegitimate deal. Because the whole tribe had never agreed to sell the land, the deal was never completed and the deed was fraudulent.[44]

That point hardly mattered to John Morin Scott. He suggested a more pressing reason to decide favorably for the Philipses. Besides providing a basis on which Indians throughout New York could claim land, a decision for the Wappingers would have strengthened the positions of insurgents who argued that they had bought land from the Indians and had improved it. Scott urged the governor's council to reassert the authority of titles from the crown as the primary basis for property claims to protect the landholdings of New York landlords and to preserve New York's political and social hierarchy. Scott advised the council that admitting that the Wappingers legitimately possessed the land because they were the primary occupants of the land "will be of a Dangerous Tendency." "'Twill open a Door to the greatest Mischiefs," he continued, "inasmuch as a great part of the Lands in the Province are supposed to lied under much of the same Scituation."[45]

The resolution of the case reveals that it was really over before it started. Officials denounced the Wappingers' claims and denied insurgents any greater political power. At one point early in the trial, an exasperated Cadwallader Colden had heard enough and "told the Indians to go home." He had heard the Wappingers' arguments before and disagreed, and they had failed to improve their case enough to make Colden change his mind. Governor Henry Moore and the others of the council agreed and determined that the "Indians now Living of the Wappinger Tribe, have no Right, Title or Claim to the Lands granted aforesaid by Letters Patent to the said Adolph Philipse." In their eyes, the deed of 1702 was valid. A few days later, Munro paid the price for his persistent opposition to landlordism. New York officials arrested him for rioting and threw him in jail where he sat, uncharged, for over a year.

Nimham refused to give up his fight. In 1767, he and a group of Wappinger and Stockbridge Indians traveled to London to present their case to the king, but the king's advisors referred them back to Henry Moore and his unsympathetic council. In the end, after years of dispute and upheaval, the governor's council put the issue to rest by dismissing the case and ordering the Indians and their tenants either to leave the territory or to submit to the proprietary authority of the Philipses.[46]

The dispute between the Wappingers and the Philipses starkly reveals that conflicts over land were also disputes over what entitled people to own land. The Wappingers based their more communal notion of property ownership on the understanding that all members of the group had a stake in the tribe's land. One or two members of the tribe could not speak for the entire group. At the same time, the Wappingers clearly wanted to make money from the land by either renting it to or selling it to European farmers. In that way, the Wappingers, like the Stockbridge Indians to the north, facilitated white settlement of the region. The Wappingers and the white settlers made occupancy and labor on the land as important to ownership as title. The Philipses, however, envisioned a different kind of rural society. They thought they should own the land alone, and, while they endorsed white settlement of the region, they wanted all migrants to the region to become their tenants. Tenants could stay as long as they acknowledged the Philipses' authority over the land. That they helped tenants settle and farm the land supplemented the Philipses' title to the land but did not supplant it.[47]

In the southern Hudson Valley, violence waned considerably after Prendergast's trial and after the Wappingers lost their case in 1767. Some insurgents on Philipsburg may have been intimidated by the threat of Prendergast's execution. Still others may have fled the Hudson Valley and then stayed away. In the northern Hudson Valley, on the other hand, disgruntled rural people stood on the brink of violence again. Insurgency began again on Livingston Manor and Rensselaerswyck precisely because insurgents returned to their farms in late 1766 and 1767. That said, land rioters in the southern valley, like their northern brethren, had unleashed a powerful strain of anti-authoritarianism that paralleled and sometimes conflicted with the discontent that marked cities during the imperial crisis. They infused their agenda with the increasingly popular notion that people in the countryside were entitled to own the land on which they lived and worked. Furthermore, they had resurrected folk traditions that were steeped in anti-landlordism and anti-authoritarianism. Within a few short years, these rioters would combine their familiar language and traditions with new rhetoric to reshape their society from below.

Chapter Four

LAND AND THE

AMERICAN REVOLUTION

•   In January 1776, forty-seven residents of Rhinebeck near Livingston Manor signed a "List of the Kings true" subjects in which they pledged their support for Britain. Just over half of the men who signed the list, twenty-seven, either were tenants or had the same surname as tenants. These twenty-seven men were approximately one-fifth of the local tenant population during the Revolution. Although Revolutionaries were unaware of the farmers' oath, they learned of farmers' reluctance to join their cause and decided to force them to stand against the king. Six months later, the local committee of correspondence "cald there menite men to gether from all parts to compel" the farmers in Rhinebeck to "disclaim and renounce all allegiances to the King and crown of great britain" and to help establish "liberty and Independency of the said states in opposition to the arbitrary claims, wiked usurpations and hostile invasions of the king and parliament." The farmers who signed the Revolutionaries' oath did so more because the local committee of correspondence "used and punished" those who refused to sign than because they agreed with it. They "thought it best to sine for we could see no way to ascape for if we hat not [signed] we would constaintly been ruined." That said, charges of coercion were best made privately perhaps to allow these men to dodge responsibility or blame in the future. Just a few days later, however, the nine Reicharts who had signed the "List of the Kings true" subjects, and who presumably had signed the Revolutionaries' Association Oath, signed another oath in which they professed their loyalty to the king. These tenants and their families pledged this second oath in secrecy to avoid the wrath of Revolutionary officials.[1]

These farmers' actions illustrate the hierarchy of choices open to inhabitants of the Hudson Valley during the American Revolution. While landownership remained an important goal, war thrust basic survival to the top of everyone's list of objectives. Most inhabitants of the valley tried to remain alive by staying out of war amidst political and military conditions that required people to make decisions that put them at risk. The British army and Revolutionary troops rumbled through or near the Hudson Valley several times in the first few years of the war, and neither mili-

tary group tolerated indecision or neutrality. Both armies supported themselves in part by plundering the belongings of enemies and neutrals, forcing many inhabitants to make a stand to protect their freeholds, leaseholds, goods, and families. Tenants and freeholders in the valley made
choices that resembled those of the farmers in Rhinebeck. They swore allegiance to one side or the other, and sometimes to both, to shield themselves from physical harm and to protect their farms in case either army
won control of the area. But they were playing a dangerous game. If they
declared their political loyalties prematurely, they risked losing everything
to the other side.

Historians who have studied the Revolutionary War in the Hudson Valley have focused on this kind of tenant participation. Staughton Lynd, on
one side, contends that most tenants opposed landlords in the hopes of
getting land; Philip Ranlet, on the other, insists that "most likely, few of
the tenants were really Tories." Both versions have difficulties. They tend
to conflate disgruntled tenants with loyalism in the northern Hudson Valley, but these groups were not always connected. Ranlet also perpetuates
the idea that New Englanders instigated land riots in the northern Hudson
Valley and that they rekindled rural discontent during the Revolution. But
New Englanders who attacked tenancy and landlordism during the Revolutionary War, like discontented tenants, hoped to replace manors in the
Hudson Valley with a community of yeoman farmers who governed
themselves free from the constraints of landlords and British imperial
rulers.[2] The portrait of the Hudson Valley during the Revolutionary War,
however, cannot be painted in broad strokes. Valley residents based complex political choices on their desire to survive the war, to join the winning side, and to keep what property they had. If possible, they hoped to
expand their claims or to gain a freehold. And they often made their decisions under great duress. Armies from both sides pressured tenants to
join them, and tenants usually retaliated by joining neither side. When
armies refused to take no for an answer, people on the ground often
based their decisions on which side they thought was most likely to let
them keep, or get, land.

As it did nearly everywhere else in British North America, the Revolution divided the inhabitants of the rural Hudson Valley. In Westchester
County just north of New York City, the Revolutionary War spiraled into a
brutal civil war that ravaged the countryside, and many of the inhabitants
simply hoped to survive the war by staying out of it. In Poughkeepsie, a
short distance away, roughly 50 percent of the people openly opposed the
Revolutionary cause, but the rest split between supporting the Revolution
and staying neutral. On Livingston Manor and Rensselaerswyck, tenants
utilized several strategies to stay alive and on their farms. Some tenants
staunchly defended their farms and families against anyone who put
them at risk. Others tried to take advantage of Revolutionary conditions
to gain land and political power. When they could muster enough support

to bolster their shaken confidence, militant rebels pushed for change, but they resorted to outright violence against landlord Revolutionaries only after they had exhausted all other options. Violence was almost always the last resort. Most tenants in the northern Hudson Valley preferred to avoid military conflict entirely, and, if they took up arms at all, many did not stay in arms for long. Finally, some inhabitants of the northern Hudson Valley actively supported Ethan Allen, who fought as much for Vermont's independence from New York as he did for colonial independence from Britain.[3]

In these cases, some disgruntled people made their deep-rooted disputes with landlords part of the Revolutionary movement. They infused their desire for land and their growing dissatisfaction with their rulers into the broader political contest with Britain. By using the war to meet their aims and by invoking Revolutionary rhetoric to voice their goals, they made their specific ambitions part of the more general goals of the Revolutionary War. In the process, they changed the meaning of the Revolution, and of their land riots, forever.[4]

TENANTS AND REVOLUTION IN THE SOUTHERN HUDSON VALLEY

In general, landlords in the southern Hudson Valley became Loyalists. That decision cost them their estates. Beverly Robinson, Frederick Philipse, James DeLancey, and Roger Morris all joined the crown early in the war, and all lost their property. Most of their tenants, on the other hand, preferred to remain out of harm's way during the war as official and unofficial armies marched through the region nearly continuously from 1776 through 1782. The British and Revolutionary forces refused to let anyone stay neutral and tried vigorously to convince rural people in the region to join them, turning the Revolution in the southern Hudson Valley into a bloody civil war.[5]

Revolutionary conflict started in the southern Hudson Valley soon after the fighting at Lexington and Concord. Almost immediately, Revolutionaries and Loyalists in the region started tallying their supporters. Neither side, however, could win over the rural populace completely and quickly decided to settle for less-than-complete support. In late April 1775, Revolutionary leaders in Westchester County noted an astonishing rush of people joining the fight against the British. Just a few days later, leaders of the county met to organize a local committee to oversee Revolutionary activities and to select representatives for an upcoming meeting of the Provincial Congress. Despite the flush of Revolutionary fervor, so many people stayed away that the local committee decided to ferret out anyone who had not announced his or her allegiance to the Revolution and demanded that everyone sign association oaths pledging their support for the cause.[6]

Administering an association oath was a public ritual designed as much to evoke loyalty to the Revolution as it was staged to compel others to join. Signers pledged to join an economic boycott of British goods, to abide by the authority of local committees of correspondence and safety, and to support the war in whatever other ways they could. Thus, the ritual was a moment for people to choose sides, making it fraught with peril. Signing or not signing association oaths was dangerous because the signers' choices were revealed publicly. Boycotters often persecuted people not on the lists as potential, or likely, friends of the British and barred them from buying or selling goods from boycott supporters. For the British, the lists provided the names of their opponents.

These strong-arm tactics produced unexpected results. Store owners and merchants found themselves in dire straits when the army they supported left or fled. When either army left an area, its supporters had to endure the wrath of the enemy. A number of Revolutionary officials and militiamen, for instance, demanded that Francis Pemart store goods for the army and thus forced him to choose sides against his will. Alone, worried about his business, and in fear that his family would pay the price of his bad choices, there was little he could do. Soon after, British soldiers drove Revolutionary forces out of the area, leaving Pemart without protection. British soldiers confronted Pemart, accused him of storing supplies for the Continental army, and sacked his store. Rather than put his store, his life, and his family's welfare in jeopardy again, Pemart joined the British. Others made their choices under similarly challenging circumstances but decided the Revolutionaries were more powerful.[7]

Loyalists likewise met with varying success. After Frederick Philipse and Beverly Robinson joined the British, their first task was to convince their tenants to join them. They had mixed results. The differences suggest that living conditions, security on the land, and exploitative relationships influenced tenants' decisions more than ethnicity or politics. In April 1775, Philipse asked the inhabitants of his estate to sign the "Protest of Inhabitants and Freeholders" to oppose the calling of the Second Continental Congress. The tenants who joined Philipse generally paid low rent and had probably grown secure on their leaseholds even if they were not well-off. Indeed, security on the land may have mattered more to poorer tenants on his estate. They lived closer to the edge of poverty, hunger, and despair than did their better-off neighbors. Risk of any kind terrified all tenants because it threatened consistent production, but it particularly threatened those tenants on the brink of despair. Philipse's request required tenants to take a risk, and most did so grudgingly if at all. Only seventy-six tenants from Philipse's estate, roughly 27 percent, joined him with the British. The rest either do not appear in records for either side or joined both sides.

Robinson fared even worse. He had riled his tenants to violence in the 1760s by restructuring their leases and forcing tenants who had held long leases to take short ones. Worse, he then raised rents, and he consistently charged interest on the debts his tenants owed him. Poorer tenants on his land could not live for long under changing lease conditions, and they certainly could not save enough to buy a freehold if Robinson constantly raised their rents. Middling tenants bitterly knew that higher rents were always coming and that they might not be able to afford them the next time. All of this combined to antagonize his tenants long before Robinson made any choices regarding the Revolution. Not surprisingly, few tenants forgot his oppressive behavior, and fewer still seemed willing to pay him any allegiance during the Revolution. Only 19 of Robinson's 146 tenants, 13 percent, joined him as Loyalists. In contrast, nearly one-third of the tenants on Cortlandt Manor, or 60 of 180, joined the British army. They may have joined the British to snub Pierre Van Cortlandt, who became a leading Revolutionary early in the crisis, but their precise reasoning remains a mystery.[8]

In general, only men could decide to join one army or the other, and their decisions dramatically affected the families they left behind. When men left to fight, they left their families to endure the depredations that rendered most inhabitants, as Sung Bok Kim rightly notes, "confused and oblivious to the moral issues of the Revolution."[9] Continental and British forces alike ravaged the southern valley, throwing the remaining families into a state of desolation and apathy from which they did not emerge until after the war. Soldiers from both sides took cows, sheep, food, clothes, ammunition and guns, and blankets from locals to support the war effort. The victims must have considered it all a plundering assault on their livelihood. Each time an army took their goods, farmers were thrust closer to the precipice of despair and starvation.

By 1777, two years of raiding began to take its toll on the local population. Timothy Dwight ministered the Continental army in Westchester County that year and witnessed the people's growing desperation firsthand. His account provides an agonizing reminder of the pain of the Revolutionary War, and of war for every community that endures it. Dwight described the inhabitants as beaten, "obsequious," and "subservient." "Their furniture," he noted, was "plundered or broken to pieces." The cattle had been taken and their crops reaped. "Weeds and wild grass" grew where wheat had filled the land before the war. "The world was motionless and silent," he continued, "except when one of these unhappy people ventured upon a rare and lonely excursion to the house of a neighbor, no less unhappy; or a scouting party, traversing the country in quest of enemies, alarmed the inhabitants with expectations of new injuries and sufferings." The armies of war had destroyed people's houses, crushed their futures, and turned the once productive region into a wasteland.[10]

In the face of such hardships, and the promise of greater ruin for joining the wrong side, most tenants tried to remain neutral. Nearly half of Philipse's tenants, and two-thirds of Robinson's, did not fight for either side during the Revolution. Even on Cortlandt Manor, where one-third of the tenants joined the British, approximately one-third stayed out of the fighting altogether. Why some men refused to fight remains somewhat of a mystery. Perhaps they were too old or too ill to fight, but others wished only to remain alive and to provide for their families in the grim hope that they could outlive the war and, possibly, get the land they lived on and improved.[11]

These grim circumstances inspired apathy in the inhabitants of the countryside. In 1777, Revolutionaries tried to slow spreading indifference and creeping opposition by enacting a state constitution that offered farmers a bit more say in government. One observer noted that a state constitution favorable to the rural populace, and especially to tenants, might "give the finishing strokes to pacify all opposition" to the Revolutionary cause. The constitution of 1777, however, fell short of the tenants' ideals. It did not address landlordism in any substantive sense, and it did not directly tackle tenants' basic political concerns. While the constitution reduced property qualifications for voting, it retained higher property qualifications for holding office, giving many people the vote for the first time but keeping many rural people out of political office. Voting, however, meant little if tenants continued to cast their votes publicly and in front of agents of their landlords, and the new constitution made no provisions for secret ballots. Even that basic goal remained unfulfilled.[12]

The new state constitution frustrated elite Revolutionaries too. The Livingstons, for instance, had been guaranteed a seat in the assembly since 1714, but the new constitution revoked it. Thereafter, the Livingstons would have to stand for election in Dutchess County, and they were outraged at such an affront to their name, status, and power. Walter Livingston argued that the seat was his family's *"unalienable right"* and should not fall prey to changing political attitudes. His Jeffersonian language notwithstanding, Livingston and his kin worried that uncontrolled tenant voters might take advantage of their new political power and elect anti-landlord candidates. He was right. Tenant voters, some voting for the first time, took the opportunity to put their own men in power. By 1778, Abraham Yates Jr. and Dirck Brinkerhoff had gained seats in the state assembly that they would not relinquish for the rest of the war. Both men were at best middling, and they had long opposed landlords. Manor lords in the northern Hudson Valley might have kept their estates and some political power, but the elections of Yates and Brinkerhoff hinted at what was coming.[13]

When it became clear that the 1777 state constitution did not address tenancy, disgruntled tenants in the southern Hudson Valley forced state legislators to confront the issue directly. Tenants and insurgents who lived in southern Dutchess County had heard rumors that Revolutionaries in other states intended to auction off confiscated Loyalist property. In October 1778, 448 "freeholders and others" demanded that New York Revolutionaries do the same thing. The petitioners threatened that any lengthy delays on a bill authorizing such sales would "occasion universal uneasiness and in all probability produce tumults and insurrections, and tend to a domestic tyranny and confusion as much to be dreaded as the evils brought upon us by our connections with Great Britain." The assembly tried to quiet these sentiments, but approximately one year later, Simon Calkins and "Others" from the area sent a similar petition to the state assembly. These same petitioners had appealed to the king for land in 1763 and 1764, arguing that their labor and occupancy on the land entitled them to own it. Two years later they rioted for land and suffered at the hands of the British army. By 1778, they were equating landownership and economic viability with citizenship and independence in the new state and country and began pressing Revolutionaries to redistribute confiscated Loyalist land in affordable lots to allow dependent tenants to become independent freeholders. After all, independent freeholders made independent citizens. In that way, Calkins and the other petitioners urged the assembly to take up the responsibility for social and political change. A year later, pressure came from within the Revolutionary movement when members of the Claverack Convention in Albany County strongly urged the state legislature to confiscate and sell Loyalist land. The assembly grudgingly obliged.[14]

Legislators had initially discussed a plan to sell confiscated Loyalist estates in 1778, and after receiving the petitions and hearing from the Claverack Convention, state assemblymen sought to take the opportunity to gather more support for the Revolution. They knew that if neutral tenants had the chance to buy the land they inhabited, these new freeholders might join the Revolution and Revolutionaries might well win the war. New Yorkers were hardly the vanguard. Instead, they were following the examples set by their neighbors. By 1778 and 1779, Revolutionaries in Pennsylvania, the Green Mountain territory, and New Jersey had already confiscated Loyalist property and sold it to shore up their support.

Pressure to confiscate and sell Loyalist estates, however, put landlord Revolutionaries in a conundrum, so they proceeded cautiously. A large chunk of the land in question was owned by landlords Frederick Philipse, Beverly Robinson, and Roger Morris. If landlord Revolutionaries opposed the sale of Loyalist property or sold it only to speculators, they risked their control of the state and put the Revolution in jeopardy. On the other hand, if they made confiscated land widely available, tenants would turn property into power and vote more of their own men into office. Landlords feared that these new men would turn the fight for a republic into a headlong rush to democracy. Worse, tenants might press that more democratic state legislature to dismantle estates in the north and sell that land too. None of these options was entirely appealing, and each contained risks, but manor lords knew that these were their only choices and that they would have to live with the consequences. In 1778, however, landlords and their agents were unwilling to enact the bill just yet and defeated it.[15]

When another bill was introduced in 1779, State Assemblyman Egbert Benson and Chancellor Robert R. Livingston, the son of Justice Robert R. Livingston, opposed it too. Both men firmly opposed lawless land rioters in the 1760s and again during the Revolution. Livingston opposed them for fairly obvious reasons; Benson did so because he was politically beholden to the Livingstons for his political seat. Benson supported the Livingstons, and, like them, he worried that the Revolution might spiral into chaos if the legislature made land too widely available by cutting Loyalists' property into small lots. But after he stalled the bill twice, Benson started to read the political landscape differently. His political allies could oppose the bill without fear of losing their position. Benson could not. The people in his county, Dutchess, greatly supported confiscation and had made their opinion clear. Although Livingston derided him for compromising on the issue, Benson finally supported confiscation in 1779, but he did not advocate wholesale redistribution.

Benson and the assembly revisited the issue because Dirck Brinkerhoff refused to let it die. If the political contest in Revolutionary New York could be reduced to two men who represented different constituents and who wanted to take New York politics in opposite directions after the war, Benson and Brinkerhoff were these men. While Benson found support among some of New York's wealthiest and most powerful men and sought to keep power in the hands of the landed elite, Brinkerhoff got his backing from the most ordinary people in the state. Brinkerhoff had led riots for land in the 1760s and rode that support to an assembly seat during the Revolution. If Benson acted as the landlords' representative, Brinkerhoff served farmers and tenants. Unlike Benson, Brinkerhoff desperately pushed for confiscation and redistribution of land and thereby threatened the very root of his opponents' political and economic power. Despite their differences and although they stood on opposite sides of New York's political world, these two Revolutionaries turned political rebellion into social upheaval for at least some New Yorkers.[16]

Under the men's direction, New York's assembly passed laws in 1779 and 1780 that authorized the sale of confiscated land and provided the people who lived on it the first chance to buy or lease it. While the bill described how people could lease land, it concentrated on how confiscated land should be sold. Qualified tenants could preempt the public auction of land if they could prove that they had stayed loyal to the Revolution and that they lived on the land. Anyone who wanted to buy unoccupied land, or land occupied by tenants who were ineligible because of their suspect loyalties, took part in open auctions that the government advertised six weeks before the sale. Buyers secured purchases by paying one-third of the cost of the land at the point of sale, and they had to pay off the rest in one year. Buyers also had to clear all their debts because Revolutionary landlords refused to let tenants escape the debts they owed, even to Loyalists. It would have set a bad precedent for landlords who kept their estates, and it would have thrown into debate the validity of other kinds of contracts made before and during the war. The assembly, however, did not explain how commissioners in charge of the sales would verify legitimate possession of the land. While requiring people to prove their allegiance to the Revolution to register a proper claim to the land, Benson also incorporated the arguments of land rioters into the act, making institutional what had been radical. When no title was available, he wrote, "Possession must be . . . sufficient Evidence of Right" ownership.[17]

Although legislators intended to redistribute land to rural people, several wealthier Revolutionaries took advantage of the bill to buy the trappings of status formerly owned by wealthy Loyalists. Lieutenant Governor Pierre Van Cortlandt, for instance, bought the DeLancey mansion in Westchester, and William Beekman bought up thirty valuable lots in New York City. Chancellor Robert R. Livingston enhanced his status by purchasing Oliver DeLancey's prestigious front pew at St. Paul's Church in New York City. Thereafter, everyone in church would have to watch Livingston, his family, and his guests walk to the front row before church and then would have to wait for them to leave.[18]

Despite indulgences, the bill performed as designed. Many tenants took advantage of the bill to purchase their leaseholds. In Dutchess County, Beverly Robinson and Roger Morris had owned 414 of the 496 lots put up for sale, and 401 different people bought 455 lots in Dutchess County. Most buyers paid approximately £100 for the land and bought lots under the five-hundred-acre limit. Only twenty of Robinson's tenants bought their leaseholds. Most of the others could not pay off their debts to their former manor lord. More tenants tried to buy their leaseholds in 1781. That year, 94 more of Robinson's 146 tenants tried to buy their land but shortly thereafter told the senate that they could not pay off their debts. Abraham Payne was one of them. He bought his leasehold under the law of 1780, but he owed Robinson approximately £300 and could not raise the cash necessary to pay off the sale and the debt within the year. As a result, Payne and the others had to "Quit their different Houses and Lands on which they have liv'd for a Number of Years, which by their Industry is brought to some degree of perfection in which consists their little all." Others preferred tenancy to starving or homelessness, and in March and April 1782, eighteen former tenants rented land from the Commissioners of Sequestration, which leased land for the state.[19]

Not all tenants stayed on their leaseholds even when they could buy them. In 1783 and 1784, 1,561 people, nearly 20 percent of Dutchess County's population, petitioned the state legislature to settle townships in the western part of the state, and, with petitions in hand, they left. They knew they could not raise the money to buy their leaseholds and to pay off their debts. These former tenants decided to take their chances on land Revolutionaries had expropriated from the Iroquois, who had, according to Revolutionaries, given up their claim to the land by siding with the enemy. Speculators often beat settlers to land in central and western New York and either sold it at high rates or tried to keep the land to create new estates. William Cooper, for instance, bought land and required would-be buyers to become tenants. Cooper, like the Livingstons and Van Rensselaers, turned his investment in land into a fortune.[20]

Changes in confiscation laws late in the war, and after it, enabled more tenants in Westchester County than in Dutchess County to buy and keep their leaseholds. The changes may have resulted from Egbert Benson's desire to lead his political opponents away from wholesale redistribution. Benson, after all, wrote most of these laws. Despite his efforts to lead, Benson was being led by men like Dirck Brinkerhoff, who represented many of the people who wanted to buy confiscated land. Brinkerhoff and his allies in the assembly forced Benson to draft laws that undermined landlords' power in the state. The new laws, like the old ones, linked citizenship to property ownership. Under the new laws, buyers had to demonstrate that they were loyal to the Revolution, that they had lived on the land throughout the war, and that they could pay one-third of the price at the point of sale. Buyers then had to pay off the rest in one year, and they had to continue to support the new nation. By 1784, tenants with a lease for the land, including tenants who had signed one- to three-year leases or who had made verbal arrangements with Frederick Philipse, had the first chance to buy the land, and they took advantage of the opportunity.[21] Of the 287 people who purchased land confiscated from Frederick Philipse, 194, or 68 percent, bought their leaseholds. On average, they bought 175 acres and paid approximately £600 for it. How much land they bought and how much they paid for it differed greatly. Alexander Ellaire's widow, Maria, bought 190 acres for £1,900, but George Coombs, a blacksmith, bought a one-acre plot for £40.[22]

These people bought their leaseholds to escape tenancy. The tenants' distaste for their subordinate status and for landlords emerged in earlier rioting, and insurgents made these feelings part of the Revolution in the southern Hudson Valley. Tenants expressed that outrage in 1783 when they learned that the Philipses intended to get back some of the land they had lost during the war. The Philipses' rumored return threatened the political and land gains many tenants had made during the Revolution. For tenants who had stayed neutral or who had supported the Revolution, independence meant freedom from landlordism, and they assured Frederick Philipse that they would defend their newly acquired land as vigorously as they had fought to get it. They had, after all, "purchased it with the price of their best blood" and vowed to "never become your vassals again." "They will not," they continued, "submit to become Tenants *at will,* to you or to your son, nor, to any other *enormous landholder, on such base terms.*" They had fought a Revolution, they concluded, so that "a Philipse or a Vanhorn, a Livingston or a Delancey" would never be their "master." "No," they insisted, "they had been fighting for freedom, and will enjoy [it]."[23]

DISAFFECTED TENANTS AND MILITIA DELINQUENCY ON
LIVINGSTON MANOR AND RENSSELAERSWYCK

While landlords in the southern Hudson Valley made their Revolutionary choices relatively quickly, landlords in the northern region struggled
more openly with their decisions. And their choices came with a price.
Robert R. Livingston soberly debated the merits of choosing one side or
another for weeks, knowing that he might lose everything if he chose
badly. Livingston's in-law, William Smith, also deliberated over these difficult questions before siding against the Revolution. He spent the war under house arrest on Livingston Manor and later lived in exile. But while
on the manor, Smith offered the manor lord a constant, living reminder
of how a man's choices could shape the rest of his life. Philip Schuyler, a
prominent landowner and an in-law of the Van Rensselaers, chose Revolution almost immediately, and he became a general in the Continental
army. At one point early in the war, he personally funded some of the troops
in his command. Later in the war, however, Schuyler endured the stinging
barbs of more egalitarian Revolutionaries who unfairly questioned his allegiance to the cause. While Livingston struggled with his decision and while
Schuyler may have regretted his choice, they did fight for independence from
Britain. These men fought to throw off parliamentary fetters and monarchical
tyranny to preserve their estates and political power. For them, land and
power equaled independence. The independence they sought combined
landownership with citizenship, making allegiance to the Revolution more
complex in the northern Hudson Valley.[24]

Landlords in the southern valley sided with the king in part to preserve
their land and power. Landlords in the northern valley joined the Revolution for the same reasons. Like their southern counterparts, the Livingstons, the Van Rensselaers, and Philip Schuyler knew that they needed
their tenants' support to win. As a result, they entered the fracas hoping to
persuade their tenants to join them. The war quickly showed them that
few tenants were willing to put their lives in jeopardy for either side. In
war, however, no one can stay neutral, and landlords eyed their neutral
tenants suspiciously. They often and mistakenly interpreted tenants' disaffection to mean loyalty to the king.

Robert Livingston Jr. profoundly distrusted his tenants. From the start,
he thought they were all Loyalists, and he was sure he knew why. In July
1775, Livingston lamented that the Revolution might fail even before Revolutionaries could declare independence because so many of his tenants
refused to join the local militia. Tenants stayed home for good reason.
Who, they asked, would farm the land? And who would reap the crops to
pay rent? Their families must assuredly "want when they are killed." Despite his concerns that his tenants had all joined the king, Livingston's
tenants had not joined either side. It did not matter; to Livingston, neutrality meant opposition, and he lumped these disaffected in with outright

Loyalists. According to Livingston, tenants who did not stand with Revolutionaries "stand by the King as they have called it, in hopes that if he succeeded they should have their Lands."[25]

In this respect, tenants on Livingston Manor shared the position of Indians and African Americans. When forced to choose, many members of these groups sided with whatever faction appeared the most likely to grant them the autonomy they sought. While Indians hoped to retain their sovereignty and land and African American slaves wanted freedom from bondage, tenants in the northern Hudson Valley wanted to own the land they labored on and occupied. But local circumstances changed rapidly and often dramatically, forcing tenants to rethink their choices. That said, their ultimate goal remained landownership, and many figured the best way to achieve that goal was to put off irrevocable wartime choices until absolutely necessary. Many tenants were willing to wait out the war right where they sat to hold onto their leaseholds and improvements. Their willingness to put off wartime choices contributed to the complexity of the Revolution in the northern valley and heightened the anxieties of everyone.

In the spring of 1775, nervous Revolutionaries like Livingston began hunting out the neutral inhabitants of the region and labeling them disaffected. As Ronald Hoffman noted, the disaffected in any given region were "probably more numerous than either Whigs or Loyalists," and that was particularly the case in the Hudson Valley. Revolutionaries in the region, and throughout the state, feared that the high number of disaffected people might undermine the war against Britain. So they tried to reduce the threat by forcing disaffected inhabitants to go in front of local committees of correspondence and declare their allegiance for the Revolution. Committees of correspondence and, later, committees of safety acted as the local arm of the Revolutionary movement. The committees sought out "disaffected" people and compelled them either to pledge their loyalty to the Revolution or to sign a bond for their good behavior for the duration of the war.[26]

Landlord Revolutionaries in the Hudson Valley worried feverishly about the behavior of their tenants because opposition to the Revolutionary cause solidified rapidly nearby. By the summer of 1775, for instance, it appeared that the Iroquois were going to side with the British. The Indians' decisions shaped the choices of tenants in western New York. They feared Indian attacks as much as, if not more than, raids by either army. Early in 1775, Sir John and Guy Johnson, the sons of Sir William Johnson, encouraged the Iroquois to fight with the British against the upstart colonists. By March 1775, the Johnsons and local officials from Tryon County, notably Walter Butler, who later led raiding parties up and down the Mohawk River, announced their loyalty to the king. They did so knowing that British general Thomas Gage approved of their attempts to convince the Iroquois to join the king against the Revolutionaries. Gage had already urged them to try to influence the political choices of the Iroquois.

At one point, Gage instructed them to tell the Iroquois that "the New England men with the People to the Southward wanted to draw them into a War against the King and were therefore continually deceiving them."[27] Many tenants in the region joined the Loyalists too. Their survival depended in large part on a good relationship with their landlords and an alliance with their Iroquois neighbors. These tenants likely worried that Revolutionaries would confiscate and sell the Johnsons' estate and throw them off the land, but they may have joined the Loyalists because they would not survive long on the land if they joined the Revolution. Together, the Iroquois, the tenants, and the Johnsons formed a powerful force on the Tryon County frontier that rallied around support of the king, or at least their dislike for Revolutionaries.[28]

While some Iroquois groups established their loyalties early in the war, others put off their decisions, inspiring great concern on both sides as the British and the Revolutionaries struggled to figure out Indians' loyalties. Guy Johnson initially convinced only four tribes from the powerful Six Nations to join the British. The others joined the British in July 1777 as General John Burgoyne marched south toward Fort Stanwix. Still, infighting plagued individual tribes. A group of Oneidas, for example, split from the rest and refused to join the British. They fought staunchly for the Revolutionaries in the fierce battle at Fort Stanwix in August 1777. Closer to Livingston Manor and Rensselaerswyck, Stockbridge Indians began breaking away from the political control of the Mohawks, who had joined the British early in the conflict. Many Stockbridge Indians were initially uncomfortable fighting for either side and preferred to stay out of the war, but their Revolutionary neighbors pressured them to enlist. When asked to join the Revolution in April 1775, the Stockbridge replied that, although they never fully "understood the foundation of this quarrel," the Revolutionaries would soon find Stockbridge Indians willing allies ready to "revenge my brothers' blood."[29]

Even though Stockbridge Indians pledged to fight the British, and did, external threats from Iroquois attacks heightened landlords' concerns for their tenants, and landlords continually pressed committees of correspondence to compel tenants to join the Revolution. As a result, the committees on Livingston Manor and Rensselaerswyck spent the bulk of their time looking for disaffected people and forcing them to swear oaths of allegiance to the Revolution or to sign bonds of surety for their future good behavior. If a person broke an oath or bond, he or she was fined, jailed, or expelled from the state.

Revolutionaries started the hunt for Loyalists close to home and quickly suspected well-known antagonists. If people had opposed landlords once, they might well do it again. Former rioters such as Daniel Hallenbeck (Michael Hallenbeck's son), Nicholas Luyck, and Abraham Lake, among others, were all forced to pledge their allegiance to the Revolution. Some former insurgents appeared before the committee more than once.

William Prendergast stood before the committee at least three times between 1775 and 1779. Although Prendergast was a well-known former rioter, Revolutionaries also questioned him because his oldest son, Matthew, had joined a group of Loyalists headed by James DeLancey. Early in the war, Matthew Prendergast declared his support for the king. As with the suspicions raised by former land rioters, Matthew Prendergast's reasons for joining the king were as equally historical. He became a Loyalist because the king had spared his father's life in 1766. At the end of the war, he and other Loyalists escaped to Nova Scotia. Matthew Prendergast returned to New York sometime in the 1790s but wore his hair in a British army regulation queue until he died in the 1830s. He never completely relinquished loyalty for the rulers who saved his father.[30]

From the Revolutionaries' perspective, the Prendergasts were not unique. Loyalty to the king was likely a family affair. Dozens of people had their allegiance questioned not because they were behaving suspiciously but because a relative had chosen the wrong side. Between 1776 and 1781, approximately 210 people in the northern Hudson Valley were labeled as disaffected; they came from 126 different families. Revolutionaries interrogated at least five Coens, six members of the Dennis family, and six Rypenberghs. The surnames of the people targeted by Revolutionaries also reflected the region's ethnic makeup. Of the 210 people tagged as disaffected, 95, or 45 percent, had Dutch or German surnames. The remaining 115, or 55 percent, had English, Scottish, Irish, or Welsh surnames.[31]

The disaffected people brought before the committees were usually poorer than the Revolutionaries who questioned them. Sixty-seven disaffected people who appear on assessment roles in 1779 (32 percent of the disaffected listed) lived on farms with an average realty valued at £113. In comparison, the average Livingston Manor tenant lived on a leasehold valued at £127, and the average Rensselaerswyck tenant lived on a tenancy assessed at £260. Thomas Denton, the poorest on the list of disaffected tenants, lived on a leasehold valued at but £12. While Denton may have been one of the poorer tenants, Johannes Dings was likely one of the wealthier ones. Dings topped the list of disaffected people for 1779 with a leasehold assessed at £200. Only 6 percent of the tenants on Livingston Manor and one-fifth of those on Rensselaerswyck lived on leaseholds valued at £200 or above. The men who investigated the disaffected and comprised the Livingston Manor Committee were better off. The poorest of the committeemen was likely Jacob Shaver, who lived on realty valued at £200. Three others—Samuel Ten Broeck, Walter Livingston, and Peter Livingston—possessed realty valued between £1,400 and £2,500, approximately ten to fifteen times the value of the realty leased by most of the disaffected people they interrogated.[32]

After examining people with a history of antagonism toward landlords, Revolutionaries investigated anyone who refused to serve in locally organized militias. Resistance to militia service had a long and distinguished history in the countryside that surrounded the northern Hudson Valley.[33] Although militia delinquency did not necessarily equal loyalty to the king and was a lesser offense than disaffection, it hampered the Revolutionaries' war effort. In the fall of 1776, Henry Livingston, who admittedly saw tories everywhere he looked, bitterly complained that he was unable to scrape together fifty men willing to march to Lake Champlain. He concluded, like other Revolutionaries, that most people in the area would not fight in a war they did not support. Despite Livingston's grumblings, not all delinquents were disaffected or Loyalists. In December 1777, the committee of correspondence questioned the 102 men who refused to march to Newcastle with the local militia and found that only 17 men should be labeled "disaffected." While all these men worried about being killed in battle, few of them declared their loyalty to either side. Most of them were either simply tired or hoped to avoid service without choosing sides.[34]

When questioned, these delinquents could hardly admit to hoping simply to survive the war and stay on their land, so some offered more personal excuses. It was far less threatening and dangerous to appear apolitical, poor, and pathetic than as a political opponent. Men like Harme Best had "Many excuses" for not fighting, such as being "Infirm." Others moaned that they were "Alone" on the land and would lose everything if they left. Worse, some were "Alone and Infirm." Some of those unable to serve in the militia, however, evidently served the Revolutionary cause in other ways. John Kortz stayed home because he was "Alone" on his farm, but he contributed to the Revolution the best he could. Kortz, and three other men who stayed home because they were "Alone," spent their spare time "making shoes" for soldiers.[35]

That kind of service mattered little to Revolutionaries like Henry and Robert Livingston Jr. They wanted soldiers in the field, not shoemakers alone and infirmed on their farms. From their point of view, men like John Kortz and Harme Best kept the manor from providing its share of men for the war. Here, however, Revolutionaries likely overstated their anxieties. To be sure, plenty of men refused to march with local militias in the northern Hudson Valley, but plenty of others did march. Approximately 280 men from the area served in local militias long enough to qualify for land bounty certificates. Revolutionaries started granting land bounty rights for militia service in April 1778. Each "class," initially defined as fifteen men but later expanded to thirty-five, received money when all members were present and fully armed. Revolutionaries tried to entice more men to join by offering each "class" land in addition to money. Whether these 280 men joined the militia for land, money, or independence remains unclear, but the offer of land bounty rights in return for militia service was an effective recruitment tool, and it suggests why some poor men joined the militia.[36]

Despite the number of men who fought for the Revolution, or who at least supported it, Revolutionary leaders in the northern Hudson Valley continued to focus on people who did not join the cause. By the end of

1775, their paranoia was slowly getting the better of them, and the mere presence of delinquents and disaffected people frayed already-taut nerves. The more delinquents and disaffected people they uncovered, the more landlord Revolutionaries worried about the success of the Revolution, about keeping their estates, and about staying alive. Worse, it was becoming quite clear to them that some malcontents hoped to use the upheaval of the Revolution to pull apart the great estates of the Hudson Valley. Revolutionary leaders hoped to diffuse that tension and to preserve their position and power by increasing the pressure on militia delinquents, disaffected people, and neutrals to join their side. But they faced a conundrum. To win over their tenants, landlords had to relinquish the very estates they were fighting the Revolution to protect. This was a step they were unwilling to take. Thus, Revolutionary landlords could not muster much, if any, backing in the twelve months after April 1775. By the spring of 1776, whatever support they had was dissipating.[37]

NETWORKS OF MILITANT TENANTS IN THE NORTHERN HUDSON VALLEY

In May 1776, Loyalists fired on a Revolutionary militia unit near George Wheeler's house, killing a horse. The Revolutionaries had marched to the area from nearby Claverack to quiet growing opposition to the Revolution. Shooting erupted when the two sides confronted each other in the Taconic area of Livingston Manor, very near the spot where land rioting had erupted in 1765. During the first rush, Revolutionaries drove the Loyalists back and wounded Nicholas Brussie Jr., a tenant on the manor, and took him prisoner. Within a few hours, the Revolutionaries had then marched to tenant Isaac Spoor's house in Taconic, on the eastern portion of Livingston Manor, where they again "found several Torys whoe opposed our men on which a fireing Inseued." Revolutionaries took several more prisoners along the way and wounded Nicholas Brussie Sr. Loyalists initially backed down, but only to summon additional forces. Fighting continued the next day when a party of approximately twenty Revolutionaries confronted one hundred Loyalists near George Wheeler's house "where a smart fireing happened." The Revolutionaries retreated, regrouped, and attacked again later that day, taking another seventeen men prisoner. The outcome of the battle was indecisive.[38]

The skirmish represented Revolutionary landlords' worst fears. Since the beginning of the war, landlords had been worrying that disgruntled tenants were organizing militant networks to strike quickly at Revolutionaries to help the British get control of the region. Conspiracies of tenants pledging their loyalty to the king had swirled about the countryside for months and stymied Revolutionary landlords. The conflict and the conspiracies illustrated how, in the beginning of the war, local circumstances led people to choose different paths to their goals, producing murky divisions among the inhabitants. War, however, quickly over-whelmed the northern Hudson Valley, and larger political and military forces compelled more regular alignments. While anxious Revolutionary landlords undoubtedly manufactured an epidemic of fear based on these alignments, by the time a Revolutionary militia unit traded shots with Loyalists at George Wheeler's farm, it was increasingly clear that a network of militant tenants was real.[39]

By the spring of 1776, British agents and Loyalists in and around the northern Hudson Valley were busy convincing as many rural people as possible to join them. The depth and breadth of British efforts to influence tenants, however, emerged slowly and became apparent to Revolutionaries only while interrogating disaffected people and militia delinquents. The Livingston Manor Committee of Correspondence uncovered one such group in September 1776 while investigating the loyalties of George Wheeler's relatives. At much the same time, they also learned that Jury Wheeler had recently threatened to shoot the captain of his local militia unit, John Elliot, if forced to march. Like other disaffected people, Jury Wheeler was not necessarily announcing his political loyalties. Instead, he simply refused to leave his family and leasehold. He offered the oft-heard excuse that his family might not survive if he was killed in battle. Whatever his reasons or motives, Jury Wheeler's friends, relatives, and alliances had already aroused the committee's suspicions. The committee questioned Wheeler for being a militia delinquent and for his links to a "Number of Disaffectd persons" who intended to strike "some Blow" against the Revolution at the "Very first Favourable Opportunity." Here was a man Revolutionaries dared not trust. They ordered Wheeler to swear allegiance to the Revolution and kept close watch on him and the people around him for some time.[40]

Further investigations only stoked Revolutionaries' fears. Andries Reese revealed that he apparently had heard that Jury and Nicholas Wheeler were organizing an imminent attack on Revolutionaries. According to Reese, Adam Kilmer, presumably a member of the Wheelers' group, announced that "if the Regulars should come up in the Country they would be rejoiced." At least two Kilmers, John Pulver, Teunis Vonck, Peter Butler, Hendrick and Casparus Lantman, and "Several More" had all allegedly vowed to support the king over Revolutionaries and had signed a "Kings Book" to prove it. These men and their families had lived in the north-eastern portion of Livingston Manor for well over a decade. Although each man later swore there was no "Kings Book" or that anyone in the countryside was trying to arouse loyalty to the king, anxious Revolutionaries sent fifty militiamen to quiet any disturbance before it exploded into open rebellion.[41]

Rensselaerswyck tenants had also established groups to oppose forced service in the war. In the summer of 1776, approximately four hundred tenants on Rensselaerswyck marched in arms to protest serving in local militia units. Like their Livingston Manor counterparts, they feared their families might lose their land and be thrown into irrevocable poverty if they died. While Revolutionaries condemned them for being Loyalists, the insurgents had not necessarily chosen sides in the political battle. That became clearer after Revolutionaries captured one of the rebels, John Van Den Bergh, who confessed that the rioters refused to fight for either the British or the Revolutionaries "if they can help it." Instead, they had organized to protect themselves, their families, and their farms and assaulted anyone, British and Revolutionary alike, who tried to take their land or goods. Adam Shufelt, caught later, was more forthcoming. He complained that New York Revolutionaries, Massachusetts Revolutionaries, and the British army all tried to undermine tenants' stability on the land. In part, he was right. While New York Revolutionaries sought to keep their estates and appease tenants, New Englanders sought to drive landlords and tenants out of the Hudson Valley so they might claim the region for themselves. According to Shufelt, the tenants in the area had been organizing themselves right from the start of the war. They knew, he insisted, that they had to stand together to defend "Property against all persons especially Yankees, who as they were informed, would burn their Houses & property, in Case they should be beat by the British Troops."[42]

Shufelt, the alleged signers of the "Kings Book," and men such as the Wheelers shared common goals. They wanted to survive the war and, if possible, join the winning side. Some people made their decisions far earlier than others, and each had reasons for either jumping in or for waiting. If they survived the war and joined the winning side, Hudson Valley inhabitants also hoped to get land. After almost two years of conflict, Revolutionaries and Loyalists finally realized this—rural people wanted to be safe and to own land—and they began rethinking what they offered people who joined their side. Toward the end of 1776, both sides began explicitly offering land as a reward for service.

An incident involving Aernout Viele illustrates how the British used land to entice tenants to side against landlords and the Revolution and shows the price Viele ultimately paid for helping the British. In June 1777, Viele confessed to swearing "several Persons to Secresy & to bear Faith & Allegiance to the King of Great Britain." He was not, he pleaded, guilty of joining the British himself, or of helping them create a web of militant tenants. Instead, he had only read the oath to enlist other "Men into the Service of the King of Great Britain." Viele was apparently recruited by Loyalists to read the oath because he "Could Reed Good English and Explane it to [others] in Dutch." He may have lied about taking the oath himself to escape the death sentence that awaited him, but too many men took the oath from him for Viele to deny the other charges. And not all of them swore it in Dutch, undermining his contention that he acted merely as a translator. After Viele confessed, he petitioned the General Court Martial of Officers of Militia to spare his life. He insisted he was "unexperienced in

Politicks and Law," making it easy for "insidious and evil meaning men to draw him into the snare that has proved his Ruin." He was young and confused, but no Loyalist. Several noted inhabitants of the region endorsed Viele's petition, including Cornelia Livingston, the wife of Walter Livingston, and she begged the court to spare his life. But the court rejected the petition and found Viele guilty. He was sentenced to death and was hanged on July 4, 1777.[43]

Viele may not have mentioned land in his confession or in his petition, but the oath he was hanged for administering specifically prescribed land as the reward for helping the British. The oath, issued by General William Howe and Sir John Johnson, requested that a battalion of volunteer soldiers be established in Albany County for the "Preservation of their Lives & properties & more Especially to Shew their Loyalty & Affection to his Majesty." Loyalists raised in the area would then help the British army quash the Revolutionaries. Above all else, these men had to maintain secrecy for the plan to work. In return, Howe and Johnson promised that "Each Officer & Private Volunteer, will receive the same Pay, Clothing, Arms & Accoutrements, as any other enlisted American Volunteer, & to be intitled to [the] same Lands as any regular Soldier." William Agnew, who swore that same oath in the hills outside the city of Albany, had "heard that Such Persons as joined the Regulars should have 100 Acres of Land."[44]

Although the British may have intended to settle their supporters in western New York, John Watts encouraged the British to strike closer to the hearts of Revolutionary New Yorkers. Revolutionary landlords knew tenants might well base their military choices on who promised them land, and they started offering land to soldiers at much the same time they were wrestling with plans to redistribute Loyalist land in the southern valley. But they really had little to offer tenants in the northern valley other than promises of what passed for independence in a society in which tenants were still ruled by landlords. For tenants, the prize was hardly worth the risk. John Watts read the situation accurately and suggested to the British that they could swing tenants to the king's side if they offered tenants the chance to own the land they inhabited. Watts had witnessed the land rioting of the 1760s and was well aware of insurgents' goals. Their condition had not changed dramatically in the intervening ten years, and he rightly figured that insurgents' aspirations had not likely changed either. Thus, Watts recommended that the British ministry should proclaim "all the present tenants be free from their vassalage, and that every one may be a freehold, of such farm and premises which he now holds for ever." Such a measure, he maintained, would "instantly bring at least six thousand able farmers into the field" for the British. Watts greatly exaggerated how many tenants might fight for the British, or for anyone, but his plea struck a chord with landlord Revolutionaries in the region who refused to give up their estates to their tenants to increase their chances for victory over the British. The British, Watts knew, could improve their chances in the war by offering disgruntled tenants the very thing landlords were unwilling to relinquish.[45]

Loyalist Beverly Robinson had made the same connection. In March 1780, Robinson seized the land issue by suggesting to Ethan Allen and the Green Mountain Boys that, if "the people of Vermont take a decisive and active part" against Revolutionaries, Parliament would separate the region from New York. Any inhabitant whose ownership of land was in dispute would become a freeholder. Robinson's offer was tempting. Allen and the Green Mountain Boys had been fighting against New York landlords since the late 1760s and by 1780 appeared only slightly closer to realizing their dream of independence from New York.[46]

Conflict between the Green Mountaineers and New York landlords had begun in the late colonial period when Ethan Allen led a group of settlers north from Connecticut. By 1774, New Yorkers were winning their dispute with Allen's Green Mountain Boys and the Bennington Boys. In February that year, the New York colonial assembly charged the Green Mountaineers and the Bennington Boys with subverting order and good government. The assembly set up a court to collect mounting debts, to issue eviction notices, and to establish New York's legitimate rule of the territory. By the end of the spring of 1775, the New York assembly had not successfully done what it had set out to do. Resistance to New York had coalesced under Ethan Allen's leadership, and by the time British and Revolutionaries fought at Lexington and Concord, Allen and his men began attacking New York justices of the peace and calling anyone who opposed Green Mountaineers "Tories." Right from the start, Allen was making the fight with New Yorkers over land an integral part of the Revolution.[47]

As military activity increased, Green Mountaineers beseeched the Continental Congress to resolve their dispute with New York. To win Congress's support, they pledged to fight the British, but only under Allen's command and only if Congress promised them independence from New York. Just two months before publication of the Declaration of Independence, Allen made his case explicitly. He informed John Hancock that the Green Mountaineers would join the Revolution if they could do so "without fear of giving our opponents any advantages" in their ongoing land dispute. In this instance, Allen was referring to New York landlords-turned-Revolutionaries, whom he distrusted immensely and regarded as potent enemies of the Green Mountaineers. Beverly Robinson had hoped to capitalize on that distrust to convince Allen that the British could help him get what he wanted. Allen, however, was as unwilling to help Robinson as he was to submit to New York rule. Allen set his priorities and used Robinson's overtures to pressure the Continental Congress to let the Green Mountain Boys separate from New York; and he bolstered his value to Revolutionaries by playing an important role in their fight with the British in the northern Hudson Valley. Revolutionaries ultimately acknowledged

Allen's desires, in no small part due to his military success, but the dispute between New York and the Green Mountaineers remained unsettled until 1790.[48]

A short time after Watts and Robinson made their overtures, two unhappy Livingston Manor tenants, Nicholas Rouwe and Christian Cooper, tried to convince British officials that their discontented neighbors were willing to join the king if the British guaranteed them the land they inhabited. In 1781, Rouwe estimated that roughly "Sixteen out of Twenty" tenants on Livingston Manor "would cheerfully" fight Revolutionaries. Cooper likewise maintained that he and other discontented tenants had long ago grown weary of being "most pitifully tossed about, by the Furious waves of Sedition & Rebellion without being able at present to help ourselves." Like Rouwe, Cooper promised that he and "many Hundreds" of tenants would "willingly spill our Blood in Suppressing Sedition and Rebellion." They had submitted to the "cursed tyrannical proceedings" of Revolutionary landlords for too long. The price of their loyalty was land. For Rouwe and Cooper, the pledge was too late. By 1781, the British army had effectively pulled out of the region, and Revolutionaries had solidified their control of the state, suggesting that Rouwe's and Cooper's pronouncements were likely toothless attempts to pressure New Yorkers to give concessions to tenants. They failed when both sides ignored them.[49]

However ineffective, these tenants' attempts to gain land in exchange for their allegiance were but more examples of how rural people in the northern Hudson Valley structured their goals during the Revolutionary War. While they obviously wanted to survive the war and used several strategies to do so, everyone struggled to make decisions that ensured their safety and stability. External forces such as military service narrowed people's choices. Even within that narrow framework, examples from Ethan Allen to Cooper and Rouwe make it clear that many inhabitants of the region tried to turn the upheaval to their advantage and get land. Leaders on both sides understood those aspirations and that the people on the ground could shape the outcome of the war. They tried to influence people's political loyalties with the promise of landownership.

THE UPRISING ON LIVINGSTON MANOR

Disaffected tenants, militia delinquents, and a network of militants inspired fear and paranoia among landlords in the northern Hudson Valley, who soon saw Loyalists everywhere. These militants, like many of the disaffected, shared some goals with landlord Revolutionaries. But how they sought to achieve these goals differed. While they all wanted to stay alive, insurgents sought land and thought they had to dismantle landed estates to get it. When they figured out that landlords were going to keep their estates, they reconfigured their alliances and retreated to the more attainable goal of staying on what land they had. At the same time, Revolutionaries were fighting for independence from Britain and protecting their estates from militants and disaffected people. By fall 1777, landlord Revolutionaries were defending their estates by taking the ironic step of shielding disaffected and insurgent tenants from attacks by outsiders. Once the external threat faded, however, manor lords again turned against internal insurgents. Not surprisingly, rampant attacks and shifting alliances made nearly every inhabitant anxious and wary of neighbors.

Landlords' fear was well placed. By the spring of 1777, insurgents were running out of options. Revolutionaries were successfully unearthing networks of Loyalist tenants and coercing apathetic and disaffected tenants to choose sides. Furthermore, promises of land from the British were enticing but hollow. After all, landlordism had flourished under British colonial rule, and nothing would stop the British from giving existing estates to wealthier Loyalists. Many insurgents had also hoped that the new state constitution might offer easier access to political power and that it might address tenancy in the new state. But it did neither. The constitution was written so that it left tenancy alone, and debates over it indicated that Revolutionary landlords in the northern region were the most reluctant to raise the issue and quashed the subject whenever it was raised. Landlords wanted to maintain the status quo amid the chaos of war and the political changes involved in state making. By the spring of 1777, it was rapidly becoming clear to insurgents that landlordism would survive the war unless they took more drastic actions.

Frustrated tenants may well have done nothing if they had to act alone. But rumors of a British invasion swept the Hudson Valley in the spring of 1777. The British wanted to take the Hudson River and isolate New England from the rest of the colonies. British general John Burgoyne intended to drive south from Canada to Albany, and Sir Henry Clinton (a distant cousin of New York's governor George Clinton) planned on driving up from New York City. Insurgent tenants hoped to time their rebellion against landlords with this British assault on the northern Hudson Valley. Dissident tenants, however, were poorly prepared and inadequately armed for rebellion. Muskets and ammunition were hard to obtain. Some rebels borrowed muskets, powder, and ball from neighbors under the pretext of hunting, and others stole powder that the Livingstons had stored for use by the militia or Continental army. Some even went so far as to scrape lead for musket balls from the nets strewn across the Hudson River to block passage of British ships. However resourceful they were, insurgents had only slightly improved their chances.[50]

Badly armed, insurgents also lost any advantage of surprise. Dozens of rebels going about the countryside collecting weapons and munitions invariably aroused the suspicions of local Revolutionaries, and rumors of the rebellion circulated for weeks. Revolutionaries quickly confirmed these rumors by obtaining concrete information a week or so before the insurgents planned to march. Margaret Livingston, sister-in-law of the manor lord, may have heard rumors of the rioters' "most Diabolical Intentions" to "Extirpate all the wiggs" and that they "plotted to cut of[f] men women and children" from their farms, but the Committee of Livingston Manor had learned of the plot from the lips of a "Dying Man in Ulster County who could not Die till he had communicated it to one of the Committee."[51]

When Revolutionaries corroborated the rumored rebellion, they acted forcefully but inadvertently tipped their hand. In late March and early April, they again demanded that disaffected tenants and militia delinquents declare their loyalty to the Revolution and serve in local militias. During the questioning, members of the committee asked if anyone knew anything about the uprising. Insurgents grew desperate and started the rebellion early to catch Revolutionaries off guard, and they hoped that the British would invade soon. In fact, however, the British army would not invade for many weeks, and the unexpected start hampered the uprising because not all the rebels took up arms at the same time. Still, although people disagreed over the number of people in arms, enough took up arms to frighten men already stretched to the limit by war. William Smith Jr. estimated that approximately four hundred to five hundred insurgents entered the field, but Smith's loyalty to the crown may have prompted him to overstate the number of people who turned out against Revolutionaries. As a result, it appears likely that fewer people marched at any one time. The Revolutionaries, however, did not wait to count. They turned their information and muskets against their opponents and routed them.[52]

Revolutionary landlords called out a militia composed of tenants drawn from Livingston Manor and Claverack to quiet the rebellion. Revolutionaries also called on some militiamen from western Massachusetts, who ostensibly fought for the Revolution and against the rebels. New Englanders, however, had long harbored animosities toward landlords, and they saw insurgent tenants as a dual threat. As tenants, insurgents represented landlordism even if they opposed it. As insurgents, they undermined the Massachusetts militia's efforts to win the war against Britain. The New Englanders quickly turned on Revolutionary landlords and attacked tenants indiscriminately in the hopes of defeating both landlordism and Loyalism. By the first week of May 1777, alleged Loyalist rioters were turning to Revolutionary landlords for protection from predatory Massachusetts militiamen. Landlords were thus forced to defend their estates by guarding both otherwise peaceful tenants and tenants who had joined the uprising. That move only fueled the ire of landlords' opponents, who uncharitably accused them of being Loyalist sympathizers. By the second week of May, the rioters were so badly overwhelmed and outmaneuvered that they began surrendering to save themselves and to stay on their leaseholds.[53]

How many people joined the uprising and who participated in it remains hotly contested. On one side, historians insist that few tenants took up arms and that fewer still joined the British. They argue either that New Englanders, once again, instigated violence in the northern Hudson Valley, that the few tenants who took up arms were Loyalists, or that the uprising of 1777 was, essentially, much ado about nothing. Historians on the other side maintain that tenants stood against their landlords. Thus, if tenant rebels appeared to be Loyalists, it was because their landlords had joined the Revolution and not because the tenants sided with the king.[54]

Both sides tend to paint with too broad a brush. Many tenants, for instance, took up arms against landlordism that spring, even though the number was likely lower than William Smith's estimate. Revolutionaries certainly worried that "almost everybody in the upper manor . . . appears to have engaged with the enemy" and responded by putting roughly three hundred rioters into the jails in Albany and Dutchess counties. The jails swelled so rapidly that the state assembly ordered Revolutionaries to prosecute only one in ten rioters and to release people who seemed ignorant of the political motives for the rebellion and those who appeared sufficiently contrite. Nearly 140 people sat in jail that summer awaiting trial for rioting. Some were freed after they signed oaths of allegiance to the Revolution and gave bonds of surety for their future good behavior. Others, like Jury and Mary Wheeler, stayed in jail for years. They either could not raise the money to pay the bond or Revolutionaries considered them too dangerous to release. In Jury Wheeler's case, the Revolutionaries were right to worry about what he might do if freed. In the fall of 1778, over a year after being put in jail, Wheeler appealed to his captors for his release. He was, he contended, too sick to stay in jail and hope to survive much longer. Revolutionaries acted compassionately and set him free. Wheeler betrayed their trust almost immediately. Just one month later, he stood before the county committee of safety for attacking Revolutionaries in nearby Claverack. This time, his pleas for leniency because of his condition fell on deaf ears, and he was jailed again. Why Mary Wheeler was kept in jail, however, remains a mystery. Perhaps Revolutionaries figured she could take care of Jury Wheeler, or maybe they saw her as a threat to their political control.

By late May and early June, Revolutionary officials had gained control of the rebellious tenants. Once the rebellion was effectively over, tenants and their families began looking for ways to stay on their leaseholds. In those few weeks, the committee of safety for Livingston manor received a flood of requests from women who sought amnesty for rioters still hiding in the woods. These women ran farms while their husbands hid, suggesting that men were generally prosecuted even when entire families opposed militias and landlords. Invariably, wives wisely asked that Revolutionaries allow their husbands to return to head the tenant households and provide for the occupants. These women invoked the language of conventional femininity and masculinity to appeal to judges even though their own lives belied their dependency.[55]

As landlords had in the 1760s, landlord Revolutionaries faced the problem of reasserting control without inspiring greater antagonism. Revolutionary leaders, however, knew better than to underestimate the political acumen of the people who took up arms against them. The Revolution may have added new critical elements, but land rioting was familiar. Landlord Revolutionaries handled land rioters in 1777 in much the same way they had dealt with them in the 1760s and for the same reasons. So, although 140 men stayed in jail for some length of time, landlords and officials dared not prosecute them all. Only fourteen or so men stayed in jail for more than a few weeks. The Wheelers, in that light, illustrate what happened to the most notorious rioters. What was different in 1777 was the imminent threat of a British invasion of the Hudson Valley. That difference required even greater delicacy and political skill. Thus, Revolutionaries proceeded carefully, explaining in large part why they only tried those rioters they could definitively target as leaders. To do otherwise might have provoked a British invasion and thus new riots that, together, would have threatened everything landlord Revolutionaries hoped to achieve.

Despite the quick defeat of the rioters, the uprising deeply upset Revolutionary landlords and their families. The events of spring 1777 underscored the risks they were taking. Margaret Livingston worried that the rioters might overthrow and kill the manor lord, Robert Livingston Jr. She also worried that rioters would make it to her house, so she demanded that Philip Livingston, her nephew, come home from the Continental Congress to protect the family, which she thought should be his first obligation. He could serve his country when his family was safe. Philip Livingston disagreed and stayed at his political post. While Margaret Livingston tried to rally her family around her, Peter Livingston, the manor lord's son, prepared bundles of provisions that he and his family could carry if they needed to flee from the combined forces of rioters and redcoats.

Robert Livingston Jr., however, appeared the most distraught of all. After enduring assaults on his estate for nearly twenty-five years, he made the difficult decision to become a Revolutionary, throwing his family's safety and wealth into jeopardy. Within two years, he faced the impending attack of his homeland by one of the greatest armies in the western hemisphere. To make matters worse from his perspective, hundreds of people in his own backyard took up muskets, hoes, and sticks to defeat the Revolution, to topple his estate, and to kill him if possible. His world was rapidly spinning out of control, and the effort to keep it together was beginning to take its toll. Grim circumstances provoked extreme emotions from this otherwise stoic man. By the time of the uprising of 1777, Livingston apparently "did not utter a Sentiment which he did not contradict" immediately, and he frequently expressed his complete exasperation with the rural people who opposed him. The anxiety drove the mighty landlord to "Temerity," and he wished that the rioters might "all be hanged and [their] children starved."[56]

Livingston was upset because the Revolution made the insurgency of 1777 qualitatively different from previous land riots. If previous land uprisings had threatened to restructure part of colonial society by taking some land and power from landlords, fights over land during the Revolution revealed conflicting views of what New York's society should become. For landlord Revolutionaries, independence meant more than just liberty from Britain. It meant preserving the preexisting social and political order. Rural insurgents saw the Revolution differently. The rebels aspired to take part in what Benjamin Quarles called the "contagion of liberty" that exploded during the Revolutionary War. In the same way that liberty meant one thing for slaves and another for slaveowners-turned-Revolutionaries, insurgents in the northern Hudson Valley interpreted independence quite differently than landlords who guided the Revolution.[57] For insurgents, independence meant freedom from landlordism and an autonomous political voice. The community they wanted to build had no room in it for landlords. That insurgents, marginalized as "Loyalists" by landlord Revolutionaries, had become social revolutionaries is not simply an irony; it was one of the unintended consequences of revolution when civil society was deeply divided by politics and class.[58]

Early in the war when Revolutionary control of New York was far from solid, people's behavior varied considerably in ways that defy the stark patterns of anti-landlord on one side or anti–New York/anti–New England on the other. Some men clearly supported the crown, but they stood shoulder to shoulder with men who fought more against landlordism than against Revolutionaries. Others joined local militias to protect their homesteads and to avoid service in the regular armies, which many considered far more dangerous. Some, like the residents of Rhinebeck, pledged their loyalty to both sides, hoping to join the winning side when the dust of war finally settled. Others fought when they could, and still others preferred not to fight. In the countryside, however, these people often sought common goals. Primarily, they hoped to avoid being killed in war. If they chose to fight, or had to fight, they fought only as long as needed. Going to war put families at risk too. Men at war could not provide for the household, and the death of a male head of household could well decimate the family. Many also hoped to use the Revolution to get land. All of these goals were hard to achieve, and the inhabitants of the northern Hudson Valley could not count on obtaining any of them.

BANDITRY AND SOLIDIFYING THE REVOLUTION

Victory over rioters in May 1777 coupled with the defeat of the British army at Saratoga in the fall later that year helped Revolutionaries secure control of the northern Hudson Valley. They solidified and legitimated their political power by adopting the constitution of 1777. The two men who did the bulk of the drafting, John Jay and Abraham Yates Jr., came to the constitution with different political views and goals, but both agreed that the final version would be good for the state. However much the Revolution and the state constitution opened politics to new men, the old rulers were reluctant to give up too much power. Philip Schuyler, for instance, derided his political opponent George Clinton's lack of the heritage and status neces-sary to "entitle him" to high political office.[59] Schuyler's opinions were symptomatic of the landed elite in the northern Hudson Valley. Whatever the political climate, men like Schuyler and Robert Livingston Jr. refused to let internal differences keep them from protecting themselves from preda-tors from below. As Staughton Lynd noted, rich men usually set aside their differences to defeat "efforts of the lower classes to obtain their own ends for themselves by violence."[60]

The constitution of 1777 sanctioned their rule, but elite Revolutionaries needed to stick together. Disgruntled rural people on Livingston Manor and Rensselaerswyck had gained some power in the new government as ris-ing land values and constitutional changes offered more tenants a political voice. Outside the walls of political establishments, insurgents threatened the Revolutionary movement with violence again in 1778. These uprisings, how-ever, were far more dispersed and far less organized than the riot of 1777. Re-gardless, the crowds, drawn from inhabitants of both manors and from de-serters from both armies, were quick to defend their farms by force from all threats, real and perceived. Revolutionaries tried to marginalize the insur-gents by calling them "wicked tories," but they were more interested in pro-tecting their households and farms than with jumping into the political melee of the Revolution. When protecting their farms, insurgents increas-ingly found themselves squaring off against wealthier men. By the summer of 1778, they began targeting wealthy men, specifically Revolutionaries, for at-tack. In doing so, insurgents became bandits.[61]

The keys to this banditry may be found in the rituals they invoked, how they symbolized themselves, the oaths they forced their enemies to swear, and who they attacked. Although they resembled militia delin-quents by refusing to take part in the war, there were no real connections between them. Instead, bandits fashioned themselves as defenders of their farms and families. They attacked anyone who harassed farmers and ten-ants in the region, but their activities reveal their agenda. Revolutionaries may have been easier to catch because they were more numerous, but these bandits made Revolutionaries their targets far more often than they attacked Loyalists or British soldiers. But stating that the bandits simply attacked Revolutionaries reduces their motivations to a political agenda they had little interest in pursuing. Bandits targeted Revolutionary militia officers who fined tenants for militia delinquency. And the bandits as-saulted members of local committees of correspondence for coercing rural people to swear oaths of allegiance to the Revolution. When they captured Revolutionary militiamen, bandits turned the ritual of oath-taking on their victims, forcing prisoners to swear oaths of neutrality for the dura-tion of the war and threatening to attack those who violated them.[62]

Although not as widespread as the riots of 1777, these attempts to un-dermine the Revolutionaries' war and to flout their authority were taken seriously. The Revolutionaries may have gained some semblance of control of the region, but the war against Britain was far from over, and Revolutionaries could not afford to give up any ground they had won. In June and July 1778, Peter R. Livingston complained that the bandits were ruining the war effort, and he begged Governor George Clinton for a company of rangers to chase them down. Worse, according to Livingston, the bandits were increasingly choosing their victims based more on wealth than on politics. Livingston accused them of turning a political rebellion into a social revolution and insisted that they had to be stopped. He carped that several "well Affected and most Loyal Inhabitants" of the region had already been "despoiled and Plundered of all their arms and great part of their Ready money cloathing and Valuable Effects." "Every man," he groused, "fears it will be his turn next."[63]

By August 1778, leaders of several towns in the southern section of Livingston Manor echoed Philip Livingston's call for help after they suffered at the hands of bandits. Governor Clinton responded quickly and sent in an army of men to search for the perpetrators. While the insurgents seemed to be everywhere, Revolutionaries had a hard time finding them. They simply melted into the countryside as tenants throughout the region "Secreeted and Concealed" them, perhaps because tenants supported the insurgents or perhaps because the bandits threatened to burn the houses and farms of any tenants who named names. On the other hand, peaceful tenants may not have stepped forward because they did not think the Revolutionaries were going to win the war. Like others before them who chased these bandits, the army had very little luck.[64]

For all their efforts, Revolutionaries only arrested William McRea. He was a blacksmith who lived on a small farm in Ballstown in Albany County, but he had been trained as a commissioned officer in the state militia and had served with his unit through the end of 1777. McRea also had been a member of the Albany Committee of Correspondence. But sometime in late 1777 and early 1778 he became disenchanted with the Revolutionary movement, or perhaps just with leading Revolutionaries, and he joined one of the roving bands of insurgents. Banditry was one thing, but treason was something far more serious. Revolutionaries tracked down McRea more because he looked like a traitor than because he had become a treacherous bandit. Once captured, McRea was charged with "not having the Fear of God in his Heart nor weighing the Duty of his Allegiance" to the Revolution, and he was accused of bringing a "miscerable Slaughter among the Subjects of this State." Although the charges amounted to treason, a capital offense, McRea's fate remains unknown.[65]

Banditry grew as opposition to the Revolutionaries' rule declined and as Revolutionaries solidified their power. Landlord Revolutionaries took advantage of their growing power and security to preserve their estates. They did it, in large part, by drawing up new state boundaries that put most of the historically disputed territory in New York. The new boundaries also forced disgruntled rural people to argue within a geographic and political framework that favored Revolutionaries, and especially New York Revolutionary landlords, over others. The legislature appointed Egbert Benson, James Duane, and John Morin Scott to draw up boundaries of the state that would appease both New Yorkers and New Englanders. All of these men had connections to or were beholden to landlords for their positions. In their report, they concluded that the "native proprietors" had ceded or surrendered their land to the Dutch government, which then granted the land to landlords. The men then traced overlapping claims from very early grants for New Netherlands to grants made for New Hampshire in 1629, and then to grants made after the English took control of the colony in the late seventeenth century. Although the committee strongly suggested that New York's legitimate boundaries began at the western bank of the Connecticut River, the men rightly suspected that the Continental Congress would not support an outcome that would perpetuate old problems and likely inspire new ones. To avoid having their report either dismissed or revised, Benson, Duane, and Scott fixed a more acceptable boundary for New York and New England. They ran their line west of the Connecticut River between the Housatonic and Hudson rivers.

The report clearly favored Revolutionary landlords and validated their claim to most of the disputed land in the region. More ominously, for insurgents, the report firmly established the land claims of the Livingstons, Van Rensselaers, and Philip Schuyler. Rural people who lived on the land described in the report either had to leave without compensation or had to submit to the landlords' authority. So many people moved during the period that it remains difficult to determine exactly how many left rather than submit to landlordism, but some must have left for precisely that reason. Farmers who lived on land outside the boundaries of these estates needed to register their claim with whatever state they inhabited. Farmers who wanted to stay on their land even though they found themselves in New York on the estates of others had to knuckle under to the proprietary whims of landlords. Despite widespread opposition to landlordism, the report ensured that it would be a fixture in the northern Hudson Valley in the post-Revolutionary period.[66]

AT WAR'S END

Landownership held many advantages in eighteenth-century North America, and this was particularly true in New York. During debates over the sale of confiscated land, Revolutionaries had tied landownership to allegiance to the Revolution and made it a fundamental component of citizenship in the emerging nation. People who owned land in the new nation could participate fully in the politics of it. Those who did not were restricted, to varying degrees, from enjoying the same kinds of political opportunities. The Revolution certainly changed how the political process worked, but, more to the point in the southern Hudson Valley, the Revolution changed who participated in the political process. In Dutchess and

Westchester counties, the political rebellion became a social rebellion as well. What is striking is that landlord Revolutionaries enacted the social rebellion that they so greatly feared and against which they so fervently fought in their own region. Although it may seem ironic that they helped pass laws that redistributed land and widened participation in the political process, they could do little else. The concomitant forces of pressure from below, conflicts with Loyalist landlords, debates among emerging rulers of the state, and the military conflict all forced Revolutionary landlords to give up some political power and status to preserve their estates and, most importantly, to win the Revolutionary War.

Once done, it could not be undone. New people entered the political process for the first time during the Revolution, and the makeup of representatives for the southern Hudson Valley moved socially down and away from the political leanings of men like Robert Livingston Jr. and Philip Schuyler. No one can question the impact of Dirck Brinkerhoff in the legislation, or the changeover of Melancton Smith and Ephraim Paine for Philip Livingston and Beverly Robinson. Only after the Revolution could a former store clerk and farmhand replace two mighty landlords as leading officials in Dutchess County, and they could have done so only with the support of tenants-turned-freeholders. The state's constitution may have broadened suffrage laws, but these people only became political actors when land was redistributed, making freeholders and voters out of former tenants. Like land redistribution, once new men entered politics they were not easily removed. Men like Philip Schuyler complained that these new men, such as Governor George Clinton, did not have the "family and connections" to "entitle him to so distinguished a predominance," but there was little Schuyler or others could do about it outside their home counties.[67]

Schuyler, the Van Rensselaers, and the Livingstons did not relinquish everything. While they opened up the Revolution in the southern region, they did so to maximize their chances of winning and to minimize their losses in their own counties. They knew their victory would exact a price. They simply wanted to limit what they had to relinquish to win the war. Thus, the Revolution had mixed results in the Hudson Valley. If some tenants in the southern region gained freeholds and access to politics, tenants in the north did not. Furthermore, many tenants in the northern Hudson Valley found themselves marginalized in their communities because of their alleged political choices during the war. Militant rural people remained tenants, and, although they reaped some of the political benefits of the Revolution, they could not fully claim the independence that only a freehold could guarantee. Insurgents in the north continued to fight for freeholds in the post-Revolutionary period, and they continued to do so against a powerful landed elite in a community, and in a nation, where political independence hinged on landownership but did not assure it. At war's end in the northern Hudson Valley, neither landlords nor insurgents entirely got what they wanted, setting the stage for yet more violence.

Chapter Five

THE REVOLUTIONARY SETTLEMENT

• In November 1785, Stephen Van Rensselaer celebrated his twenty-first birthday and became lord of Rensselaerswyck in the manner of his class. The Van Rensselaers, Livingstons, Schuylers, and other wealthy New Yorkers feasted inside the Van Rensselaers' newly completed mansion five miles north of Albany in Watervliet. The guests and family sat on imported chairs in parlors lined with mahogany bookshelves and warmed themselves in front of fireplaces adorned with ceramic tiles imported from the Netherlands. As in Mary Philipse's wedding nearly thirty years before, an observer would immediately notice the difference between landed and landless, rich and poor. Affluent guests such as Philip Schuyler stayed inside for the festivities. They were attended to by servants, and they ate and drank from the best china and crystal the Van Rensselaers could offer. Van Rensselaer's tenants and their families, on the other hand, ate and drank outside, battling the fierce winds of that cold November day. Nonetheless, according to a friend of Van Rensselaer's, the tenants played their part in the ritual by deferring to their manor lord when he finally stepped out onto the balcony of his mansion late in the afternoon.

When he spoke to them from the balcony, Van Rensselaer made it clear that he was going to be dramatically different from his predecessors. In the late colonial period, the Van Rensselaers, like their landlord neighbors, were moving away from an informal relationship with their tenants toward a standardized economic arrangement. Stephen Van Rensselaer hammered that point home when he stepped out onto the veranda to warn tenants that if they did not start paying their rent on time he was going to take the unprecedented step of suing them for it. Previous manor lords had been unwilling to go so far, but the new manor lord figured that he did not have many other options. He needed to reassert his control over his tenants to stabilize and then increase his family's income. If litigation did not work, he threatened to evict tenants who refused to pay.[1]

Van Rensselaer's speech may have fatally disrupted a public ritual designed to show that he was only the latest in a long line of manor lords. However politically inept the speech may have been, Van Rensselaer was worried about his family's declining income. Tenants had stopped paying rent during the Revolution and had not resumed. Just a few months before his birthday, Van Rensselaer demanded that tenants resume paying rent, but few did. A few weeks after that, Van Rensselaer again ordered them to pay; still, many refused. By his twenty-first birthday, Van Rensselaer knew that the economic and political world around him had changed enough that he had to risk upsetting his coming-of-age ritual with a blatant assertion of his power and authority.

Van Rensselaer's friend and biographer Daniel Dewey Barnard did not regard the manor lord's threats as too harsh. Barnard barely remembered the warning at all. Instead, he recalled that the celebration resembled similar festivals he had attended at the Van Rensselaers' manor house before 1776. But the 1785 party was different, and Barnard knew why. The Revolution may well have enabled people in the southern Hudson Valley to get land, and it offered Vermonters the chance to create a new polity, but, according to Barnard, the Revolution was best measured by the freedom with which tenants on Rensselaerswyck expressed their "joy, and their affection" for their new landlord. Evidently, before the Revolution tenants did not feel free enough to act quite so deferentially to their landlord. Although the Revolution may not have offered them land, it had offered tenants, Barnard noted, the freedom to express their love for and devotion to their manor lord.[2]

On the other hand, Van Rensselaer may have threatened his tenants simply to avoid formal legal proceedings against them, believing it was in everyone's best interest to settle these disputes informally. Many tenants, however, simply could not pay. War had devastated their farms and their families. In August 1785, for instance, tenant John Devoe contacted the overseer of the estate, Abraham Ten Broeck, pleading that the recent request for rent "could not hardly . . . ment me." Devoe lived on the west side of the Hudson River in an area marked by steep cliffs, sloping meadows, and sandy pine barrens. Poor weather, bad land, and war had kept him from growing enough food to feed his family. Devoe had little chance of meeting the dual responsibilities of all tenants, to feed his family and to pay rent, and so he had asked for some relief. While he wanted a temporary release from rent, he vowed to meet the landlord's demands. Even then he thought he could do so only "with the help of God." Other tenants were less optimistic. Rather than be evicted and humiliated, Ezekial Sayles sold the improvements he made to his leasehold to pay off his mounting debt to Van Rensselaer. He explained that many members of his "large family" had been "Somethin Sickly" over the past several months. Still, he intended that "no one should be the loser by me." Hopes and intentions were not rent, so Van Rensselaer pocketed what rent he received and issued stronger threats.[3]

These readings of Van Rensselaer's birthday celebration and his ascension to manor lord reveal the complexities of the Revolution in the northern Hudson Valley. To the north and south, people had gained freeholds as a result of the Revolution. The new freeholders contrasted starkly with the manorial tenants who had tried, yet failed, to use the Revolution to get land. Their inability to get land, the war, land disputes, and land redistribution in the surrounding areas either kept tenants from paying rent or prompted dissident tenants to subvert landlordism again by not paying rent. The Livingstons and the Van Rensselaers saw the result of those forces every time they looked at ledger books that showed decreasing rent income. Furthermore, the Revolution offered disgruntled tenants on Livingston Manor and Rensselaerswyck a new language steeped in recent political culture to legitimate their long-standing desires for land. In that vividly different political and economic situation, Van Rensselaer resorted to new, harsher methods to reestablish his position, and that of landlords, atop New York's social and political hierarchy.

The world was different for insurgents too. The Revolution had changed the political and cultural world, but tenants' relationship to the land had remained largely unchanged. As a result, tenants could not fully participate in the new world around them. Although tenants had gained some increased access to politics during the war when Revolutionaries lowered property requirements for voting and office holding, political independence eluded them because they did not own land. Moreover, landlords continued to assert their control over the goods tenants produced. To fully reap the political and economic rewards of the Revolution, insurgents had to subvert landlordism. Insurgents took up that fight immediately after the Revolutionary War. Their goals mirrored those of the colonial period: Insurgents wanted to take land from landed tycoons and give it to the people who lived and labored on it. In renewing their struggle for land, rebels in the northern Hudson Valley, like land rioters that haunted the Massachusetts and Pennsylvania backcountry, undermined whatever success Revolutionaries had won.

Insurgent tenants thought their labor and occupancy on the land entitled them to own it and that they should be able to keep the profits made from their labor. Landlords, however, insisted that tenants' labor and occupancy proved the landlords', not the tenants', titles. These arguments presage those used by laborers and industrialists in the mid-nineteenth century. While wage laborers maintained that they should be able to at least share the profits derived from their labor, industrialists rebuked them by noting that workers improved raw materials industrialists owned and that workers could freely take their labor elsewhere. Although these arguments became critical issues as industrial capitalism emerged and then dominated the United States in the late nineteenth century, they inevitably transcended economic issues, especially for tenants, because in the post-Revolutionary period property ownership equaled independence and liberty.[4] As a result, by using Revolutionary rhetoric, insurgents made land disputes as much about social and political independence as about getting freeholds, making the uprisings in the post-Revolutionary period qualitatively different than rebellions before it.[5]

THE POST-REVOLUTIONARY MANORIAL ECONOMY

The Revolutionary War had thrown the manorial economy and land-lordism into turmoil. The acreage owned by landlords in the southern Hudson Valley decreased significantly during and after the Revolutionary War. Revolutionaries sold off the estates of landlords-turned-Loyalists, and manor lords who became Revolutionaries faced mounting anti-landlord sentiment in the region. Sometimes landlords responded by selling land to tenants. The state legislature followed suit by outlawing primogeniture, entail, and feudal tenures. Despite these attacks on manorialism, the Van Rensselaers and the Livingstons held fast to their Hudson Valley estates after the Revolution. Newly available land in the west eased tensions by offering dissatisfied people the chance to start over, but not everybody moved. Many preferred to take their chances with landlords and stay on land they had worked for years rather than pit themselves against antagonistic Indians and roaming bands of British soldiers. Landlords in the northern Hudson Valley also kept their estates by obtaining powerful seats in a state and federal political system that inhibited government's ability to attack property rights any further.[6]

How successfully they managed their estates remains questionable. Rent income collection declined on both Livingston Manor and Rensselaerswyck during the war. The amount of wheat paid to the Livingstons, for instance, dropped from a high of approximately 3,680 bushels in 1774 to a low of 1,342 bushels in 1779, far below even the worst year in the decade before independence. Although that number started to go up slowly after 1779, the Livingstons did not reach prewar income levels until the middle 1780s. Thereafter, they collected on average approximately 70 percent of the rent owed. Rensselaerswyck saw similar dips in income so dramatic that Stephen Van Rensselaer started pressing his tenants for back rent the day he became lord of the manor. Like the Livingstons, the Van Rensselaers saw slow progress and reached pre-Revolutionary levels by the early 1790s. So many tenants either refused or failed to pay rent to Philip Schuyler that he tried to sell off some of the land in Rensselaerswyck that he administered for his wife. In the early 1790s, he offered it to disgruntled tenants at what he thought were reasonable rates, but they refused.[7]

Despite low returns, landlords watched happily as the number of tenants on their estates increased after the war. Tenancy boomed in the northern Hudson Valley after the war as migrants moved onto the uninhabited regions of Rensselaerswyck and Livingston Manor. They moved into the region for many of the same reasons that people became tenants in the Hudson Valley before the Revolution. Landlords enticed migrants with long, developmental leases, fairly good land, and comparatively low rent. In fact, the Livingstons and Van Rensselaers issued the same printed, standardized leases after the Revolution that they had used before it. The

Livingstons gathered up the unused leases, scratched out any phrases that mentioned the king or Britain, and substituted more appropriate Revolutionary dates and references. These new tenants paid higher rent than earlier tenants—rent on Rensselaerswyck rose from roughly ten to thirteen bushels of wheat per one hundred acres—but they agreed to the same kind of stipulations that characterized leases in the northern Hudson Valley before independence. Still, they acquired relatively good land cheaply. Like prospective tenants before them, these postwar migrants became tenants because they did not have the money to buy freeholds either in the southern Hudson Valley or in central New York. While some of these migrants moved onto leaseholds vacated during the war, others moved into unimproved leaseholds. Some probably hoped to sell the improvements they made to the land and buy a freehold somewhere else, but others intended to stay put. In the roughly two decades after the Revolution, the population of Livingston Manor increased from approximately 4,600 people to nearly 7,400.[8] The same thing happened on Rensselaerswyck, but more dramatically. Between 1779 and the end of the century, approximately 3,336 new tenants signed leases for land in the western and northern portions of the manor.[9]

The new tenants settled towns such as Claverack, Petersburgh, Stephentown, Watervliet, Rensselaerville, Bethlehem, and Greenbush. As the Hudson River flows south from the Adirondack Mountains into Albany County, the valley opens between the Helderberg and Catskill mountains on the west and the Taconic Mountains to the east, offering farmers near the river fairly good soil. Away from the river, however, tenants found less inviting territory. On the east side of the river, tenants who lived in Claverack, Hillsdale, and Hudson, all formed after 1770, tilled undulating ground of loamy soil in the west, but the farmland grew rockier as one moved east toward Massachusetts. North of these towns and near the river, in Greenbush, tenants rented generally flat and fertile land that ran up away from the river to the hills that dominated Stephentown, Berlin, and Petersburgh. In Stephentown and Petersburgh, formed after the Revolution, tenants tried to farm the rocky valleys or the steep hills that jutted up to barren mountains nearly two thousand feet above the river. On the western side of the river, in Bethlehem, founded in 1793, tenants lived on rolling terrain that ended in steep cliffs near the river. The nearby towns of Watervliet, formed in 1788, and Rensselaerville, formed in 1790, both contained the rich soil found between the Hudson and Mohawk rivers. While Watervliet was primarily flat, Rensselaerville grew rockier and hillier as tenants moved west until they abutted, and then moved into, the steep hills of the Helderberg region.[10]

While some tenants who moved into these towns groaned at the increase in rent, they openly opposed onerous stipulations like the quarter sale. New and long-standing tenants begged the manor lord to stop collecting the quarter-sales fee. Perhaps new tenants erroneously believed that they could sell their improvements as one might sell a freehold, or perhaps they thought, again incorrectly, that they might eventually pay off the land and get freehold title to it, but Van Rensselaer did not intend for tenants to own their leaseholds, and the leases did not imply that they would. When Van Rensselaer flatly refused to get rid of the quarter-sales stipulations, many tenants ignored it. Reeve Huston rightly points out that "for the next three generations, many tenants simply neglected to inform the manor office when they sold their farms." In a survey of 768 leases that matured in the last twenty years of the eighteenth century, only 45 percent, 348, changed hands with the landlord's knowledge. The rest, 55 percent, remained with the heirs of the original lessee, or the tenant or heirs sold off the improvements without telling the Van Rensselaers. If sold, the sales of these improvements went unrecorded, and the tenants often were not prosecuted by the landlord, making these acts of noncompliance an effective form of resistance. As in the colonial period, tenants came and went, but some remained on the estate for a long time and joined with longer-term tenants who were either loyal to the manor lord or disparaged him.[11]

Old problems such as debt still plagued the manors after the war. On Rensselaerswyck, many tenants had not paid rent since the Revolution, and they had fallen far into debt. Worse, from the landlord's perspective, many tenants who signed leases in the late 1770s and 1780s did not start paying rent when their leases matured. Van Rensselaer wanted to recoup those losses and, as he showed several times, was willing to compel tenants to pay up. By the end of the 1780s, his hard tactics were starting to pay off, and tenants were settling their debts. Regardless, unpredictable weather and poor crops conspired to keep tenants from paying rent regularly, and most continued to owe a year or two in back rent. Van Rensselaer, like other manor lords, was usually willing to overlook these problems if a tenant otherwise paid rent consistently.[12]

Although rent payments fluctuated, Van Rensselaer usually collected approximately three-quarters of the rent due, and his income skyrocketed. In 1792, for instance, Stephen Van Rensselaer received 13,925 bushels of wheat (worth approximately £4,800), 2,226 fowls, and 550 days of labor from his tenants. The following year, he received 14,893 bushels of wheat, 2,362 fowls, and 581 days of labor from his tenants. Four years later, in 1797, his income rose to 25,216 bushels of wheat, 4,342 fowls, and 1,075 days of labor from tenants. Even though he collected only a portion of the rent owed to him from 1792 to 1797, Van Rensselaer's income rose from approximately £4,800 to £8,000.[13]

As in the earlier period, tenants in the Hudson Valley did not always deliver what landlords expected. New tenants in the hills of Rensselaerswyck, for instance, did not frequently pay rent with wheat, the commodity landlords preferred because of its market value downriver. Instead, new tenants, and plenty of long-standing ones, too, paid rent with wood. Lumber harvesting suggests that these leaseholds, or parts of them, were at the start of the production cycle. It also indicates that tenants, and freehold farmers, dramatically changed the way the countryside looked. Many newer tenants rented land in the rocky and sloping hills west of Albany and may have had problems turning hillsides into land fit for wheat production. Longtime tenants were likely clearing new land for producing wheat. Wheat cultivation was more productive on newly cleared land, and fertility declined quickly. Tenants closer to the river who lived on richer bottomland fared better but still had to clear new acreage every few years to accommodate wheat production. In either case, tenants knew the Van Rensselaers would accept lumber as rent. Before the war, the landlord may have had a harder time finding a market for lumber, but after it inhabitants of New York City needed the wood to rebuild the parts of the city the British army had burned. Moreover, New York City was expanding, and people needed the building supplies. Tenants' lumber production satisfied that market.[14]

Despite the increase in lumber payments, new and established tenants diversified production as much as possible, and they tended to rely on the labor of family members and neighbors instead of on agricultural wage labor. Farm labor and techniques in the Hudson Valley did not change dramatically in the second half of the eighteenth century. Thus, tenants worked alongside their neighbors and family members to grow various crops. Besides cutting wood, tenants grew wheat, barley, oats, and fruit, and they herded sheep, cattle, and milk cows. They produced many different goods for several reasons. First, diversified crop production reduced the risk of going hungry if one or two crops failed. Second, farmers were limited more by what they could harvest than by what they could plant. Varied production meant tenants spread their labor out over the entire year and could manage harvests more effectively. Finally, these crops, and tenant production in general, required very little cash investment, something that was always in short supply in freehold farm households and especially in tenant households.[15]

In the post-Revolutionary period, tenancy spread well beyond the Hudson and Mohawk valleys into western New York, where men set out to establish new estates. New proprietors, like Hudson Valley landlords, aspired to generate income from people working on their land. James Duane, for instance, had accumulated approximately thirty thousand acres northwest of Albany before the Revolution, but he did not fill it with 250 tenants until after the war. Similarly, William Cooper launched his estate and town roughly fifty miles west of Albany. Like the landed tycoons of the Hudson Valley, Cooper preferred to lease land to tenants rather than to sell it to prospective settlers. Even longtime landlords started new estates on the frontier, but they did not necessarily administer them the same way they operated their Hudson Valley estates. Robert Livingston, the chancellor, operated his family's Hudson Valley estate as his predecessors had, but he bought and then sold land on the frontier to finance new endeavors. He used some of that money to fund Robert Fulton's experiments that led to the steamship *Clermont,* named for a portion of Livingston's estate. Philip Schuyler was an exception among longtime landlords in the Hudson Valley. While Schuyler offered to sell some Hudson Valley land to quiet disgruntled people, most landlords kept their estates in the Hudson Valley in the post-Revolutionary period. The land generated too much money to give up.[16]

The post-Revolutionary manorial economy illustrates how industrial capitalism was rooted in agrarian capitalism. Livingston's investment in Fulton's steamship shows how landlords transformed the agricultural goods they collected from their tenants into commercial goods and finally into broader endeavors. Livingston was hardly alone. Philip Schuyler planned on investing the profits he reaped from tenants' income in bigger business activities. Schuyler had long dreamed of building a canal that would run along and sometimes into the Mohawk River to link the fertile land in western New York with Albany. From there, goods would flow down the Hudson River to New York City and beyond. But Schuyler never lived to see his vision completed. The Erie Canal was finally built some twenty years after he died.[17]

Landlords expanded their endeavors and prospered because Rensselaerswyck and Livingston Manor profited financially. But years of unrest among a significant portion of tenants who simply refused to pay was politically dangerous. Landlords wanted to regain the political positions and power that they had lost during the Revolution. They had, as Edward Countryman pointed out, "misread the state when they wrote the constitution." Rising land values and revitalized antagonism toward landlords pushed tenants either to avoid the voting place or to vote against the Livingstons, Schuylers, Van Rensselaers, and their agents. By the end of the Revolutionary War, lower-sort men such as Jacobus Swartout and Dirk Brinkerhoff had gained seats in either the state assembly or the state senate, and men like Philip Schuyler found themselves peering in at these new faces from the outside.[18]

Schuyler and the others quickly realized their mistakes, and they took steps to control their tenants' votes. The state constitution offered them one easy way to influence tenants. Until 1787, voters cast their ballots the old fashioned way—they announced their selections publicly. Voters could stay home rather than vote, but landlords and their agents made sure their tenants voted, and voted properly, by threatening to sue nonvoters for back rent or to collect the other fees and fines tenants invariably owed. Thus, tenants in the post-Revolutionary period found themselves subjected to the same kind of bribery and bullying they endured during the colonial period. Even with secret ballots, landlords browbeat tenants to vote for them. Tenants picked candidates by handing different kinds of paper through a screen to a monitor, who then wrote down the tenant's name and vote. Other tenants found themselves handing their ballots directly to an agent of the landlord, who read them and recorded the. tenant's vote. But the political rebellion offered some changes. By 1777, of the 290 men elected to the assembly, only 6 had served in the colonial legislature, and 161 men gained political office for the first time. The trend continued in 1781 and 1782 when voters in the northern Hudson Valley again sent new men to sit in the legislature. They did not send any Livingstons, Van Rensselaers, or Schuylers. Landlords, however, had worked hard to preserve their estates and power, and it was apparent that after the Revolution they would have to defeat impulses from below that threatened their vision. They finally started to win back their lost seats by 1785 when Robert Livingston Jr. crowed that "Gentmn. of property in the County . . . carried this Election to a man." Regardless, they spent the remainder of the period reclaiming lost ground.[19]

PEACEFUL PETITIONS FOR LAND

Discontented inhabitants of the northern Hudson Valley resisted landlords' resurging political power while they worked to slow down encroaching landlordism. Their language of discontent reflected the new world in which they operated. While the insurgents' aspirations had remained consistent, they now used language steeped in Revolutionary rhetoric. In much the same way that yeoman South Carolinians understood their political status in terms of property ownership, disgruntled tenants in the northern Hudson Valley knew that landownership led to political and economic independence. As long as tenancy predominated, and for as long as they remained tenants, leaseholders remained politically and economically beholden to their landlords. Manor lords, however, went the other way. For them, citizenship, patriotism, and economic independence grew out of property ownership. In the post-Revolutionary period, the rights of property versus the rights of citizens became one way in which social conflicts played out ideologically.[20]

Disgruntled tenants and squatters who lived on Livingston Manor and Rensselaerswyck renewed their land disputes immediately after the war. As in the earlier period, dissidents initially tried to achieve their goals peacefully. In February 1784, James Spencer, Simeon Roulee, and others petitioned the new state government for land in Columbia County, New York. The new county was created in 1786 and lay just north of Dutchess County on the east side of the Hudson River. It contained much of Livingston Manor. The petitioners echoed the reasoning of rebels in the colonial period: The landlords' ancestors had duped Indians into selling off their lands or had simply taken it and had reconfigured the boundaries of otherwise small grants to make their estates much larger. Discontented tenants were again petitioning for ownership of the land they leased and not for ownership of unimproved land nearby or for equitable redistribution of all land. The petitioners attested that they "had honestly acquired" the land by virtue of their "many years hard Labour" for "support of themselves and Familys." Spencer and Roulee hoped that the government would recognize their claim and fulfill the promise of the Revolution. At first, the assembly appeared sympathetic. The members instructed the petitioners to present to "either house of the Legislature at the first meeting . . . a bill for granting them [the petitioners] relief from the Grievances Complained of in their petition relative to the Lands they Occupy." The legislature, however, rejected the petitioners' bill, leaving them again to "fall a Sacrifice to the Mercinary and unjust Views of their Adversaries, unto which fate until some further hearing on the matter they can by no means submit."[21]

The Van Rensselaers, Livingstons, and state officials tried to thwart future complaints of this kind by settling the boundaries between New York and New England. They all remembered various and sometimes violent disputes that grew out of unclear boundaries, and few officials anywhere wanted to relive those adventures. Settling the boundaries meant that both sides would have to give up some land, but it was better to lose some land than to enhance chances of upheaval by leaving boundaries unclear. In 1787, commissioners from New York and Massachusetts surveyed and outlined their common border. They began their investigation with the boundary report written during the Revolution. Commissioners negotiated the new border in July 1787, and Philip Schuyler, one of New York's commissioners, submitted the new plan to both states at the end of the month. The report reaffirmed the boundaries established during the Revolution, and the new boundaries were accepted.[22]

If the boundary report was supposed to avert rebellion, officials in both states misread the conditions that facilitated discontent. The report settled the dispute between Massachusetts and New York, but it failed to address or resolve the real issues that provoked disputes. The boundary report was a diplomatic success but a political failure. Disgruntled tenants had hoped that a new boundary line would put the disputed region in Massachusetts. They figured they stood a far better chance of getting title to their land from that state than from New York. But insurgents refused to relinquish their claims to land simply because they found themselves dealing only with New York after 1787. Their claims for ownership depended on occupancy and labor, conditions that transcended political boundaries.[23]

The survey inspired a new round of petitions. In 1789, Roulee and Spencer and roughly two hundred others submitted at least two more petitions to the state assembly. These later petitions followed the pattern of the earlier one. Petitioners again impugned the Van Rensselaers for their predicament, and they allied with the victims of attacks in 1766 by British soldiers, who had "laid Waste their Habitations killed their Cattle & destroyed their crops to the great Injury & irreparable Loss of many of your Petitioners and their helpless Families." For landlords and state officials, however, titles to land remained the litmus test for conflicting land claims. Landlords argued that by protecting their estates they benefited the overall community, and they presented their service during the Revolution as further evidence of their honorable actions: Property ownership had roused landlords' allegiance to the Revolution. These well-known and well-respected Revolutionaries knew that few if any rural rebels could counter with tales of their own extensive Revolutionary service. The petitions went nowhere.[24]

THE MURDER OF A SHERIFF

Armed with new state boundaries that legitimated their estates and recent defeats of petitions for land in the assembly, landlords again pressed tenants for rent. Stephen Van Rensselaer restated his threats to evict tenants who did not pay rent, but his strong-arm tactics did not always work. Some tenants clearly could not pay. They had not made their farms productive enough, or they had not recovered from the war yet. While these tenants worried Van Rensselaer, he was far more concerned with those tenants who flatly refused to pay. Regardless of how often or seriously he threatened them, these dissidents rebuked him at every turn, and the new manor lord spent the ensuing decade hounding them.[25]

Philip Schuyler tried a different approach. He sought to appease some of the more discontented tenants on land he administered for the Van Rensselaers. He managed the part of Claverack that belonged to his wife, Catherine, the daughter of John Van Rensselaer. The region contained the notoriously unruly towns of Hillsdale (formerly Nobletown) and Spencertown. According to Schuyler, many of the tenants in the region had not paid rent since the end of the war, and he wanted the money they owed him. While he sought to collect rent in arrears, he recognized the limited potential for earning profits from these tenants. Many of them had been resisting tenancy since at least the end of the war, and others had been fighting landlordism and tenancy far longer. Schuyler also knew that they were angry that some of their neighbors had already been evicted, and, while he hoped to make some money, he ardently wished to keep peace in the countryside.

To achieve his somewhat contradictory goals, Schuyler proposed two plans. First, anyone who wanted to stay on the land they had improved had to buy it from him for 18s. per acre with a five-year mortgage and the cancellation of all back rent. Second, those who chose to remain tenants could eradicate all rent in arrears by paying one year's rent. Schuyler considered these conditions gracious because they resembled, and in many ways bettered, the stipulations put on tenants who bought land confiscated from Loyalists. His proposal represented a dramatic change in how he interacted and dealt with his tenants and suggests at least one way this otherwise staunch and largely conventional man thought of the Revolution. Schuyler tried to democratize landholding on a portion of Rensselaerswyck he administered, and he believed that most of the disgruntled people would take the deal. He was wrong; most refused to pay him anything for land that they thought should be theirs anyhow. Their labor on the land and their allegiance to the Revolution had solidified their claims to the land they occupied.[26]

Thus spurned, Schuyler acted more decisively. Like other landlords and officials, he targeted the leading men who stood in his way. In the middle of October 1791, Schuyler directed the deputy sheriff of Columbia County to appraise John Arnold's farm, to evict Arnold and his family, and to sell the improvements they had made to the land. Arnold had been a notorious rioter for years and was a known leader of rural insurgents. Moreover, he had probably not paid rent for a long time, if at all. When the deputy sheriff arrived at Arnold's farm, he noticed that many of the local inhabitants had already "assembled and with threats deterred the deputy from proceeding with" Schuyler's order. The deputy left. A few days later, the sheriff, Cornelius Hogeboom, visited Arnold's farm with a county judge, his relative Stephen Hogeboom, and with the same deputy sheriff. While these men waited for another deputy to deliver the eviction papers, disgruntled rural people began congregating ominously in nearby woods. The sheriff and his party wisely tried to leave, but Arnold, incensed that his farm was being sold from under him, drew his pistol and fired into the air. At the signal, thirty to forty men painted and dressed to look like Indians ran from the nearby woods and chased the sheriff and his companions.[27]

Most of these "Indians" just wanted to keep officials from selling Arnold's farm. They rode and ran around the clearing, shouting at the sheriff and his men and shooting their guns into the air. The maneuver worked, and the sheriff and his men began to disperse. John Arnold and Thomas Southward, on the other hand, had far more sinister motives. They trapped Sheriff Cornelius Hogeboom, and Southward shot the sheriff fatally in the chest. Stephen Hogeboom and the other men retreated to the nearby town of Hudson, where they organized a posse to capture the other rioters, who had fled into the nearby countryside to hide at Peter Showerman's farm. Hot on the heels of the rioters, the posse captured thirteen men and charged them with felonious rioting and second-degree murder. Arnold hid for weeks before he was captured and charged with murder. Southward was captured at much the same time and was charged with capital murder, indicating that he and not John Arnold had killed the sheriff. Peter Showerman was charged with abetting the rioters for letting them hide in his farm, but he evidently died before he could stand trial. His role in the riot remains a mystery. Four other rioters escaped capture entirely by boarding a boat headed for Nova Scotia, which had served as the primary destination for the rural lower sort who had sided with the British during the Revolution.[28]

Why the rioters dressed as Indians remains somewhat unclear. Plenty of rioters throughout the region disguised themselves to avoid prosecution. Participants in the classic rite of rough music, or charivari, often hid their identities to escape detection or to avoid being targeted later by officials. But dressing as Indians suggests other agenda. The rioters may have been trying to identify themselves as citizens in the new nation by disguising themselves as people clearly recognized as outsiders. The irony of the new United States was that it was a nation without nationalism in which citizens identified themselves by marginalizing others. At the same time, the rioters may have been trying to invoke New Yorkers' perception of Indians as ruthless allies of the British. The Iroquois had sided with the British during the Revolutionary War, and some of the fiercest fighting in the state took place between white New Yorkers on one side, and the British army and the Iroquois on the other. In that way, rioters may have tried to deflect culpability for the violence they perpetrated by casting themselves as fierce and violent people of another race. Or perhaps the rioters donned Indian garb to make a better claim to the land. Indians were widely regarded as the first occupants of the land, and rioters considered Indians' claims superior to landlords'. They thought the state should too. By dressing as Indians, rioters may have been trying to assume the role of the first and legitimate occupants of the land, thereby invalidating the claims of landlords and strengthening their own.[29]

In the ensuing weeks, debate over the killing revealed how social differences of new men in power contributed to the rise of political dispute. Partisan politics had divided the ruling factions of New York's elite for a long time, but these groups usually joined forces to defeat social rebellion from below in the colonial period. While elite politicians had disagreed over how they wanted to rule, they generally agreed that they should command their social inferiors, and they presented a unified front against anyone who threatened New York's political and social hierarchy. After they reasserted themselves in the mid-1780s, landlords and their agents continued to condemn any and all attempts at social rebellion from below. But the Revolution had opened politics, especially at the state level, to new men who were reluctant to denounce social rebellion categorically. Men such as Matthew Adgate, Dirk Brinkerhoff, and Abraham Yates entered the fray and tended to side with disgruntled rural people against landlord politicians. Brinkerhoff, for instance, championed the redistribution of Loyalists' land to make it possible for tenants to buy the land they inhabited and improved. Others like them included a social agenda in their direct political attacks of the growing power of wealthy men in their community, making the political gap a social one as well. In the process, they made politics in New York intensely partisan and socially driven.[30]

Abraham Yates especially drew parallels that heightened the conflict between politics and social standing. He knew that the "middle sort" like himself stood at odds with the social elite such as the Livingstons and Philip Schuyler. He also divided his fellow politicians in New York when he criticized the United States Constitution of 1787 as a conspiracy designed to usurp the liberties of the people. According to Yates, the elite "propagate[ed] among the People [the theory] that the Confederacy was defective, that too Much power remained in the hands of the People and the several state Legislatures." The advocates of the Constitution insisted that only a strong, centralized government that reduced the power of middling men could remedy these problems. For Yates, that was precisely the issue. The Constitution was an attempt by monied men to reduce the political influence of middling men who had made headway into state politics at the expense of the elites in their communities. These elites wanted their power back, and they were willing to sacrifice the political liberties of common people to get it.[31]

The subsequent trial of the rioters heightened these lingering political tensions by revealing the cracks in New York's political foundation. Outside Columbia County, Anti-Federalists and Federalists alike thought the rioters represented a threat to the order of the new nation. Rural riots and attacks on state officials heightened fears of disorder in the new nation, and political leaders of all stripes worried that violence in the countryside would upset the country's newly obtained, but tenuously held, stability. These officials wanted the court to mete out swift and severe punishment. Governor George Clinton himself severely criticized the rioters because they dared to threaten the "laws and authority of the government."[32]

Inside Columbia County, officials were more divided. While they wanted to punish the offenders, keep the peace, and diminish chances for future rioting, how and why officials wanted to achieve these goals differed greatly. Stephen Hogeboom, who was a Federalist in 1788 but returned to Clintonian alliances before embarking on a Republican future, wanted to restore order and, understandably, to punish rioters for killing his relative. Federalist Henry Livingston feared that harsh retribution might incite further rebellion. He hoped calmer heads would seek peace instead of simple vengeance. Anti-Federalists in the county also disagreed with each other. Anti-Federalist John Livingston chastised judges regardless of their political affiliation. He criticized them for not proceeding quickly enough against the rioters and for not protecting the landlords' property rights. According to John Livingston, the other Anti-Federalists should follow the path taken by Peter Van Ness, who took a hard line against the insurgents and murderers.[33]

Van Ness was one of many men who presided over the trials of the rioters. In New York, judges, like elected officials, were also divided by party affiliation and by their opinions of the rioters. Seven judges—Peter Livingston, Peter Van Schaack, Samuel Ten Broeck, Jacob Ford, Robert Yates, Stephen Hogeboom, and Isreal Spencer—may be identified as Federalists in the early 1790s. Six others—William B. Whiting, Matthew Adgate, Philip Frisbie, Seth Jenkins, Peter Van Ness, and John Lansing—may be recognized as Anti-Federalists or, later, as Democratic Republicans, who were not necessarily descendants of Anti-Federalists but who also opposed the Federalists. The other judges—Claudius J. Delameter, David Lawrence, and David Pratt—can not be adequately categorized. That Philip Schuyler was a staunch Federalist may well have prompted some overtly political judges to let their political views influence how they administered the trials. They may not have acted in the best interests of peace or of justice, something their opponents would have greatly resented. While not every judge heard every case, such political division among jurists saturated a local murder with elements of a national political debate that some in the courtroom may have wished either to ignore entirely or to forget for the time being.[34]

Although the judges presided over the trials, jurors decided the fate of the rioters. Jurors in New York at the time were neither as rich as nor as politically powerful as either landlords or judges and were almost certain to be, if not sympathetic to the rioters, at least reluctant to alienate neighbors. Some jurors, such as David Bonestadt, were tenants or former tenants, and most if not all of the jurors lived in the region near Arnold's farm. Even before the juries sat down to hear the cases, they probably favored their neighbors over landlords and Federalist state officials. The jurors made their predilections quite clear, and the rioters benefited by being tried by a jury of their peers. While Southward and Arnold were tried separately because of the seriousness of the charges against them, the other rioters stood trial together. None of it mattered. What mattered more was that the jurors were unwilling to support landlords' attempts to evict tenants even if a tenant had determinedly refused to pay rent for years. Landlords made enemies among tenants, even among those who had paid rent faithfully, when they used the force of law to evict rural insurgents to make more money. By evicting tenants, landlords were attacking the rights and liberties of all the inhabitants of the countryside. From a juror's point of view, landlords sacrificed the rights of rural people to live securely on the land and to provide for their households so they could make fortunes from their tenants' labors. One by one, all of the rioters were acquitted.

The acquittals rocked the state and the county. While the juries used this opportunity to condemn violence against land rioters and to denounce landlordism, opponents accused the jurors of throwing out the order of law and government that Revolutionaries had fought for and were fighting to preserve. Landlords in the region felt particularly betrayed. They had put their lives and fortunes at great risk during the Revolution, but rural dissidents attacked them with an arm of the very government Revolutionary landlords had created. Despite the audacity of the verdicts and the uproar over them, the Hudson Valley changed very little as a result.[35]

A RETURN TO PETITIONS

In the summer of 1792, the fervor over the trials began to wane, but Thomas Witbeck, who managed Rensselaerswyck, was still uneasy. He worried about more violence, and he insinuated as much to Stephen Van Rensselaer whenever he could. Witbeck overstated his fears, however. Insurgents were not clamoring to take up arms again. They knew that Thomas Southward had barely escaped execution, and few wanted to get that close to the noose. But disgruntled farmers did not hide. If anything, the not-guilty verdicts inspired them to try to get land again but to use more peaceful methods this time. Disgruntled tenants on Rensselaerswyck resumed petitioning the state legislature, pleading that the new government should address their complaints and solve the ongoing, and now decades-old, dispute between insurgents and landlords. They returned to petitions, rather than nonpayment of rent, because they worried about more evictions and more violence. Petitions were a legitimate method of complaint, unlike rioting, even though insurgents expected the petitions to fail. The new state government had shown that it was as unlikely as any colonial government to parcel up Hudson Valley estates.[36]

By the end of 1792, insurgents had submitted at least four petitions to the state legislature for land in and around the towns of Kinderhook, New Canaan, Hillsdale, and Claverack. Petitioners reiterated previous complaints. The Van Rensselaers' titles did not include the disputed land, and the Van Rensselaers had fraudulently expanded their estate at the expense of Indians. Jonathan Havens, an assemblyman, thought the issues were "of a nature so alarming, as to require the serious attention of the Legislature." In the same breath, however, he worried that there was "little prospect of having the said controversies determined in the ordinary course of law." The assembly faced a dilemma. If members supported the petitioners, they would irritate men of standing in New York and throw the state's hierarchy into disarray. Yet, if they acted against the petitioners, they risked rekindling violence.[37]

New York officials worried about widespread violence in the countryside because it appeared to be erupting all around them. By the early 1790s, squatters in the Susquehanna River valley and inhabitants of the Massachusetts backcountry had taken up arms against their political rulers. Disputes over land along the northern branch of the Susquehanna River closely resembled aspects of the dispute playing out in the northern Hudson Valley. Squatters from New England—Connecticut in this case—had started settling land occupied by Delaware Indians in the late colonial period. While some Pennsylvanians wanted the land set aside for the Delawares, others wanted the land parceled out and sold to settlers and speculators, some wanted to sell it or give it to the Iroquois, and still others sought to settle the land themselves. These disputes became part of the Revolutionary War in the Susquehanna Valley and led to vicious fighting between people who chose sides based more on their relationship to the land than on their political allegiances. Fighting over the land, on the ground and in court, continued into the post-Revolutionary period and threatened to spill over into nearby states. Rural insurgence in western Massachusetts struck even closer to the heart of nervous New Yorkers. In 1776, insurgents there struggled to get a voice in the newly emerging state government. Just a year later, other backcountry people took up arms to protest currency legislation that threatened their welfare. By the middle 1780s when Daniel Shays led his rebellion, the rural inhabitants of the state had a long history of violent protest, and they drew on that heritage again when they demonstrated, and then rioted, against what they considered to be unfair taxes.[38]

What matters more than what happened in these rebellions is what New Yorkers of all classes thought was happening. Conspiracies of widespread frontier rebellion may have been a bit far-fetched, but they were not new in the 1790s, and they were not entirely unfounded. In August 1771, a "Gentleman at Pennsylvania" complained to a friend that an internal war in the Wyoming Valley might, if unchecked, "prove as dangerous as the Regulators of North Carolina." What he really worried about was that if officials could not stop the rioting, "one general Chain will be form'd of them throughout the whole Continent, as the Views and Conduct of them are all similar."[39] In post-Revolutionary New York, officials and landlords did not need to imagine any connections between Hudson Valley insurgents and their counterparts in the Wyoming Valley, Vermont, and western Massachusetts. Insurgents and revolutionaries such as Ethan Allen and Thomas Young had moved through these regions during the Revolutionary War, spreading anti-authoritarianism and anti-landlordism as they went. In the 1780s, Philip Schuyler, the Livingstons, and the Van Rensselaers all worried incessantly that Shaysites would likewise travel through upstate New York, spreading rebellion wherever they traveled. In September 1787, a Connecticut newspaper summed up their fears by concluding that "We see . . . *banditties* rising up against land and good order in all quarters of our country."[40]

What did the rural inhabitants of upstate New York, tenants and insurgents alike, know of these matters? Surely, the landlords and political elite were not the only ones who knew of land riots in other places. But showing what tenants knew remains difficult. Lower-sort Americans lived in a largely oral society in which they received their news via rumors and gossip, and social exchanges of information, stories, and prejudices could not be easily dismissed or invalidated. Some of the insurgents in the northern Hudson Valley, however, may well have met the very man who personified the dangerous insurrection officials and landlords feared most. Daniel Shays, along with many discontented New Englanders, moved onto Rensselaerswyck in 1790, just before Arnold and Southward attacked Cornelius Hogeboom. Although no concrete evidence links Shays with either New York rioter, it remains unlikely that his neighbors did not know of his troubled past. Shays moved on after only a few years.[41]

Whatever inspired insurgents in the Hudson Valley to act, fear of widespread rioting and legislative infighting incapacitated the New York assembly. Officials were unlikely to pass political initiatives that undermined the authority and order they had struggled to establish. But officials also worried about explicitly condemning the petitions and inciting more riots. At the same time, legislators could not work out a solution that satisfied any of the parties involved, making the issue simply too hot to handle politically. More than that, legislators were fighting among themselves for control of the state, enabling landlords and their agents to take advantage of partisan politics to at least push the petitions off the political agenda for the time being. In the end, either despite the turmoil or perhaps because of it, the legislature did nothing.[42]

The assembly did not merely throw out every petition that came its way. Officials considered the merits of each before making a decision. The four rejected petitions were unfounded, but the assembly decided favorably on a petition submitted by other inhabitants of Hillsdale. Disputes over the tract began in the 1750s when a group of migrants moved to the area from East Haddam, Connecticut. A series of ongoing court cases investigated who owned the land. The Massachusetts assembly argued that the region was part of that colony while the Van Rensselaers insisted that it was part of Rensselaerswyck and was marked by Kinderhook Creek. Opponents continued to press the issue in large part because of the vague boundaries of that part of the estate. To ease the pressure in 1773, John Van Rensselaer, the proprietor, finally settled the disputes. To get an unassailable title to the rest of his land, Van Rensselaer gave up approximately sixty-six thousand acres of the land in question. The inhabitants of that land spent the ensuing twenty years either embroiled in the Revolution or trying to get titles to their plots. In February 1793, these inhabitants petitioned the assembly for the land. Jonathan Havens read an act to grant them that land. The act was put down, and according to legislative procedure a second reading was ordered. An act had to be read at least three times before it was finally abandoned or passed. The next day, John Livingston put the bill before the assembly again. He and a committee had gone over it, changed its name, and resubmitted it. The bill "was again read, and agreed to by the house." What made this petition different from the rejected ones? The assembly was not really doing anything new. It was simply granting land to the petitioners that the Van Rensselaers had already given up in 1773.[43]

Petitioners on Livingston Manor, however, had no such luck. After the death of Robert Livingston Jr. in 1790, Henry Livingston began administering the part of his father's estate that contained the region beset by land rioting over the past half century.[44] What he saw when he looked out over his new tenants was hardly encouraging. Almost immediately after taking control, Livingston learned that Petrus Pulver had expanded his leasehold. Pulver's initial lease was for 217 acres, but, according to Henry Livingston, by 1790 Pulver farmed "much more" than that, and he had not paid rent at all since 1775. Pulver was not the only one. Livingston bemoaned that a majority of his tenants had "extended the Boundaries mentioned in their Leases" without telling him or his father, and most had not paid rent since the Revolution. To remedy the problems, Livingston and William Wilson, who managed the Livingstons' holdings in Columbia County, planned to return tenants to their original leaseholds. But he also worried that these already-antagonistic tenants might violently rebuke his attempts to regain some control over the estate, so Livingston also intended to draw up new leases for tenants who wanted to stay on their expanded tenancies. Although he certainly figured he had few other options, he was surprisingly reluctant to come down too hard on people he knew might well reject his concessions. His best strategy was to recognize the illicit leasehold extensions tenants had made over the previous years, increase their rent, and profit from their labor.[45]

From late 1792 through 1793, insurgents tried to circumvent Livingston's attempts to reorganize their leaseholds by again petitioning the state assembly for the land they inhabited. Like other petitioners, they relied on long-standing arguments and received some inconsequential support from sympathetic assemblymen. In March 1794, for instance, Andrew Wheeler, whose relatives had rioted against the Livingstons in 1776 and 1777, joined one such petition. Approximately one week after receiving the petition, a committee from the assembly declared that the petitioners had a legitimate "title to a considerable portion of the said lands, in the town of Livingston." The committee then ordered the state to conduct a survey to determine the proper boundaries of the manor, and the towns in it, to settle the dispute. The members, however, refused to go much further than that and left unresolved the proper boundaries of either Livingston Manor or the towns in the region. While the matter was hardly under their jurisdiction, they wanted to sidestep a potentially explosive political topic. Regardless, this marked at least the third time in less than a decade that the assembly had acknowledged the petitioners' position but decided not to take any action. That kind of fence-sitting enabled the assembly to appear sympathetic to petitioners without directly addressing their claims. The result was that the assembly tacitly reaffirmed the landlords' claims.[46]

Less than one year later, in January 1795, Petrus Pulver headed yet another group of petitioners who asserted their rights to the land. Again, the signers reiterated previous arguments. This time they justified their claims in relationship to the government formed during and after the Revolution. Furthermore, they embedded their perception of land use inside their interpretation of the Revolution. In the new petition, Pulver and 214 others contended that the first manor lord, Robert Livingston (1654–1728), had bought his land under "false and fraudulent pretences" from local Indians and that the family had illegitimately expanded boundaries of the grants they received from colonial governors. The land, the petitioners argued, should revert to the state in much the same way that the state government had claimed the property of Loyalists during the Revolutionary War. The petitioners contended that they were willing to pay the state a fair price for the land in exactly the same way that tenants bought confiscated Loyalist land. They left to the state to figure out how to compensate the Livingstons for their lost land. By adopting this last strategy, the petitioners proposed a policy that had already worked in the southern Hudson Valley and that petitioners thought should be implemented in the rest of the region. The critical difference, however, was that the landlords in question in the north had all supported the Revolution, and they, or their agents, sat in the assemblies that debated these measures. Not surprisingly, these men refused to divide their estates or the estates of their benefactors, and the legislature's attitude toward these petitions remained unchanged.[47]

The ethnically diverse petitioners shared material conditions, aspirations, and the common tradition of the American Revolution. Slightly less than one-third of the petitioners had English, Scottish, Irish, or Welsh surnames. The others had Dutch or German surnames. They lived near the site of the British attack of rioters at Nobletown in July 1766 and near a Dutch Reformed and a Lutheran church. Of the 214 petitioners, 98 placed a mark near their names, including Catrina Michel, who was probably the widow of Johannes Michel. Approximately half of the signers were tenants on Livingston Manor. Fifty of the signers appeared on the 1779 tax list as residents of the manor. The wealthiest petitioner was rated as having £225 in realty, and the poorest lived on a leasehold valued at only £10. The average signer's leasehold was rated at £119. While that was slightly below the average of the tenants on the manor, it was less than 1 percent of the realty owned by the landlord at the time. At least forty-seven others shared family names with tenants; and twelve more had become tenants in the 1790s. At least eight of the twelve new tenants had signed leases to avoid eviction in the late stages of the war or immediately after it. They accepted tenancy over the perils of starting over on the frontier. Pulver, for his part, asserted that most of the signers were tenants, but he also plainly stated why they opposed the Livingstons in the first place. Tenants on the manor, and everywhere in the Hudson Valley, lived under "Terms and Conditions oppressive and burthensome to the last degree."[48]

The New York assembly reviewed Pulver's petition. As it had for petitions in 1789, 1792, and 1793, however, the assembly ordered yet another investigation of the boundaries of Livingston Manor. Here assemblymen struck a familiar chord. They found problems with the Livingstons' title but again decided not to intervene in the dispute. Petitioners and insurgents had consistently claimed that their physical labor on the land, not simply their occupancy, entitled them to own it. They had cleared forests, removed stones, plowed fields, planted crops, reaped the harvests, fenced in their leaseholds, and built houses and barns. They had improved the land with their hands. The state, however, expressed a different rationale and sided definitively with the landlords. Any decision that affirmed the petitioners' logic undermined the legitimacy of labor contracts throughout the state. As a result, the assembly concluded that the Livingstons turned wilderness into property by living on it and administering it for more than one hundred years. The legislature declared that "after such a length of possession it would be improper in the State to resume lands for any real or supposed defects in the original grants under which such lands may have been held." Furthermore, during their possession the Livingstons had filled the land with tenants who then labored on it. In a truly radical pronouncement, the assembly then used the petitioners' arguments to affirm landlords' titles. Tenants' labor on the land, as a result, remained an important component of landownership, but not in the way the petitioners had hoped. According to the assembly, tenants' labor on the land did not legitimate their claims of ownership but instead validated the landlords' title to the land.[49]

A CITIZEN SPEAKS OUT

In the winter and spring of 1795, "A Citizen" spoke out in favor of the tenants. In several essays in *The Albany Gazette* that spanned three months, "A Citizen" accused Stephen Van Rensselaer of, among other things, jeopardizing the welfare of tenants by restricting their access to fuel and building materials on uninhabited common land. The dispute was hardly a trivial one economically, and it carried enormous symbolic weight. Van Rensselaer and insurgents were debating whether longtime residents of the estate had a customary right to the resources found outside the boundaries of their leaseholds. In England during enclosure in the sixteenth and seventeenth centuries, use of the commons for fuel, foddering, and building material sparked endemic disputes that often turned violent. Landlords could and did charge tenants and small landholders with the capital crime of poaching.[50] Although New York tenants in the late eighteenth century were unlikely to be well versed on this particular subject, they likely had a clear sense of customary rights, and they strongly opposed landlords who apparently took everything. The influx of new tenants into Rensselaerswyck after the Revolution brought the issue to the forefront, but it was not a new problem. In 1762, Abraham Yates levied the same kinds of criticisms at the Van Rensselaers, and it appeared that he was doing it again thirty years later.[51]

Yates had long shown himself to be a critic of wealthy men running politics. While he openly criticized landlords in the 1760s, he drew their ire again during the Revolution for pushing for social rebellion. In 1778, Philip Schuyler derided Yates as the very representative of the new kind of man entering politics during the Revolution. According to Schuyler, these new men, like Yates, were self-made and rose from mechanic to assemblymen and then to senator. That was exactly what irritated Schuyler. Men like Yates, whom Schuyler mocked as the "late Cobbler of Laws and Old Shoes," lacked the pedigree to be effective rulers. Schuyler's class prejudices notwithstanding, by 1784, Yates had blossomed into such an irritant to men of wealth that Thomas Tillotson, the brother-in-law of Robert R. Livingston, scorned Yates as an "old booby."[52] Still, Yates stood firmly against a wealthy oligarchy. In 1789, he criticized the United States Constitution as a conspiracy of monied men to usurp the liberties of the people and allow men like Philip Schuyler and Alexander Hamilton to "erect a Nobility."[53]

Yates again took up his pen to expose oppression after Thomas Witbeck warned tenants that anyone caught cutting "down or carrying away timber or firewood" from Van Rensselaer's uninhabited land would suffer "pain of being prosecuted for trespass." The warning signified another change in Van Rensselaer's policies concerning his tenants. Van Rensselaer and previous lords of the estate had allowed tenants to glean firewood and lumber from uninhabited regions. In the post-Revolutionary period, however, timber became a more valuable commodity as New Yorkers rebuilt their city. Van Rensselaer, for one, did not want to lose potential profits to tenants who poached his lumber. At the same time, he worried that prospective tenants might demand lower rent for land already cleared by poachers who had taken a commodity new tenants relied on while they made their farms productive. Finally, the move indicated that Van Rensselaer was shedding the last layer of veneer of paternalism that had characterized previous manor lords. He was clearly more concerned with profits than with his tenants. This was the acid test; a man who would put his profits ahead of the welfare of his tenants would, according to "A Citizen," put his personal interests before those of the nation.[54]

"A Citizen" did not restrict his criticisms to changing customary rights. He quickly addressed the more familiar issues of conflicting land claims and, as Yates had done before, championed the cause of those rural people who wanted to dismantle the great estates that survived the Revolution. By the mid-1790s, the argument resonated among people who had been making the same case for nearly forty years. "A Citizen" contended that Indians had "made a grant of part" of the region around Albany to the "original settlers." The Van Rensselaers, however, subsumed that land into their manor when they fraudulently expanded their estate. To turn back encroaching English settlers and to encourage Dutch colonization of the area, the Dutch government legitimated the Van Rensselaers' claims by granting them a patent to the estate. The Van Rensselaers' grant measured two miles north and south from Albany along the banks of the Hudson River and extended up to twenty-four miles east and west. The Van Rensselaers, and others who subsequently received large tracts of land, wanted to fill their estates with tenants who would pay rent. To achieve their goals, "A Citizen" contended, these landlords usurped the power of the Dutch West India Company and forced their opponents to move. Thereafter, the region had "no other name, but that of the colony of Rensselaerswyck."[55] "A

Citizen" drew on and expanded similar opinions made by Yates, Thomas Young, and Daniel Nimham. While Yates, Young, and Nimham pondered these issues with a colonial institutional framework, "A Citizen" used these disputes to publicly assess developing power relationships within the state and nation. In this way, "A Citizen" criticized the state's attempt to restrict ordinary people's pursuit of happiness.[56]

The members of the assembly turned deaf ears to Pulver's petition and to the criticisms of "A Citizen." But the rebuke held two possibly unforeseen consequences. First, in rejecting Pulver's petition, the assembly argued that tenants' labor confirmed and validated landlords' ownership of the land. In doing so, the assembly adopted the widely held belief that use and occupancy entitled people to own land and directly addressed ongoing disputes over land and power during the Revolutionary settlement. How the assembly handled these conflicting claims hinted at what became one of the keys to the prominence and power of American democratic capitalism in the nineteenth and twentieth centuries. The assembly adroitly turned alternative ideas into mainstream rhetoric by using them against the people who espoused them. Rebellion waged from the center hardly threatened, or threatens, the structure.

Second, the assembly laid the foundation for future insurrections. By 1795, the Livingstons, Philip Schuyler, and the Van Rensselaers had spent the better part of a decade fighting a two-front battle to keep their land. On one side stood several hundred disgruntled rural people who consistently declared that their labor and occupancy on the land entitled them to own it. On the other side, landlords faced off against middling men and state officials, especially members of the assembly, who were arguing over the distribution of land and power in the new state. Landlords tried to convince their opponents that preserving Hudson Valley estates would help protect stability in the new state. They may not have been as successful as they wanted, but in the 1790s only a few men were willing to risk order by attacking landlordism or by questioning a landlord's power. When it decided against Pulver's petition, the assembly effectively closed its doors to future petitions for land, compelling insurgents to take more dramatic steps.[57]

A RETURN TO VIOLENCE

Approximately one year after the assembly stifled their petitions, insurgents again resorted to violence. From the spring through the fall of 1797, insurgents on and near Livingston Manor prevented Henry Livingston from surveying new tenancies. Livingston wanted to survey the land to mark out new leaseholds and to obtain accurate measurements on existing ones. If a tenant claimed more land than his lease outlined, Livingston intended to increase the tenant's rent. Tenants agonized that Livingston intended to evict any tenant who would not or could not pay the rent due on the extra land. They were right to be worried. Surveyors returned with men who carried eviction notices, and the insurgents attacked them. "The Devil has got into my people here," Livingston lamented. When they "heard I was going to Survey (which was not the fact)" they "muster'd (in disguise) a number to prevent me." Livingston confided to William Wilson that "all things are Hostile here."[58]

The tenants' attacks worked, but only to a point. "One brand of fire would injure me materially," Livingston complained, and so he decided to try to settle "in all cases" even if he lost money. But he quickly changed his mind. After several small skirmishes with surveyors, the local sheriff, and the landlord's agents, the rioters traveled to Henry Livingston's house, where they taunted him with cheers. When Livingston tried to survey new leaseholds in September 1797, rioters again attacked the surveyors. Livingston responded by trying to evict the leaders of the rioters, and the rioters again attacked and beat men who delivered eviction notices. The rule of law was breaking down.[59]

In February 1798, Governor John Jay tried to restore order and begged the state senate to send out troops to quash the rebels. Jay insisted that the insurgents had attacked state officials and had thus threatened landlords' inviolable titles. If the challenge was successful, Jay contended, New York's political order, and that of the new nation, faced an improbable future. In short, for the Federalist Jay, the rioters proved "very offensive to justice and [were] subversive of good order." Jay spoke to a largely understanding audience. Many of the Federalists in the senate sympathized with the landlords, were landlords, or considered the rebels a threat to New York's stability. Unlike Federalists, Republicans were split over the uprising. Some supported it while others decried it. Two days after Jay's plea, the state legislature resolved to use force to suppress land rioters on Livingston Manor. In doing so, the legislators followed a path taken by their predecessors and mirrored similar steps taken by other states in the 1780s and 1790s. Like their neighbors, New York assemblymen worried more about preserving their positions and restoring order than about taking the Revolution any further.[60]

Livingston had cautioned others to avoid excessive force for fear of inciting widespread rebellion. But he followed cues from the legislature and took a harsher stand. He knew that the state would support his measures, or at least would suppress riots that erupted in response to his activities. And, like the rioters he opposed, Livingston had tried nearly everything else. Pleas, petitions, rebukes, threats, and some conciliation had all failed. For Livingston, outright force appeared to be the last best chance to get what he wanted. If he thought that way, so did insurgents. In the spring of 1798, Henry Livingston made it known that any tenant who could not or would not pay back rent would be evicted and sued. His hard tactics backfired and stirred dissidents to mount their last "obstinate Resistance to the Law" of the century. In May, dissidents responded to Livingston's demands and threats by setting fire to the Livingstons' iron furnaces in Ancram. The furnaces only survived because of the quick action of the people who lived and worked in the buildings that were set ablaze.

In October, after a summer of skirmishing, Petrus Pulver and Livingston Manor tenant Ambrose Latting organized insurgents for a face-to-face meeting with Henry Livingston. Livingston, however, was so afraid that he stationed trusted allies to watch his "Barn and horse this night." While his fears never materialized, his concerns inhibited good negotiations. The talks went nowhere, and the insurgency in the countryside faded. Perhaps the insurgents did not attack any further because they worried how the government might retaliate. Rioters in Massachusetts and Pennsylvania had recently been beaten down by powerful federally organized troops, and New York's legislators made it clear that they would support military force to quash rioters in the Hudson Valley. On the other hand, insurgents may have simply tired of fighting a battle it appeared unlikely they would ever win given the assembly's unwillingness to back them. Whatever their reasons, insurgents in the Hudson Valley did not mount another rebellion that decade.[61]

IN THE END

What began as a series of petitions exploded violently with the murder of a sheriff, attacks on political officials, arson, and a formal call for the use of troops to suppress land rioters. Insurgents, however, became rioters only after they had failed to sway the legislature with petitions. At the same time that rioters were trying to grab land and to secure political power, landlords were busy solidifying their position in the new state and nation. Where landlords succeeded, insurgents generally failed. By 1798, land rioters in the new nation, like their predecessors, found themselves confronting politically powerful landlords who had the support of the military and other officials. During these disputes, however, both sides had infused their rhetoric with language drawn from the Revolution. And each side interpreted that Revolutionary language in their own way and used it to espouse far different goals. By the late 1790s, the opponents had blended the previously separate and often conflicting vocabularies so much that future disputes over land became contests over liberty, independence, and freedom.

From 1783 through 1798, New York landlords, state officials, and rural insurgents argued and then fought because they held conflicting perceptions of what entitled people to own land. In the Hudson Valley, land made liberty, independence, and freedom possible. By the end of the Revolutionary War, officials of the new state government had incorporated the populist notion that labor and occupancy on the land added to one's claim to it. Tenants' labor, however, did not entitle them to own the land they lived on and improved. Instead, rulers of New York turned that labor theory of value against the laborers, arguing that tenants' occupancy and labor legitimated land-lords' ownership of the land. Legislators also made citizenship and political participation in the new state and nation dependent on property ownership. Thus, a landlord's property claims were validated by his title, his occupancy of the land, tenants' labor on it, his good service to the Revolution, and his status as an active citizen and ruler. But insurgents on the ground came at these issues from the opposite direction. After the Revolution, insurgents increasingly insisted that allegiance to the Revolution and then good citizenship should entitle them to own the land they lived and labored on. In that way, insurgents combined labor, occupancy, allegiance to the Revolution, and citizenship to legitimate their land claims. In the end, their arguments were important. Insurgents shaped the course of the history of the northern Hudson Valley but not in the ways they would have chosen had they won landownership and, thus, independence.

CONCLUSION

• Insurgents renewed their attempts to get land in the 1810s after the political atmosphere had swung in their favor, and they continued until landlordism was finally dismantled in the middle of the century. By 1793, the Upper Manor Livingstons had allied with the Clintonians for a brief period, but they had returned to the Federalists by the end of the eighteenth century when new men began exerting their influence over Republicans in the state. These new men wanted to eliminate landlords from New York politics without necessarily turning the Hudson Valley's social hierarchy upside down, and they listened closely to insurgents' appeals for land to gain a political advantage. One of the noteworthy men in this group, Martin Van Buren, began his political career by supporting dissident tenants in the early 1800s. He used their support to defeat Edward P. Livingston for a state senate seat a short time later.

Insurgents thought they could take advantage of that changing political climate by again petitioning the state legislature for land. In 1811, Benjamin Birdsall and 153 other "Dam'd Rascals at the Manor of Livingston" petitioned the New York state legislature for land. Like petitioners before them, these nineteenth-century insurgents argued that their labor and occupancy on the land entitled them to own it. But Birdsall went one step further, illustrating how post-colonial petitions qualitatively differed from colonial ones. He pointed out that by refusing to let tenants claim their leaseholds as freeholds, landlords and state officials were denying tenants the very independence that was the natural right of all Americans. Birdsall's petition suffered the same fate as most of the others; it was denied. Insurgents were denied title to their leaseholds, and the independence they sought, for the ensuing thirty years. Disputes over land in the northern Hudson Valley culminated with the Anti-Rent wars of the 1830s and 1840s. By then, however, debates over landownership had taken on new meanings derived from ongoing debates over labor, capitalism, expansion, and abolitionism.[1]

Anti-Renters added that new language to the unmistakable rhetoric developed by insurgents in the eighteenth century. Disgruntled rural people began developing their anti-landlord rhetoric in the 1740s when landlords in the Hudson Valley were making their estates profitable. Landlords made their manors lucrative by establishing and then maintaining a symbiotic but unequal relationship with leaseholders that resulted in the dramatic transference of agricultural goods from tenants to landlords. Leases issued by landlords were the contract for that relationship, and they created stark class differences. They drove a wedge among inhabitants of the colonial Hudson Valley, dividing landed tycoons from propertyless tenants.

While most tenants made do, and some even fared well, landlords grew fantastically rich. Indeed, landlords prospered by profitably expropriating and then selling the agricultural goods produced by their tenants. They legitimated their position, in part, by upholding a set of political and economic rituals and practices—often called deference, paternalism, or both—designed to suggest the care of subordinates without actually providing it. Landlords glossed over the exploitative nature of the manorial economy with a thin coat of paternalism. Moreover, whatever gestures landlords offered were momentary acts made by men who had successfully turned their economic standing into traditional authority by creating and maintaining gross inequalities in access to, and use of, markets and power. A system based on such inequality, and that produced great disparities of wealth, generated so much antagonism among the inhabitants that they nearly destroyed it. Thus, at much the same time that landlords established themselves politically and economically, they found themselves assailed from below by insurgents determined to dismantle the root of their power—their estates. Redistributing land, however, would have meant more than just changes in who owned the land. It would have dramatically altered the political structure and economic hierarchy of New York. While elite men would have continued to dominate politics, they would have contended with a far more politically active, and independent, yeomanry. Despite efforts from below to force that change in the late colonial period, landlords entrenched their brand of authority by defeating the insurgents at every turn.

An incredibly diverse group of people opposed landlords. This point can no longer be reduced to geographic divisions that mask complex cultural and material relationships among people on the ground.[2] English, Dutch, Scots-Irish, German, and Welsh tenants were joined by Stockbridge and Wappinger Indians and by settlers and squatters from New York and New England. What bound these diverse groups was their relationship to the land and a common desire to own the land they inhabited and improved. In fact, the shared goals of these diverse crowds led to interesting alliances that suggest that historians should reinvestigate that world with these relationships in mind. The most important, and previously the most overlooked, relationship is the one between River Indians and European settlers. While Indians have generally been portrayed as antagonistic to white settlement, the Stockbridge and Wappinger Indians instead facilitated white settlement because it solidified their claims and weakened those made by New York landlords. In the post-Revolutionary period, after Europeans had marginalized Indians, European insurgents made crowds at least appear as racially diverse as they had been in the colonial period by dressing up as Indians when they rebelled.

Disputes over land invariably pitted landed elites who controlled political institutions against either landless insurgents or against insurgents who became landless if they lost. Insurgents usually tried to settle their disagreements with New York's landed elite in courts or assemblies. But landlords dominated these institutions, and they lost every battle. After several defeats and in the face of increasingly long odds in court, insurgents resorted to violence. The ensuing ritualized violence enabled insurgents to grab some power in a world in which they felt powerless, provided a way for them to express their dissatisfaction with their plight, and revealed the heritage they drew on when they rioted.

During these contests, insurgents increasingly argued that their labor and occupancy on the land entitled them to own it. They built that rhetoric into their long-standing argument that landlords had obtained their great estates fraudulently. Landlords had either duped local Indians out of their land or had taken it from European settlers. Overlapping boundaries with New England only made these disputes more confusing by adding an extra layer of conflicting titles to the arguments. When they had endured these assaults for as long as they thought possible, landlords throughout the Hudson Valley called out the British army to quash rioters. Although they fell back on that tactic only when they had exhausted all others, military force also characterized the landlords' exasperation with rioters. The results, however, were often the same. As in court, landlords and colonial officials usually routed insurgents and rioters in the field. Thereafter, insurgents presented a dazzling array of peaceful and violent attacks on landlords' claims.

During and after the War for Independence, land disputes highlighted differing and sometimes conflicting interpretations of the Revolution. More than that, they illustrate how people continued to wage ongoing battles through the Revolutionary War and after it. The Revolution may have changed the language of the debates, but it did not dramatically alter the goals of the combatants. In that light, the Revolution becomes an explosive event in a chain of cultural discord, social disputes, and political conflicts that shaped the Hudson Valley throughout the second half of the eighteenth century. The long life of the disputes indicates that the Revolution in New York was one part of an important battle fought by the economic and political elite of New York, on one side, and people on the margins of their society, on the other, as both sides sought to secure their property rights and political independence.

Different perceptions of landownership took on new meaning during the War for Independence as landlord Revolutionaries and insurgents combined their arguments for land with Revolutionary rhetoric. In the southern Hudson Valley, landlords tended to become Loyalists. Revolutionaries confiscated their estates, divided them, and sold the lots to fund the war effort. The sale of confiscated Loyalist estates, in conjunction with lowered property limits for voting, paved the way for a general infusion of new men into politics and democratized landholding and politics in the southern region. In the Green Mountain region, insurgents led by Ethan Allen fought for the Revolution and used their position to compel the Continental Congress to take the region from New York and give the land to the people who lived on it and improved it.

In the northern Hudson Valley, most of the landlords became Revolutionaries. They opposed the king to protect their estates and to secure their political power. Disgruntled rural people had hoped that landlord Revolutionaries would fulfill the promise of independence and redistribute land to the people who lived and worked on it. They simply wanted the same opportunities to obtain land being offered to tenants in the southern Hudson Valley. When it became clear that landlord Revolutionaries were not going to give up their estates without a fight, some insurgents again resorted to violence. They struck particularly hard in the spring of 1777. They had hoped to time their rebellion with a British invasion of the region, but the British came too late. Revolutionaries knew of their plans, and the insurgents were badly prepared, and, not surprisingly, quickly dispatched. Landlord Revolutionaries spent the remainder of the war protecting their estates from attacks by insurgents, predatory New Englanders, and British troops, all of whom threatened to dismantle landlords' estates. At the war's end, landlord Revolutionaries in the northern Hudson Valley had fended off these attacks. They had kept their estates and had maintained a powerful, if somewhat diminished, political voice.

The Revolution was a critical turning point in the land riots in the Hudson Valley, but it had, at best, mixed results. Political rebellion had paved the way for social rebellion in the southern Hudson Valley and in the Green Mountain territory. But landlords in the northern Hudson Valley kept their estates largely intact, and tenants remained subordinate and propertyless. The irony was that landlords in the northern valley only kept their estates by enacting the very legislation they feared most. While men like Philip Schuyler and Robert Livingston did not want any government to have the power to claim their estates and then sell off that land, they had to give that power to the legislature so it could confiscate and then sell Loyalist land in the southern valley. But these same men staunchly refused to make any such provisions regarding their own estates in the northern Hudson Valley. They had joined the Revolution to protect their estates and power, and they had no intentions of giving either away. Once they parceled out the estates of Loyalists in the southern valley, they fretted that Revolutionaries would push for more of the same in the northern valley, turning the political rebellion into social upheaval. In this respect, landlords' goals differed markedly from the desires of insurgents, who wanted to survive the war and get land even if it meant taking it from landlord Revolutionaries.

The legacy of the Revolution was, for insurgents, largely rhetorical. In the post-Revolutionary period, insurgents incorporated Revolutionary language into the petitions for land that they sent the new state government.

Some petitioners drew comparisons between land disputes in the colonial period and those in the post-Revolutionary world, but they used new language to do it. By using the new language, insurgents made their disputes part of a larger debate over national politics that suggested how people outside the Hudson Valley interpreted the Revolution. The trials after the killing of Cornelius Hogeboom in 1792 offer one example, but the language also emerges clearly in the petitions insurgents sent to the assembly in the 1790s. How the state rejected Petrus Pulver's petition in 1795 reveals how completely landlords, state officials, and insurgents viewed the relationship between property ownership, labor, and the Revolution. Pulver, like other petitioners, argued that an inhabitant's allegiance to, or at least neutrality to, the Revolution, occupancy of the land, and labor on the land combined to entitle the person to own it. The Livingstons had lived on their estate, or at least occupied it, for nearly one hundred years by the 1790s. While long occupancy suggested that they owned it, their property ownership inspired them to serve the public and to support the Revolution. But the state did not stop there. Instead, the assembly turned the petitioners' logic against them, proclaiming that the tenants' labor did not confirm their claims to the land but rather validated the landlord's claim. The pronouncement legitimated landlordism in the northern Hudson Valley, making property ownership the litmus test for independence of all kinds in the new nation. Landlords had gained their independence, but insurgents would have to wait decades to win theirs.

In the second half of the eighteenth century, rural insurgents developed a rhetoric that was increasingly based on the notion that labor on the land, occupancy of it, and service to the Revolution and then to the state and country entitled people to own the land they lived and labored on. Land rioters expressed their themes somewhat crudely in the late colonial period, but articulated them far more clearly by the 1790s after they infused their arguments with Revolutionary rhetoric. In doing so, they laid the foundation for the rioting in the region in the 1830s and 1840s. By that time, land rioters' rhetoric had taken on new elements of national disputes over the expansion of the country, slavery, and capitalism. Yeoman farmers figured that slavery threatened the ability of farmers and free laborers everywhere to provide for their households. Thomas Devyr, the editor of the newspaper for the Anti-Renters in the 1840s, maintained that his paper "will be devoted . . . to the abrogation of all FEUDAL TENURES existing in new York." He further proposed a solution to slavery. Devyr wanted property distributed to those who needed it so they could make their own way. His world had polarized, and he wanted to bring greater equality to it by dedicating himself to the "diffusion of Equal rights, and a Freehold Soil . . . securing to each destitute laborer and mechanic an Independent Freehold, on which to labor for the support of his family." Insurgents from William Prendergast to Robert Noble to Petrus Pulver would have agreed.[3]

NOTES

ABBREVIATIONS

AAS American Antiquarian Society, Worcester, Mass.

AIHA Albany Institute of History and Art, Albany, N.Y.

ALC American Loyalist Claims, Great Britain, Public Record Audit Office, Microfilm Collections, New York volumes, David Library, Washington's Crossing, Pa.

CCHS Columbia County Historical Society, Kinderhook, N.Y.

CCCH Columbia County Court House, Hudson, N.Y.

CHA Joel Munsell, ed., *Collections on the History of Albany,* 4 vols. (Albany, N.Y., 1876)

DHNY E. B. O'Callaghan, *The Documentary History of the State of New-York,* 4 vols. (Albany, N.Y., 1850–1851)

DRCNY E. B. O'Callaghan, ed., *Documents Relative to the Colonial History of the State of New York,* 15 vols. (Albany, N.Y., 1853–1887)

JAH *Journal of American History*

JER *Journal of the Early Republic*

KEMPE John Tabor Kempe Papers, New-York Historical Society, New York, N.Y.

LP Livingston-Redmond Papers, 1630–1900, 13 rolls of microfilm, Franklin Delano Roosevelt Library, Hyde Park, N.Y.

MACR *Massachusetts Archives, Colonial Records,* Massachusetts Archives, Boston, Mass.

NYH *New York History*

NYHS New-York Historical Society, New York, N.Y.

NYPL New York Public Library, New York, N.Y.

NYSL New York State Library, Manuscripts and Special Collections

RRLP   Robert R. Livingston Papers, 1707–1862, 52 rolls of microfilm, New-York Historical Society

SHRL   Sleepy Hollow Restorations Library, White Plains, N.Y.

WMQ   *William & Mary Quarterly*

VCP   Van Cortlandt Papers, Sleepy Hollow Restorations Library, White Plains, N.Y.

VRMP   Van Rensselaer Manor Papers, New York State Library, Manuscripts and Special Collections

INTRODUCTION

1. William Smith quoted in Staughton Lynd, *Anti-Federalism in Dutchess County, New York; A Study of Democracy and Class Conflict in the Revolutionary Era* (Chicago, 1962), 50. I give a fuller account of the riots in chapter 3, but see *New York Mercury,* 18 August 1766; and *New-York Gazette,* 1 September 1766.

2. Irving Mark, *Agrarian Conflicts in Colonial New York, 1711–1775* (1940; Port Washington, N.Y., 1965); Sung Bok Kim, *Landlord and Tenant in Colonial New York: Manorial Society, 1664–1775* (Chapel Hill, N.C., 1978); Edward Countryman, "'Out of bounds of the Law': Northern Land Rioters in the Eighteenth Century," in *The American Revolution: Explorations in the History of American Radicalism,* ed. Alfred F. Young (DeKalb, Ill., 1976), 40–49; Edward Countryman, *A People in Revolution: The American Revolution and Political Society in New York, 1760–1790* (New York, 1989). I based the maps on maps found in Kim, *Landlord and Tenant,* frontispiece; and Staughton Lynd, "Who Should Rule at Home? Dutchess County, New York, in the American Revolution," *WMQ,* 3rd ser., 18 (1961), 342.

3. Marvin L. Kay, "The North Carolina Regulation, 1766–1776: A Class Conflict," in Young, *The American Revolution,* 71–123; Marjoleine Kars, *Breaking Loose Together: The Regulator Rebellion in Pre-Revolutionary North Carolina* (Chapel Hill, N.C., 2002); Woody Holton, *Forced Founders: Indians, Debtors, Slaves, and the Making of the American Revolution in Virginia* (Chapel Hill, N.C., 1999); Michael A. McDonnell, "Popular Mobilization and Political Culture in Revolutionary Virginia: The Failure of the Minutemen and the Revolution from Below," *JAH* 85 (1998); Terry Bouton, "A Road Closed: Rural Insurgency in Post-Independence Pennsylvania," *JAH* 87 (2000), 855–87; Thomas L. Purvis, "Origins and Patterns of Agrarian Unrest in New Jersey, 1735–1754," *WMQ,* 3rd ser., 39 (1982), 600–27; Brendan McConville, *These Daring Disturbers of the Public Peace: Agrarian Unrest and the Struggle for Power in New Jersey, 1700–1776* (Ithaca, N.Y., 1999); Michael A. Bellesiles, *Revolutionary Outlaws: Ethan Allen and the Struggles for Independence on the Early American Frontier* (Charlottesville, Va., 1993); John L. Brooke, *The Heart of the Commonwealth: Society and Political Culture in Worcester County, Massachusetts, 1713–1861* (Cambridge, 1989); Alan Taylor, *Liberty Men and Great Proprietors: The Revolutionary Settlement on the Maine Frontier, 1760–1820* (Chapel Hill, N.C., 1990).

4. Allan Kulikoff, *From British Peasants to Colonial American Farmers* (Chapel Hill, N.C., 2000), 127–36.

5. Peter Kalm, *Travels in North America: The English Version of 1770* (New York, 1987), 326–31, 335, 646–47; Richard Smith, "Journal from New York to Albany," in *History of the Valley of the Hudson,* ed. Nelson Greene, 2 vols. (Chicago, 1931), 1:9, 488–90;

J. H. French, *Gazetteer of the State of New York* (1860; repr., Baltimore, 1995), 155–57; Frederick W. Beers, *Atlas of the Hudson River Valley from New York City to Troy* (New York, 1891); Map of Rensselaerswyck, New York, Part of the Manor of Rensselaerswyck, 1798.

6. Paul Gilje comprehensively describes riots and rioters in *Rioting in America* (Bloomington, Ind., 1996), quote on 6, and chapters 1 and 2. In *The Road to Moboc-racy: Popular Disorder in New York City, 1763–1834* (Chapel Hill, N.C., 1987), Gilje writes that the crowds he studied respected "both persons and property; seldom did [they] lash out in murderous assault," vii. Gordon S. Wood, "A Note on Mobs in the American Revolution," *WMQ*, 3rd ser., 23 (1966), 635–42; Patricia Bonomi, *A Factious People: Politics and Society in Colonial New York* (New York, 1971); Pauline Maier, *From Resistance to Revolution: Colonial Radicals and the Development of American Opposition to Britain, 1765–1776* (New York, 1972); Gary B. Nash, "Social Change and the Growth of Prerevolutionary Urban Radicalism," in Young, *The American Revolution*, 3–36; Dirk Hoerder, "Boston Leaders and Boston Crowds, 1765–1776," in ibid., 233–74; Alfred F. Young, "English Plebian Culture and Eighteenth-Century American Radicalism," in Margaret Jacob and James Jacob, eds., *The Origins of Anglo-American Radicalism* (London, 1984), 185–212; Countryman, "'Out of Bounds of the Law'"; Kay, "The North Carolina Regulation"; Bill Buford, *Among the Thugs* (London, 1991); Mike Davis, *Ecology of Fear: Los Angeles and the Imagination of Disaster* (New York, 1998); Barry Glassner, *The Culture of Fear: Why Americans Are Afraid of the Wrong Things* (New York, 1999).

7. Dixon Ryan Fox, in *Yankees and Yorkers* (New York, 1940), argued that the riots resulted from cultural conflicts between Dutch New Yorkers and English New Englan-ders. Irving Mark, in *Agrarian Conflicts,* countered Fox's argument. Sung Bok Kim re-vived Fox's interpretation to refute Mark and asserted that land-hungry New Englanders started the riots by squatting on the land. The riots were not class conflict, Kim attested, because most tenants were petty bourgeois. See Kim, *Landlord and Tenant,* 374.

8. Countryman, *A People in Revolution;* Lynd, *Anti-Federalism in Dutchess County;* Lynd, "The Tenant Rising at Livingston Manor, May 1777," *New-York Historical Society Quarterly* 48 (1964), 163–77; Cynthia Kierner, "Landlord and Tenant in Colonial New York: The Case of Livingston Manor," *NYH,* 70 (1989), 137–45; Jonathan H. Earle, "The Undaunted Democracy: Jacksonian Antislavery and Free Soil, 1828–1848" (PhD diss., Princeton, 1996); Jamie L. Bronstein, *Land Reform and Working-Class Experience in Britain and the United States, 1800–1862* (Stanford, Calif., 1999); Reeve Huston, *Land and Freedom: Rural Society, Popular Protest, and Party Politics in Antebellum New York* (New York, 2000); Thomas Summerhill, "The Farmer's Republic: Agrarian Protest and the Capitalist Transformation of Upstate New York, 1840–1890" (PhD diss., University of California, San Diego, 1993).

9. Daniel Vickers, "Competency and Competition: Economic Culture in Early America," *WMQ*, 3rd ser., 47 (1990), 3–29; James Henretta, "Families and Farms: Mental-ité in Pre-Industrial America," *WMQ*, 3rd ser., 35 (1978), 3–32; Christopher Clark, *The Roots of Rural Capitalism: Western Massachusetts, 1780–1860* (Ithaca, N.Y., 1990), chapter 2; Edward Countryman, "The Uses of Capital in Revolutionary America: The Case of New York Loyalist Merchants," *WMQ*, 3rd ser., 49 (1992), 3–28; Allan Kulikoff, *The Agrar-ian Origins of American Capitalism* (Charlottesville, Va., 1992), chapters 1 and 2; Daniel Vickers, *Farmers and Fishermen: Two Centuries of Work in Essex County, Massachusetts, 1630–1850* (Chapel Hill, N.C., 1994); Cathy Matson, "'Damned Scoundrels' and 'Liber-tisme of Trade': Freedom and Regulation in Colonial New York's Fur and Grain Trades," *WMQ*, 3rd ser., 51 (1994), 389–418; Thomas S. Wermuth, *Rip Van Winkle's Neighbors: The Transformation of Rural Society in the Hudson River Valley, 1720–1850* (Albany, N.Y., 2001).

10. "Text of the events leading up to and the declaration of the Helderberg War," 4 July 1839, in the Anti-Rent Collection, NYSL, quoted in Earle, "The Undaunted Democracy," 71; Thomas Ainge Devyr in *The Anti-Renter,* 13 September 1845.

1—LANDLORDS AND TENANTS BEFORE AMERICAN INDEPENDENCE

1. Alice Curtis Desmond, "Mary Philipse: Heiress," *NYH,* 28 (1947), 26; Staughton Lynd, "The Revolution and the Common Man: Farm Tenants and Artisans in New York Politics, 1777–1788" (PhD diss., Columbia University, 1962), 38; Helen Wilkinson Reynolds, *Dutch Houses in the Hudson Valley before 1776* (1929; repr., New York, 1965), 298–301.

2. Daniel Vickers, "Competency and Competition: Economic Culture in Early America," *WMQ,* 3rd ser., 47 (1990), 3–29; Vickers, *Farmers and Fishermen: Two Centuries of Work in Essex County, Massachusetts, 1630–1850* (Chapel Hill, N.C., 1994), chapter 5; Edward Countryman, "The Uses of Capital in Revolutionary America: The Case of Loyalist Merchants," *WMQ,* 3rd ser., 49 (1992), 3–28; Cathy Matson, "'Damned Scoundrels' and 'Libertisme of Trade': Freedom and Regulation in Colonial New York's Fur and Grain Trades," *WMQ,* 3rd ser., 51 (1994), 389–418; Thomas S. Wermuth, *Rip Van Winkle's Neighbors: The Transformation of Rural Society in the Hudson River Valley, 1720–1850* (Albany, N.Y., 2001); James Henretta, "Families and Farms: Mentalité in Pre-Industrial America," *WMQ,* 3rd ser., 35 (1978), 3–32; Christopher Clark, *The Roots of Rural Capitalism: Western Massachusetts, 1780–1860* (Ithaca, N.Y., 1990); Allan Kulikoff, *The Agrarian Origins of American Capitalism* (Charlottesville, Va., 1992); Brendan McConville, *These Daring Disturbers of the Public Peace: The Struggle for Property and Power in Early New Jersey* (Ithaca, N.Y., 1999), 102–3.

3. Unless otherwise indicated, I have converted all currency to 1775 £NY. In 1779, assessors for the state rated realty and personalty in 1775 £NY. For New York currency in 1775, £165 NY roughly equaled £100 Sterling, or approximately £5 NY to £3 Sterling. I used the equations found in John J. McCusker, *How Much Is That in Real Money? A Historical Price Index for Use as a Deflator of Money Values in the Economy of the United States* (Worcester, Mass., 1992), appendix A, table A-2. Edward Countryman, *A People in Revolution: The American Revolution and Political Society in New York, 1760–1790* (New York, 1989), 344, note 7; the Assessment Rolls, 1779, Roll A-FM, N66 #71, NYSL.

4. Andrias Bergher's lease, 1737, VCP, folder v. 1942 a and b; Joseph Purdy's lease, 1737, VCP, folder v. 2194; Jonathon Odell's lease, 1749, VCP, folder v. 1697; Townsend Losey's lease, 1772, VCP, folders v. 2204 and v. 2206. Cortlandt Manor was ultimately apportioned to Stephanus Van Cortlandt's heirs between 1732 and 1734, and some of the proprietors began selling off their property almost immediately. By the end of the colonial period, they had sold approximately 37 percent of the roughly eighty-two thousand acres that had originally comprised the manor. The Beekmans kept their estate together until Gertruyd Beekman died in 1777. See Sung Bok Kim, *Landlord and Tenant in Colonial New York: Manorial Society, 1664–1775* (Chapel Hill, N.C., 1978), 180–83.

5. The Livingston Manor Patent, 22 June 1686, *DHNY,* 3:625; statements by James DeLancey and Beverly Robinson for Frederick Philipse's Loyalist Claim in Robert A. East and Jacob Judd, eds., *The Loyalist Americans: A Focus on Greater New York* (Tarrytown, N.Y., 1975), 130–35; Irving Mark, *Agrarian Conflicts in Colonial New York, 1711–1775* (1940; repr., Port Washington, N.Y., 1965), 19–49; Sung Bok Kim, "The

Manor of Cortlandt and Its Tenants, 1697–1783" (PhD diss., Michigan State University, 1966); Kim, *Landlord and Tenant*, 67–70, 118, 178–80; Countryman, *A People in Revolution*, 17–19.

6. Robert R. Livingston to Gulien Verplank, "Immigration Advertisement," December 1749; Robert R. Livingston to Robert Livingston Jr., New York City, 7 June 1764, both in RRLP.

7. For Cortlandt Manor, see Kim, "The Manor of Cortlandt and Its Tenants," chapter 5; Kim, *Landlord and Tenant*, 154–56, 172; and Rent Rolls for Beekman's Precinct for 1756, 1759, and 1779, RRLP. I hesitate to use these lists to give exact numbers of tenants on Beekman's Precinct because it is quite likely that they are incomplete. Combined, this evidence indicates that the number of tenants Beekman administered increased over the colonial period. For Philipsburg, see the testimonies of Beverly Robinson, John Watts, and John Tabor Kempe in Frederick Philipse's ALC, 12, vol. 19. For the number of tenants on the estate, see "The Philipsburg Manor Rent Roll of 1760," *New York Genealogical and Biographical Record* 110 (1979), 102–4; and "Rent Roll of Frederick Philipse's Estate (Philipse Manor), 1776–1784," *New York Genealogical and Biographical Record* 108 (1977), 74–78. For Livingston Manor, see Countryman, *A People in Revolution*, 17–23; and Florence Christoph, *Upstate New York in the 1760s: Tax Lists and Selected Militia Rolls of Old Albany County, 1760–1768* (Camden, Maine, 1992), 90–97. For Rensselaerswyck, see "A List of Indentures 1699–1744" and "Leases Granted by Stephen Van Rensselaer Esquire and his ancestors for lands," 1 September 1790, both in VRMP. See also Kilian Van Rensselaer's will, 18 June 1718, Townsend Collection, Box 1, NYSL. For a list of tenants, see "Abstract of Deeds given by Stephen Van Rensselaer Esq dec'd. with the Quit Rent due in upon each Lott Respectively," n.d., Van Rensselaer Family Papers, Mrs. Benjamin Wadworth Arnold Collections, AIHA; List of leases in Boxes 36, 84, and 86, VRMP; "The List of Tenants," Van Rensselaer Family Papers, Vlie House, Box 3, AIHA; "Record Book of Leases for Bethlehem Rensselaerswyck, 1771–1800," AIHA.

8. Although I have identified approximately 2,038 tenants in the Hudson Valley in the late colonial period, leases do not exist for all of them. As a result, my general statements on leases issued in the Hudson Valley in the colonial eighteenth century comes from my reading of 755 extant leases for Philipsburg in the Philipse Papers, PT 249, 8904 #26, SHRL; Van Cortlandt Manor leases, VCP, folders v. 2204, v. 2206, v. 2194, and v. 1697; leases in LP, rolls 6, 7, and 8; leases in RRLP, rolls 1 and 52; "Leases Granted by Stephen Van Rensselaer, Esquire and his ancestors for lands," 1 September 1790, VRMP; and the lists of leases in Boxes 36, 84, and 86, VRMP. This point corresponds with the discussion of common land in K. D. M. Snell, *Annals of the Labouring Poor: Social Change and Agrarian England, 1600–1900* (Cambridge, 1985). J. M. Neeson, *Commoners: Common Right, Enclosure, and Social Change in England, 1700–1820* (Cambridge, 1993); Roger Manning, *Village Revolts: Social Protest and Popular Disturbances in England, 1509–1640* (Oxford, 1988).

9. For specific leases that contain these conditions, see Andrias Bergher's lease, 1737, folder v. 1942 a and b, VCP; leases for Philipsburg in the Philipse Papers, Pt 249, 8904 #26, SHRL; leases for Peter Lowree (1760) and Matthyse Smith (1769), among others, LP, rolls 7 and 8; and Abraham Ten Broeck's Lease Ledger, Box 84, VRMP.

10. Quotes are from the text of Solomon Schutte's lease with Philip Livingston, 14 April 1748. I have read approximately 353 leases for the period from 1700 to 1783 for Livingston Manor, but many are damaged enough that they provide only general information. See also the leases for Peter Lowree (1760), Samuel Crumpe (1768),

Matthyse Smith (1769), Grappo Leake (1772), and Augustine Vites (1773), LP, rolls 7 and 8. For lists of tenants on Livingston Manor, see Christoph, *Upstate New York in the 1760s,* 97. See also the list of tenants and general lease requirements in Rent Rolls for Clermont and Beekman's Precinct for 1756, 1759, and 1779, RRLP, roll 52; and in the leases in Box 1, John Livingston Papers, NYSL. All of the leases I have seen for Rensselaerswyck that contain the "for ever" clause also give the Van Rensselaers power to take over a leasehold if a tenant failed to fulfill the conditions of the lease. For Rensselaerswyck tenants who signed leases before 1750, see "A List of Indentures 1699–1744" and "Leases Granted by Stephen Van Rensselaer Esquire and his ancestors for lands," 1 September 1790, both in VRMP. See also Kilian Van Rensselaer's will, 18 June 1718, Townsend Collection, Box 1, NYSL. For a list of tenants, see "Abstract of Deeds given by Stephen Van Rensselaer Esq dec'd. with the Quit Rent due in upon each Lott Respectively," n.d., Arnold Collection, AIHA; leases in Boxes 36, 84, and 86, VRMP; "The List of Tenants," Van Rensselaer Family Papers, Vlie House, Box 3, AIHA; and the "Record Book of Leases for Bethlehem Rensselaerswyck, 1771–1800," AIHA. For Philipsburg, see Frederick Philipse's Loyalist Claim, East and Judd, eds., *The Loyalist Americans,* 128–35; Philipse's ALC, 12, vol. 19; Frederick Philipse to James Hunter, 7 February 1760, and 28 December 1762, Philipse Papers, SHRL; Beverly Robinson, who administered part of the manor, issued developmental leases for two lives, but by the early 1760s he began forcing tenants to sign one-year leases (ALC, 12, vol. 21); Mark, *Agrarian Conflicts,* 131–32; Patricia Bonomi, *A Factious People: Politics and Society in Colonial New York* (New York, 1971), 220. For Cortlandt Manor, see Joseph Purdy's lease, 1737, folder v. 2194; Jonathon Odell's lease, 1749, folder v. 1697; and Townsend Losey's lease, 1772, folders v. 2204 and v. 2206, all in VCP; Rent Rolls for the "Lands in the Manor of Cortlandt belonging to the estate of the Late Mr. Peter Warren," for 1760 and 1765, both in v. 1644, SHRL; rent receipts for Philip and Pierre Van Cortlandt in 1749, 1770, 1775, and 1776, VCP; and Kim, "The Manor of Cortlandt," especially chapter 5.

11. Charles W. McCurdy, *The Anti-Rent Era in New York Law and Politics, 1839–1865* (Chapel Hill, N.C., 2001), 22–31.

12. See Vickers, *Farmers and Fishermen,* chapter 5; and Wermuth, *Rip Van Winkle's Neighbors,* chapter 5.

13. For Cortlandt Manor, see Rent Rolls for the "Lands in the Manor of Cortlandt belonging to the estate of the Late Mr. Peter Warren" for 1760 and 1765, both in v. 1644, SHRL; rent receipts for Philip and Pierre Van Cortlandt in 1749, 1770, 1775, and 1776, VCP; Kim, "The Manor of Cortlandt," chapter 5 and table 3–8; and Kim, *Landlord and Tenant,* 187–90. For Philipsburg, see Harry B. Yoshpe, *The Disposition of Loyalist Estates* (New York, 1939), table 2, 139–47; "The Rent Roll of Col. Frederick Philips's Estate (Philips Manor), 1776–1784," *New York Genealogical and Biographical Record* 108 (1977): 74–78; Frederick Philipse's ALC, 12, vol. 19; Beverly Robinson's ALC, 12, vol. 21. For Livingston Manor and Clermont, see Rent Rolls and leases in LP, rolls 6 and 7; and Rent Rolls in RRLP, roll 52. For Rensselaerswyck, including Claverack, see leases in Boxes 36, 84, and 86, VRMP; and Abraham Ten Broeck's Lease Ledger, Box 84, VRMP.

14. For Maryland, see Gregory A. Stiverson, *Poverty in a Land of Plenty: Tenancy in Eighteenth Century Maryland* (Baltimore, 1977), tables 2 and 3. For Hannover, New York, see the Assessment Rolls, 1779, NYSL. See also Allan Kulikoff, *From British Peasants to Colonial American Farmers* (Chapel Hill, N.C., 2000), 129–34; Lucy Simler, "Tenancy in Colonial Pennsylvania: The Case of Chester County," *WMQ,* 3rd ser., 43 (1986), 542–69; James *The Best Poor Man's County: A Geographical Study of Early South-*

eastern Pennsylvania (Baltimore, 1972), 89–91; and Alan Taylor, *Liberty Men and Great Proprietors: The Revolutionary Settlement on the Maine Frontier, 1760–1820* (Chapel Hill, N.C., 1990), tables 3 and 4.

15. Obediah Ackerly, ALC, 13, vol. 11 (for his changing production patterns as a tenant on Philipsburg). For a tenant on Cortlandt Manor who followed a similar pattern, see Enoch Hunt's ALC, 13, vol. 17; and the Westchester County Assessment Rolls for Cortlandt Manor, April 1779, NYSL. See also the ALC of Alpheus Palmer of Cortlandt Manor, 13, vol. 17, in which he claimed twenty-nine pigs and hogs, sixty-four sheep and lambs, six barrels of pork, one barrel of butter, eighty pounds of feathers, and five hundred weight of cheese. For Philipsburg tenants, see Joseph Orsser, ALC, 13, vol. 14; Solomon Horton, ALC, 12, vol. 18; and the comments of a tenant farmer from Philipsburg who described what he took to market in New York City in the *New-York Mercury,* 8 December 1766.

16. For leases to tenants in the eighteenth century for Beekman's Patent, see the Rhinebeck lease ledger in RRLP, roll 52; for rent payments for his Cortlandt tenants, see Kim, *Landlord and Tenant,* table 5.2, 199; and for rent payments from his Beekman Precinct tenants, see the rent rolls in RRLP, roll 52. For rent payments made to Peter Warren's estate, and to Stephen Van Cortlandt, see v. 1644, VCP; and for rent receipts signed by Pierre and Philip Van Cortlandt, see v. 1827, SHRL. For Frederick Philipse and Beverly Robinson, see Yoshpe, *The Disposition of Loyalist Estates,* table 2, 139–47; "The Philipsburg Manor Rent Roll of 1760," 102–4; and "The Comparative View of the Increases of B. Robinson's Rents from 1755 to 1777," Robinson's ALC, 12, vol. 21.

17. For Livingston Manor, see, for examples, the payments of Ephraim Reese and Frans Brusie in the Livingston Manor Rent Ledger, 1767–1784, NYHS. The ledger contains the rent information for 370 tenants, and I have calculated average rent payments from it and from existing leases and rent records for the manor found in LP, rolls 6, 7, and 8. For the Van Rensselaers, see rent payments for Jacob I. and Levinias Lansing, William Hogan, Wouter Becker, Mattys Bovie, Daniel Boss, Jacob Outhoudt, and Jacob Loock in the Rensselaerswyck Ledger A of Rents, 1768–1789, VRMP.

18. See Robert R. Livingston to Robert Livingston Jr., n.p., June 1764, RRLP, roll 1; and Frederick Philipse's Loyalist Claim, *The Loyalist Americans,* 128–35; and in ALC, 12, vol. 19. See also Beverly Robinson's ALC, 12, vol. 21; Abraham Yates Jr. to Robert Livingston Jr., Albany, 4 December 1766, LP, roll 8; Kulikoff, *From British Peasants,* 132–55; and Woody Holton, *Forced Founders: Indians, Debtors, Slaves, and the Making of the American Revolution in Virginia* (Chapel Hill, N.C., 1999), 131–88; and Hannover, Ulster County, Assessment Rolls, 1779, NYSL.

19. For Peter Warren's practices, see Kim, *Landlord and Tenant,* chapter 5. For rising wheat prices and for increased demands for bread in the West Indies, among other places, see Kulikoff, *From British Peasants,* 211–16.

20. See the leases in the Philipse Papers, PT 249, 8904 #26, SHRL. For James Hunter's lease, see Frederick Philipse to James Hunter, 7 February 1760, and rent receipt dated 28 December 1762, Philipse Papers, SHRL. For the Philipses' lease practices, see Frederick Philipse's ALC, 12, vol. 19.

21. The tenant's comments are in Richard Smith, *A Tour of the Four Great Rivers: The Hudson, Mohawk, Susquehanna and Delaware in 1769* (New York, 1906), 6. The Philipses did not own their estate as a freehold, like the Livingstons and Van Rensselaers. Thus, like tenants who could sell the improvements to a leasehold but not the land, the Philipses were not entitled to reap the full value of the estate. See Countryman, *A People in Revolution,* 17–20; Kim, *Landlord and Tenant,* 178–80; and Philipse's ALC, 12, vol. 19.

22. See Henry Beekman's leases and leases for Beekman's Precinct in RRLP, roll 52; leases in LP, rolls 6, 7, and 8; catalogue of leases for Rensselaerswyck at NYSL; and Abraham Ten Broeck's Lease Ledger, Box 84, VRMP.

23. See Elizabeth and John Shaver's entries in the Livingston Manor Rent Ledger, 1767–1784, NYHS; and in Rent Rolls for Livingston Manor, LP, roll 8. See also Robert R. Livingston to Robert Livingston Jr., New York City, 14 March 1763, RRLP, roll 1.

24. See entries for the Reeses, the Brusies, and Johannnes Kool in the Livingston Manor Rent Ledger, 1767–1784, NYHS. For correlative data on other estates, see entries for, among others, Jacob I. and Levinias Lansing, Jacob Loock, William Hogan, Wouter Becker, Mattys Bovie, David DeForest, Douwe Fonda, and Jacob Outhoudt in the Rensselaerswyck Ledger A of Rents, 1768–1789, VRMP; and Rent Rolls for Henry Beekman's estate for 1756, 1759, and 1772 in RRLP, roll 52. For Beekman's tenants on Cortlandt Manor, see Kim, *Landlord and Tenant*, table 5.2, and 198–200. See also Beverly Robinson's ALC, 12, vol. 21; and Frederick Philipse's ALC, 12, vol. 19. For diverse agricultural production in the southern Hudson Valley, see Obediah Ackerly, ALC, 12, vol. 11; Enoch Hunt, ALC, 13, vol. 17; and Alpheus Palmer, ACL, 13, vol. 17. All were tenants on Cortlandt Manor. For Philipsburg, see Joseph Orsser, ALC, 13, vol. 14; and Solomon Horton, ALC, 12, vol. 18.

25. For Livingston Manor and Beekman's estate, see the leases they issued for Beekman's Precinct in RRLP, roll 52; leases in LP, rolls 6, 7, and 8; and the Livingston Manor Rent Ledger, 1767–1784, NYHS. I base these conclusions for Rensselaerswyck on my survey of 768 specific leases issued in the second half of the eighteenth century for the manor that indicate how long tenants stayed on their leaseholds, and on the rent records for the estate found in Ledger A of Rents, Rensselaerswyck Manor, NYSL. Here I also want to refine Reeve Huston's interpretation of "for ever," in *Land and Freedom: Rural Society, Popular Protest, and Party Politics in Antebellum New York* (New York, 2000), in which he argues that tenants on Rensselaerswyck with perpetual leases became "the legal owners of their farms, subject to rents and other restrictions" (23). In a survey of these 768 leases, approximately 45 percent of the leaseholds, 348, changed hands. The land was re-leased, and the new tenants did not have the same surnames as the original tenants. It is possible that the other 55 percent of the leaseholds stayed within the families of the original lessees, or that the sons or daughters of leaseholders sold the leaseholds without the Van Rensselaers' consent. What remains clear, however, is that the Van Rensselaers did not relinquish their ownership of the land. For a discussion of how the Van Rensselaers handled tenants' debt, see Huston, *Land and Freedom,* 25.

26. Terry Bouton, "A Road Closed: Rural Insurgency in Post-Independence Pennsylvania," *JAH* 87 (2000), 855–87.

27. John L. Brooke, *The Heart of the Commonwealth: Society and Political Culture in Worcester County, Massachusetts, 1713–1861* (Cambridge, 1989); Bouton, "A Road Closed," 855–87.

28. Robert Livingston Jr. to Josiah Loomis, Manor Livingston, 17 January 1752. See also Livingston to Loomis, Manor Livingston, 4 February 1752, LP, roll 7.

29. Hannah Brewer to Philip Schuyler, Crompound, 1 December 1784; Schuyler's response, Claverack, 25 November 1785, which appears on the verso. See also James Perry to Philip Schuyler, Cortlandt Manor, 9 May 1786, Local Land Papers, Philip Schuyler Papers, roll 13, NYPL; and Schuyler's Account Book, 1769–1795, roll 15, NYPL.

30. For Beekman's tenants on Cortlandt Manor, see Kim, *Landlord and Tenant,* table 5.2, and 198–200. For his tenants in Dutchess County, see Rent Rolls for 1756, 1759, and 1772, in RRLP, roll 52. For Beverly Robinson, see the "Comparative View of the Increases of B. Robinson's Rents from 1755 to 1777," ALC, 12, Vol. 21; Frederick Philipse, ALC, 12, vol. 19; and "The Rent Roll of Col. Frederick Philipse's Estate," 74–78. For an example of the operations of grist mills on Philipsburg, see William Purdy's lease, 2 June 1761, Philipse Papers, PA 249, SHRL; and Kim, *Landlord and Tenant,* 166–69. For a description of one such mill, see Reynolds, *Dutch Houses in the Hudson Valley,* 298–301.

31. Van Rensselaer's Book of Tithes, 1758–[1770]; Ledger B of Rents for Rensselaerswyck, 1769–1789, Box 75, both in VRMP.

32. See Ledger B of Rents for Rensselaerswyck, 1769–1789, Box 75, VRMP. Abraham Ten Broeck recounted some of these figures in an unaddressed letter, 16 February 1764, Letters of Abraham Ten Broeck, 1753–1783, Box 53, VRMP. Ten Broeck administered the estate from the mid-1760s until the last patroon reached maturity in 1785. Robert Van Deusen's lease is in Van Rensselaer Papers, 10 September 1718, as cited in Kim, *Landlord and Tenant,* 168.

33. See Rent Rolls for Clermont for 1756 and 1759 in RRLP, roll 52; and, for his statement, see Robert R. Livingston to Robert Livingston Jr., New York City, 17 March 1762, RRLP, roll 1.

34. I have calculated these figures from the Livingston Manor Rent Ledger, 1767–1789, NYHS, which includes the yearly rent paid by between 266 and 330 tenants, out of 370, over the given period. The number of tenants fluctuated because tenants moved on and off the manor, and others did not pay rent, and is lower than the number of tenants on tax lists for the manor in 1779.

35. Robert Livingston Jr. to Jacobus Proper, memorandum, 1 May 1763; "Articles of Agreement" signed by Robert Livingston Jr. and Johan Barnhart Koens, 7 October 1763; sales of William Krankhyte's improvements to Philip Fells for £100, of which Livingston kept £69 to cover Krankhyte's quarter-sales fee and outstanding debt, all in LP, roll 7. For the sales of improvements elsewhere in the valley, see Solomon Horton, ALC, 12, vol. 18, October 1786; records in Abraham Ten Broeck's Debit and Credit Accounts of the Manor, 1763–1787, Box 41, VRMP; John Duncan to Ten Broeck, Hermitage, 22 September 1769, Ten Broeck Family Papers, Box 1, AIHA; Rensselaerswyck Rent Ledger B, 1769–1789, Box 75, VRMP; Beverly Robinson, ALC, 12, vol. 21; Frederick Philipse, ALC, 12, vol. 19; Kim, *Landlord and Tenant,* 255–56; Hannah Brewer to Philip Schuyler (1784), and James Perry to Philip Schuyler (1786), both in Local Land Papers, Schuyler Papers, roll 13, NYPL. See also the Schuyler Account Book, 1769–1795, Schuyler Papers, roll 15, NYPL.

36. Robert Livingston Jr., cited in Cynthia Kierner, *Traders and Gentlefolk: The Livingstons of New York, 1675–1790* (Ithaca, N.Y., 1992), 87; see also 41–43 and 92–93. Figures for wheat production are in the Livingston Manor Rent Ledger, 1767–1789, NYHS.

37. Peter DeWitt's Ledger A, 1750–1759, DeWitt Papers, Box 47, NYSL; DeWitt's Account Journal, DeWitt Papers, 1764–1789, Box 47, NYSL; Kierner, *Traders and Gentlefolk,* 96–97.

38. "A General Accot. of Goods rec'd per the Manor Sloop," 1767; "Sales of 342 tons of Pig Iron," 30 March 1767, both in RRLP, roll 16; Walter Livingston's Waste Book, 1765–1767, RRLP, roll 16; John Abeel to Robert Livingston Jr., New York City, 13 November 1766, LP, roll 8.

39. I base my figures for realty holdings in the Hudson Valley on assessments made according to "An Act for raising monies by tax to be applied towards the public exigencies of this State," passed by the New York State legislature in 1779. Assessors rated realty at one shilling per pound for all improved land, "including wood lands, kept for the purpose of fuel and timber and deemed parts and parcel of an improved farm." According to the act, realty also included houses, barns, mills, stores, and other buildings, but land made up the bulk of the assessment. Assessors rated personalty at six pence per pound of personal estate held within the state, but the legislature had resolved that the personalty of each citizen should be assessed only if it exceeded the "debts due from each respective person, or value thereof, at the time of the assessing." The assembly also provided that a "tax of one shilling per pound shall . . . be raised on the amount of all unimproved lands . . . not subject to a right of commonage of any kind whatsoever." In other words, landlords paid less for unimproved and unin-habited land. See "An Act for raising monies by tax," passed on 2 March 1779, chapter 16, *Laws of New York,* 2nd session, quotes on 103 and 108; and the re-affirmation of the act on 23 October 1779, ibid. The list is the most complete list for New York in the second half of the eighteenth century, and thus allows for regional comparisons. See the Assessment Rolls, 1779, NYSL.

40. Compare discussions of production of freeholders in Wermuth, *Rip Van Winkle's Neighbors,* chapters 1 and 2, with my discussion earlier in the chapter and with Kim, *Landlord and Tenant,* 183–202.

41. Frederick Philipse quoted in Countryman, *A People in Revolution,* 27; Reynolds, *Dutch Houses in the Hudson Valley,* 96–98, 299–301; Edward Hagaman Hall, *Philipse Manor Hall at Yonkers, New York* (New York, 1912), 208–9; Edgar Mayhew Bacon, *The Hudson River From Ocean to Source* (New York, 1902); Division for Historic Preservation, Bureau of Historic Sites, *Schuyler Mansion: A Historic Structure Report* (Albany, N.Y., 1979). For the Van Rensselaers' house in Watervliet, see Martha J. Lamb, "The Van Rensselaer Manor," *Magazine of American History* 11 (1884), 1–6; and Walter W. Spooner, *Historic Families of America Comprehending the Genealogical and Representa-tive Biography of Selected Families of Early American Ancestry, Recognized Social Standing, and Special Distinction* (New York, 1907). For the Van Cortlandts' manor house, see Joseph T. Butler *The Family Collections at Van Cortlandt Manor* (Tarrytown, N.Y., 1967). For the Livingstons' houses, see William H. W. Sabine, ed., *Historical Memoirs . . . of William Smith,* 2 vols. (New York, 1969–71), 2:passim; John Ross Delafield, "The Story of the Hermitage," *Dutchess County Historical Society's Year Book* 24 (1939), 24, 30; and Kierner, *Traders and Gentlefolk,* 138–40.

42. For Lasher's house, see Neil Larson, *Ethnic and Economic Diversity Reflected in Columbia County Vernacular Architecture* (Kingston, N.Y., 1986), 18–23; for Camer's, see ibid., 38–41. For houses of tenants and farmers elsewhere in the Hudson Valley, see the Loyalist Claims of John Freeman, ALC, 13, vol. 14; Benjamin Palmer, ALC, 13, vol. 18; Elizabeth Green, ALC, 13, vol. 16; and Samuel Bagnel, ALC, 13, vol. 17. See also the discussion of Jonathon Odell's house in Reynolds, *Dutch Houses in the Hudson Val-ley,* 298–99, plate 107.

43. Approximately 2,233 people appear on the 1779 assessment rolls for all four estates. Roughly 885 appear as tenants on assessment rolls for Livingston Manor and Rensselaerswyck in 1766 and 1767, but 1,616 appear on the 1779 rolls for the manors. Specifically, approximately 474 households are listed on Livingston Manor in 1779, but rent rolls indicate that approximately 345 people paid rent that year. Similar dis-crepancies abound for the other manors as well. Approximately 274 tenants appear

on lists for Philipsburg in 1776, and another 146 appear on a list for Robinson's portion of that manor, but only 87 appear on the assessment rolls for the manor in 1779. Roughly 530 people appear on Cortlandt Manor in the 1779 rolls. Overall, I have compiled a list of approximately 2,870 tenants who lived in the Hudson Valley from the 1740s to 1779, but here I have only included the names of people I could identify as tenants on the tax lists and in rent records or leases. The records themselves limit how many people fill all of these categories. Many Van Rensselaer Manor records, for example, were burned either partially or entirely. On Livingston Manor, I do not include names that are similar. For example, I counted Andreas Rees, Andries Riis, and Andrias Reece as one person. Taken together, my figures are, considering the extant records, rightly conservative. Thus, this is hardly a scientific or definitive evaluation of the tenant population in the Hudson Valley, and some discrepancies concerning percentages would assuredly arise from other investigations. That said, my general remarks concerning the diverse nature of the tenant population would remain conclusive. See the list of inhabitants of Livingston Manor and Rensselaerswyck in Christoph, *Upstate New York in the 1760s*. See also the list of inhabitants for all four manors in the Assessment Rolls for Counties, 1779, 1786, 1789, NYSL. See also, for example, Ledger A of Rents, 1768–1789, VRMP; Livingston Manor Rent Ledger, 1767–1789, NYHS; list of tenants given by Beverly Robinson, ALC, 12, vol. 21; and "The Rent Roll of Col. Frederick Philips's Estate," 74–78.

44. Kim, *Landlord and Tenant*, 210–12; Countryman, *A People in Revolution*, chapters 1 and 2.

45. Kim, *Landlord and Tenant*, 49–54; Countryman, *A People in Revolution*, 77; letters between Abraham Yates, the ill-fated candidate, and Robert Livingston Jr., in 1760 and 1761, in LP, roll 6.

46. For property requirements for voting in colonial New York, see Staughton Lynd, *Anti-Federalism in Dutchess County, New York; A Study of Democracy and Class Conflict in the Revolutionary Era* (Chicago, 1962), 41–42; Countryman, *A People in Revolution*, 32–33, 76–79, and chapter 1; and John C. Guzzardo, "Democracy Along the Mohawk: An Election Return, 1773," *NYH*, 57 (1976) 30–52. For voters in Westchester County, New York, see E. Marie Becker, "The 801 Westchester County Freeholders, 1763," *New-York Historical Society Quarterly* 35 (1951), 283–321. For voting requirements throughout the colonies, see Robert J. Dinkin, *Voting in Provincial America: A Study of Elections in the Thirteen Colonies, 1689–1776* (Westport, Conn., 1977), 36–40.

47. Peter R. Livingston and John Morin Scott to William Smith Jr., Sabine, *Historical Memoirs*, 2:129, 157.

48. Countryman, *A People in Revolution*, 78.

49. Kim, *Landlord and Tenant*, 49–54; Countryman, *A People in Revolution*, 77; letters between Abraham Yates Jr. and Robert Livingston Jr., in 1760 and 1761, LP, roll 6. For an analysis of voting practices in colonial New York, see Roger Champagne, "Family Politics versus Constitutional Principles: The New York Assembly Elections of 1768 and 1769," *WMQ*, 3rd ser., 20 (1963), 57–79; Dinkin, *Voting in Provincial America*, 133–36; Kim, *Landlord and Tenant*, 210–12; and Countryman, *A People in Revolution*, chapter 1.

50. J. R. Pole, "Historians and the Problems of Early American Democracy," *American Historical Review* 67 (1962), 641; Kim, *Landlord and Tenant*, 121; Richard Beeman, "Deference, Republicanism, and the Emergence of Popular Politics in Eighteenth-Century America," *WMQ*, 3rd ser., 48 (1992), 401–30.

2—PROPERTY AND POWER IN THE NORTHERN VALLEY

1. "The Memorial & Representation of John McArthur, Living on the Province Land West of Sheffield," 22 April 1755, *MACR, 1724–1775,* 6:191.

2. The general account of the shooting of William Rees comes from John Van Rensselaer's affidavit, 22 February 1755; John Van Rensselaer, "An Account of the Murder of William Rees," 28 April 1755; Robert Livingston Jr.'s affidavit, 8 May 1755; and Lieutenant Governor Oliver DeLancey to Lieutenant Governor Phips of Massachusetts, 12 May 1755, all in *DHNY,* 3:466–74.

3. Daniel K. Richter, *The Ordeal of the Longhouse: The Peoples of the Iroquois League in the Era of European Colonization* (Chapel Hill, N.C., 1992), 22.

4. Lieutenant Governor George Clark to the Lords of Trade, New York City, 24 May 1739, *DRCNY,* 6:143–44.

5. Patrick Frazier, *The Mohicans of Stockbridge* (Lincoln, Nebr., 1992), 39–49.

6. Frazier, *The Mohicans of Stockbridge,* 52–56; John Livingston to Robert Livingston Jr., New York City, 25 November 1751; William Livingston to Robert Livingston Jr., New York City, 25 November 1751, LP, all in roll 7.

7. Robert Livingston Jr. to Josiah Loomis, 17 January 1752, LP, roll 7; Robert Livingston Jr. to Josiah Loomis, 4 February 1752, LP, roll 7; "Robert Van Deusen & Johannis Van Deusen ads Josiah Loomis," 23 August through 29 August 1753, LP, roll 6. The boundary dispute between New York and New England has been well recorded. See Irving Mark, *Agrarian Conflicts in Colonial New York, 1711–1775* (1940; repr., Port Washington, N.Y., 1965), chapters 1 and 2; Dixon Ryan Fox, *Yankees and Yorkers* (New York, 1940); Philip J. Schwarz, "'To Conciliate the Jarring Interests': William Smith, Thomas Hutchinson, and the Massachusetts–New York Boundary, 1771–1773," *New-York Historical Society Quarterly* 59 (1975), 299–319; Sung Bok Kim, *Landlord and Tenant in Colonial New York: Manorial Society, 1664–1775* (Chapel Hill, N.C., 1978), chapter 7, and 415; Philip J. Schwarz, *The Jarring Interests: New York's Boundary Makers, 1664–1776* (Albany, N.Y., 1979), chapters 6 and 7; and Cynthia Kierner, *Traders and Gentlefolk: The Livingstons of New York, 1675–1790* (Ithaca, N.Y., 1992), 46–86.

8. Richard White, *The Middle Ground: Indians, Empires, and Republics in the Great Lakes Region, 1650–1815* (New York, 1991), x; Daniel K. Richter, *Facing East from Indian Country: A Native History of Early America* (Cambridge, Mass., 2001), chapters 3 and 5.

9. "Robert Livingston Jr.'s accounts of the damage done by Joseph Paine," July 1753, LP, roll 7; Robert Livingston Jr. to Lieutenant Governor Oliver DeLancey, Manor Livingston, 12 February 1754, *DHNY,* 3:458–59; Robert Livingston Jr. to Abraham Yates Jr., Claverack, 12 December 1754, Abraham Yates Papers, NYPL; "An Addendum to the Affidavit of 21 November 1755," Peter Livingston, LP, roll 7; Robert Livingston Jr. to Governor Hardy, Manor Livingston, 22 November 1755, *DHNY,* 3:486–87.

10. See, for example, the affidavits of Jan Hallenbeck (12 May 1753), Japheth Hunt (4 August 1753), Jacob Spoor (4 September 1753), Catrina Hallenbeck (4 September 1753), and Joseph Paine (4 September 1753), in *MACR, 1724–1775,* 6:118–27. See the report of the House of Representatives in Massachusetts, 11 September 1753, *MACR,* 6:139–41.

11. John Van Rensselaer's affidavit, 22 February 1755; "An Account of the Murder of William Rees," 28 April 1755, both in *DHNY,* 3:466–74; Town Meeting Minutes, 31 May 1757, Spencertown Proprietors Book, 1755–1763, NYSL.

12. See the affidavits of William White (7 February 1755) and Joseph Pixley (8 February 1755), both in *DHNY,* 3:463; the affidavits of Peter Livingston, Dirck Swart,

Timothy Dannon, Jacob Decker, and James Elliot, 21 November 1755, LP, roll 7; "Six Mile Tract Deed from Springfield, Massachusetts, A True Copy from Hampden County," Registry of Deeds, Book I, 747–49, 27 September 1756, CCHS; and Town Meeting Minutes, 31 May 1757, Spencertown Proprietors Book, 1755–1763, NYSL.

13. Petition submitted by Jonathon Darby, Andries Rees, Christiana Hallenbeck, Christopher Brusie, Henry Bradley, and Simon Burton to the Supreme Court, Council, and House of Representatives of Massachusetts, 30 May 1757, *MACR* 6:240; Robert Livingston Jr. to Abraham Yates, Manor Livingston, 14 April 1757; Robert Livingston Jr. to Abraham Yates, Manor Livingston, 9 May, 15 May, and 18 May 1757, all in Yates Papers, NYPL; John Chambers, Chairman, "Report of the Committee on a Letter of [inquiry] from the Governor of Massachusetts Bay respecting the disturbances on the Borders of the two Governments," 29 July 1757, Miscellaneous Manuscripts, "Massachusetts," 1750–1769, NYHS; Lieutenant Governor James DeLancey, "A Proclamation to Arrest Certain Rioters on Livingston Manor," 8 June 1757, *DHNY,* 3:491; William Livingston to Robert Livingston Jr., New York City, 13 June 1757, LP, roll 7; Robert Livingston Jr. to Abraham Yates, Manor Livingston, 3 July 1757; Robert Livingston Jr. to Abraham Yates, Manor Livingston, 6 July and 19 July 1757, both in Yates Papers, NYPL.

14. Robert Van Deusen to Robert Livingston Jr., 29 October 1755, *DHNY,* 3:485; Robert Livingston Jr., "Complaints to the Governor of New York," 16 November 1755, LP, roll 7; Governor Hardy to the Lords of Trade, 23 February 1756, Fort George, *DRCNY,* 7:37–38; Robert Livingston Jr. to Abraham Yates, New York City, 20 October 1756; Robert Livingston Jr. to Abraham Yates, Manor Livingston, 23 November and 15 December 1756, both in Yates Papers, NYPL; Governor Hardy to the Lords of Trade, Fort George, 22 December 1756, *DRCNY,* 7:206–7; John Chambers, "Report of the Committee on a Letter of [inquiry] from the Governor of Massachusetts Bay respecting the disturbances on the Borders of the two Governments," 29 July 1757, Miscellaneous Manuscripts, "Massachusetts," 1750–1769, NYHS.

15. Depositions of John PoskNehonnohwok and David Nannaunookkunuck, 23 July 1761, of Jacob Vosburgh, 18 June 1762, and of Jonathon Reed, 29 June 1762, in Sorted Legal MSS., Box 3, KEMPE, NYHS. See also Frazier, *The Mohicans of Stockbridge,* chapter 12.

16. Frazier, *The Mohicans of Stockbridge,* 152–55.

17. Kempe's quotes from his "Argument in Opposition to Mr John Van Rensselaer's petition for Further time to be Heard on his Caveat," 3 December 1761, Unsorted Lawsuits, V-Z, KEMPE. See also the collection of papers and depositions on this case in MSC. MSS., "Massachusetts," 1750–1769, NYHS; and Kim, *Landlord and Tenant,* 350–58.

18. "Beby and others agt Renselaer, Notes for Reply," Unsorted legal MSS.; "Argument in Opposition to Mr John Van Rensselaer's petition," both in KEMPE; Kim, *Landlord and Tenant,* 327–45, 350–58; Reeve Huston, *Land and Freedom: Rural Society, Popular Protest, and Party Politics in Antebellum New York* (New York, 2000), 34.

19. Philip Schuyler to Gouvenor Morris, 3 February 1777, quoted in Staughton Lynd, "Abraham Yates's History of the Movement for the United States Constitution," *WMQ,* 3rd ser., 20 (1963): 225.

20. Stefan Bielinski, *Abraham Yates, Jr., and the New Political Order in Revolutionary New York* (Albany, N.Y., 1975); William H. W. Sabine, ed., *Historical Memoirs . . . of William Smith,* 2 vols. (New York, 1969–71), 2:121—26 April 1777.

21. Abraham Yates Jr., "Argument in an action at law being a history of the manor of Rensselaerswyck and the rival claims of Albany and Schenectady," 1762, Yates Papers, NYPL; Yates, n.d., "Notes on Ancient Revolutions of New York," Yates

Papers, NYPL. There is no date on the "Notes," but he presents these fundamental arguments more articulately in March 1771, suggesting that he wrote the "Notes" sometime between 1762 and 1771.

22. Samuel Jones to Abraham Yates Jr., New York City, Yates Papers, Reel 1, NYPL.

23. Cadwallader Colden to the Lords of Trade, New York City, 28 February 1761, *DRCNY,* 7:456–57.

24. Robert Livingston Jr. to Abraham Yates, Manor Livingston, 13 March 1762, Yates Papers, NYPL. See also Robert R. Livingston to Robert Livingston Jr., n.p., June 1764, RRLP, roll 1; and Abraham Yates to Robert Livingston Jr., Albany, 4 December 1766, LP, roll 8.

25. Oneida Sachem quoted during an Indian conference, *DRCNY,* 6:984; "Affidavits of John H. and Genevieve Lydius," 5 April 1760, *DRCNY,* 6:987.

26. John Lydius to John Tabor Kempe, 22 January 1761, and notes for *The King agt John Henry Lydius,* in Kempe's hand, 25 April 1763, in Sorted Legal MSS., Box 3, KEMPE. David Jones wrote the decision for the court, "Information for Intrusion Special Verdict Found," 31 July 1764, *The King agt John Henry Lydius,* Henry Van Schaack Papers, Box 1, NYSL.

27. Thomas Young, *Some Reflections on the Disputes between New-York, New-Hampshire, and Col. John Henry Lydius of Albany* (New Haven, 1764), quotes on 3, 14, 15, and 19, emphasis in original; Pauline Maier, "Reason and Revolution: The Radicalism of Dr. Thomas Young," *American Quarterly* 28 (1976): 229–49; David Freeman Hawke, "Dr. Thomas Young—Eternal Fisher in Troubled Waters, Notes for a Biography," *New-York Historical Society Quarterly* 54 (1970): 7–29; Henry Herbert Edes, "Memoir of Dr. Thomas Young, 1731–1777," *Publications of the Colonial Society of Massachusetts* (Boston, 1910): 2–54. For Jefferson, see Richard K. Matthews, *The Radical Politics of Thomas Jefferson: A Revisionist View* (Lawrence, Kans., 1984), 20–24.

28. See Edmund S. Morgan and Helen M. Morgan, *The Stamp Act Crisis: Prologue to Revolution* (Chapel Hill, N.C., 1953), 119–33; Gordon S. Wood, *The Radicalism of the American Revolution* (New York, 1992), 172–75; and Edward Countryman, *A People in Revolution: The American Revolution and Political Society in New York, 1760–1790* (New York, 1989), chapters 1 and 2. See also the discussion of the Stamp Act and crowds reacting to it in Robert R. Livingston to Robert Livingston Jr., Woodstock, 1 May 1766, LP, roll 8; Robert Cambridge Livingston to Robert Livingston Jr., New York City, 29 and 30 May 1766, LP, roll 8; "Constitution of the Sons of Liberty of Albany, and Names of the Signers," *American Historian and Quarterly Genealogical Record* 1 (1876), 142–52; and "Henry Van Schaack's case respecting the abuse he met with from the traitors at Albany," Unlisted Manuscripts and Lawsuits, V-Z, KEMPE.

29. "Copy of the warrent of the Justice of Albany against [Robert Noble] and others June 1766," Rensselaerswyck MSC. MSS., NYHS.

30. Town Meeting Minutes, Spencertown Proprietors Book, 1755–1763, 31 May 1757, NYSL; G. D. Scull, ed., *The Montresor Journals* (New York, 1882), 28 June 1766, 375–76.

31. John Van Gelden and Ebenezer Smith's petition to Francis Bernard, 7 February 1767, 350–51; William Kellogg to Francis Bernard, Nobletown, 25 July 1766, 328–29, both in *MACR,* vol. 7.

32. "Copy of the warrant of the Justice of Albany against [Robert Noble] and others June 1766," Rensselaerswyck MSC. MSS., NYHS; Scull, *Montresor Journals,* 2 July 1766, 376; "Notes on the Trial of the Defs. for the Several Murthers vizt. of Cornelius

Ten Broeck, Thomas Whitney, and John Bull," NYSL; trial transcripts for *"The King agt. Alex. McArthur, Daniel McArthur, Thomas Johnson, Levi Stockwell,"* August 1766, MSC. MSS., "D," NYHS.

33. Scull, *Montresor Journals,* 1 May 1766, 363; "Constitution of the Sons of Liberty of Albany, and Names of the Signers," 142–52; "Henry Van Schaack's case," Unlisted Manuscripts and Lawsuits, V-Z, KEMPE; "Albany City Records, 1753–1783," *CHA,* 1:85–351; Countryman, *A People in Revolution,* chapter 7; Staughton Lynd, "The Revolution and the Common Man: Farm Tenants and Artisans in New York Politics, 1777–1788" (PhD diss., Columbia University, 1962), 119–26.

34. "Copy of the warrant of the Justice of Albany against [Robert Noble] and others June 1766," Rensselaerswyck MSC. MSS., NYHS; "Notes on the Trial of the Defs. for the Several Murthers vizt. of Cornelius Ten Broeck, Thomas Whitney, and John Bull," NYSL; trial transcripts for *"The King agt. Alex. McArthur, Daniel McArthur, Thomas Johnson, Levi Stockwell,"* August 1766, MSC. MSS., "D," NYHS; Kim, *Landlord and Tenant,* 405–9.

35. Peter R. Livingston to Philip Schuyler, New York City, 27 February 1767, quoted in George Dangerfield, *Chancellor Robert R. Livingston of New York, 1746–1813* (New York, 1960), 40. See also Cadwallader Colden to the Earl of Hillsborough, New York City, 25 April 1769, *DRCNY,* 7:61; Roger Champagne, "Family Politics versus Constitutional Principles: The New York Assembly Elections of 1768 and 1769," *WMQ,* 3rd ser., 20 (1963), 57–79; Robert J. Dinkin, *Voting in Provincial America: A Study of Elections in the Thirteen Colonies, 1689–1776* (Westport, Conn., 1977), 133–36; Kim, *Landlord and Tenant,* 210–12; and Countryman, *A People in Revolution,* chapters 1 and 2.

36. William Moore's poem quoted in Lynd, "The Revolution and the Common Man," 70.

37. Governor Henry Moore to the Earl of Shelbourne, Fort George, New York City, 22 December, 1766, *DRCNY,* 7:885–86. See also Walter Livingston to Robert Livingston Jr., New York City, 29 December 1766; John Schuyler to Robert Livingston Jr., New York City, 29 December 1766; and James Duane to Robert Livingston Jr., New York City, 2 February 1767, all in LP, roll 8. Governor Henry Moore to the Earl of Shelbourne, Fort George, New York City, 24 February 1767, *DRCNY,* 7:910–11; Captain John Clarke to Lieutenant Colonel Maitland, 5 August 1766, and Clarke to General Thomas Gage, 17 August 1766, Gage Papers, Clements Library; "Counsellor Dagges Opinion on the Indian Grant of Lands to William Frend & Others—as stated in a Case dated London 17 February 1770," in Van Schaack Papers, CCHS.

38. First quote from "Petition to Governor William Tryon of the Inhabitants of New Britain," 11 January 1772, New York Colonial Manuscripts, New York Land Papers, 1642–1803, 30:77, NYSL; second set of quotes from "Petition to Governor William Tryon of the Inhabitants of Spencertown," 24 November 1772, New York Land Papers, 32:114; and petition of Hezekiah Baldwin, Martin Beebe, and David Bratt for New Canaan, New Concord, Spencertown, and New Britain, 29 September 1772, New York Land Papers, 32:94.

39. Lieutenant Governor Cadwallader Colden to the Lords of Trade, New York City, 8 February 1763, *DRCNY,* 7:608.

40. "Conventions of the Inhabitants of the New Hampshire Grants in Opposition to the Claims of New York with notes and explanations," 1765, *Collections of the Vermont Historical Society,* 2 vols. (Montpelier, Vt., 1870–1871), 1:3–4; *George Clark and Peter DeLancey agt James Breckenridge,* April 1769, Unsorted Lawsuits, P-U, KEMPE.

41. Deposition of John Walworth, Albany County, New York, 8 May 1771, Unsorted Lawsuits, V-Z, KEMPE.

42. Ira Allen, "Miscellaneous Remarks on the Proceedings of the State of New York against the State of Vermont, &c.," 1777, in *Collections of the Vermont Historical Society* 1:119.

43. "Controversy Respecting the New Hampshire Grants," *DRCNY*, 4:925–1026; Michael A. Bellesiles, *Revolutionary Outlaws: Ethan Allen and the Struggle for Independence on the Early American Frontier* (Charlottesville, Va., 1993), 96–97, 99–103.

44. *Collections of the Vermont Historical Society,* 1:6–7; "A Letter to William Tryon of New York from M. Dewey and others of Bennington, Vermont," 5 June 1772; Tryon's response, Albany, 11 August 1772, both in William Slade, ed., *Vermont State Papers: Being a Collection of Records and Documents* (Middlebury, Conn., 1823), 23–24, 29–30; *The Connecticut Courant,* 22 August 1772.

45. "The Vision of Junus, the Benningtonite," *Connecticut Courant,* 22 September 1772; "Copy of Deposition of Oliver Church and Joseph Hancock," 22 March 1775, Box 6, KEMPE; "Riot and Bloodshed in Cumberland County," 23 March 1775; deposition of John Griffin, 27/8 March 1775, both in *DHNY,* 4:904–14; Bellesiles, *Revolutionary Outlaws,* 110–11.

46. I want to reiterate here the difficulties of determining origins from surnames and again assert that such a practice only allows for the general conclusion that the rioters were of diverse backgrounds. For names of the rioters, see "A Proclamation to Arrest Certain Rioters on Livingston Manor," 8 June 1757, *DHNY,* 3:491; "A Proclamation to Arrest Rioters," 31 March 1762, *DHNY,* 3:493; "Copy of a warrant of the Justices of Albany County against [Robert Noble] and others June 1766," Rensselaerswyck, MSC. MSS., NYHS; "Notes on the Trial of the Defs for the Several Murthers vizt. of Cornelius Ten Broeck, Thomas Whitney, and John Bull," in *"The King agt. Alexander McArthur, Daniel McArthur, Thomas Johnson, and Levi Stockwell,"* n.d., in NYSL and MSC. MSS., Dutchess County, "D," NYHS; petition submitted by Jonathon Darby, Andries Rees, Christiana Hallenbeck, Christopher Brusie, Henry Bradley, and Simon Burton to the Supreme Court, Council, and House of Representatives of Massachusetts, 30 May 1757, *MACR,* 6:240; Robert Livingston Jr. to Abraham Yates, Manor Livingston, 14 April 1757; Robert Livingston Jr. to Abraham Yates, Manor Livingston, 9 May, 15 May, and 18 May 1757; all in Yates Papers, NYPL; John Chambers, Chairman, "Report of the Committee on a Letter of [inquiry] from the Governor of Massachusetts Bay respecting the disturbances on the Borders of the two Governments," 29 July 1757, Miscellaneous Manuscripts, "Massachusetts," 1750–1769, NYHS; William Livingston to Robert Livingston Jr., New York City, 13 June 1757, LP, roll 7; Robert Livingston Jr. to Abraham Yates, Manor Livingston, 3 July 1757; and Robert Livingston Jr. to Abraham Yates, Manor Livingston, 6 July and 19 July 1757, both in Yates Papers, NYPL. This number does not include the 252 people who petitioned New York for land in the 1770s. See the "Petition for land in New Britain," *Calendar of Land Papers,* vol. 30, 11 January 1772, 77; "Petition for the Town of Austerlitz," *Calendar of Land Papers,* vol. 32, 24 November 1772, 114; and "Petition of Hezekiah Brown and the principal inhabitants of New Canaan," *Calendar of Land Papers,* vol. 32, 24 November 1772, 116.

47. "A Proclamation to Arrest Certain Rioters on Livingston Manor," 8 June 1757, *DHNY,* 3:491; "A Proclamation to Arrest Rioters," 31 March 1762, *DHNY,* 3:493; "Copy of a warrant of the Justices of Albany County against [Robert Noble] and others June 1766," Rensselaerswyck, MSC. MSS., NYHS; "Notes on the Trial of the Defs for

the Several Murthers vizt. of Cornelius Ten Broeck, Thomas Whitney, and John Bull," in *"The King agt. Alexander McArthur, Daniel McArthur, Thomas Johnson, and Levi Stockwell,"* n.d., in NYSL and MSC. MSS., Dutchess County, "D," NYHS.

48. Robert Livingston Jr. to Abraham Yates, 2 May 1755, Yates Papers, NYPL; "Affidavit of Robert Livingston," 8 May 1755, New York City, *DHNY,* 3:473–73. For Hallenbeck's actions and Livingston's response see the papers for 19 May 1755, 22 May 1755, and 23 June 1755, all in *DHNY,* 3:478–84. For women at the attack on Noble's farm, see *"The King agt. Alex. McArthur, Daniel McArthur, Thomas Johnson, Levi Stockwell,"* August 1766, MSC. MSS., "D," NYHS. For women rioters in other colonies, see Brendan McConville, "Conflict and Change on a Cultural Frontier: The Rise of Magdalena Valleau, Land Rioter," *Pennsylvania History: A Journal of Mid-Atlantic Studies* 65 (1998), 122–40; and Terri L. Snyder, *Brabbling Women: Disorderly Speech and the Law in Early Virginia* (Ithaca, N.Y., 2003).

49. I compared manor records, lease records, and rent records with lists of known rioters. I did not count names spelled differently in these records unless I could corroborate the misspelled names from another source.

3—DISCONTENT IN THE SOUTHERN VALLEY

1. David Akin's evidence for William Prendergast's trial, n.d., Lawsuits, C-F, KEMPE; Governor Henry Moore to the Earl of Shelburne, Fort George, New York, 22 December 1766, *DRCNY,* 7:885–86.

2. "Articles of Peace Concluded in Presence of the Mohawks between the Dutch and the River Indians," 30 August 1645; "Extract of a Letter of the Directors to Petrus Stuyvesant," 15 April 1650; "Report made by P. W. Van Couwenhoven of Information Respecting Intrigues of the English with the Wappings and Esopus Indians," March 1664, all in *DRCNY,* 13:18, 26–27, 363–64.

3. This brief description is drawn from Irving Mark, *Agrarian Conflicts in Colonial New York, 1711–1775* (1940; repr., Port Washington, N.Y., 1965), 131–34; Oscar Handlin and Irving Mark, "Chief Daniel Nimham v. Robert Morris, Beverly Robinson, and Philip Philipse—An Indian Case in Colonial New York, 1765–1767," *Ethnohistory* 2 (1964): 193–246; Georgiana C. Nammack, *Fraud, Politics, and the Dispossession of the Indians: The Iroquois Land Frontier in the Colonial Period* (Norman, Okla., 1969), 70–73; Sung Bok Kim, *Landlord and Tenant in Colonial New York: Manorial Society, 1664–1775* (Chapel Hill, N.C., 1978), 376–80; and Patrick Frazier, *The Mohicans of Stockbridge* (Lincoln, Nebr., 1992), 154–71.

4. "A Petition In a Confirmation of Our Inheritances together with our Associates," 10 November 1763; "Petition to the King," 27 February 1764, both in MSC. MSS., "D," NYHS.

5. Kempe's notes to a "Council Held at Fort George in the City of New York," 28 July 1762, Unsorted Legal Lawsuits, M-O; "Notes on the Pretensions & Suggestions of the Inhabitants of New Canaan," Box 6, both in KEMPE.

6. See John Tabor Kempe's notes on this subject in conjunction with the Lockwood and Peters cases, n.d., P-U, KEMPE; Abraham Yates to Robert Livingston Jr., Albany, 4 December 1766, LP, roll 8; and the Legal Notices in the Henry Van Schaack Papers, n.d., Box 1, NYSL.

7. Brendan McConville, *These Daring Disturbers of the Public Peace: The Struggle for Property and Power in Early New Jersey* (Ithaca, N.Y., 1999), chapters 1 and 3; Lt. Gov. Cadwallader Colden to General Thomas Gage, Spring Hill, 2 September 1765, *DRCNY,*

7:758; William Smith Jr. to Governor Robert Monckton, New York City, 8 November 1765, in William H. W. Sabine, ed., *Historical Memoirs . . . of William Smith,* 2 vols. (New York, 1969–71), 1:30.

8. Prendergast quoted in testimony of Moss Kent Sr.; testimony of George Hughson, both in *The King agt. Elisha Cole,* 13 June 1767, Sorted Legal Manuscripts, Box 2, KEMPE.

9. Foote Papers, Chatauqua County Historical Society, Chatauqua, N.Y.; A. W. Anderson, *The Story of Pioneer Family* (Jamestown, N.Y., 1936), 1–18; Patricia Bonomi, *A Factious People: Politics and Society in Colonial New York* (New York, 1971), 221–24.

10. Irving Mark and Oscar Handlin, eds., "Land Cases in Colonial New York, 1765–1767; *The King v William Prendergast,*" *New York University Law Quarterly Review* 9 (1940): 165–67; Gideon Grindle's Deposition, 28 July 1766, *The King agt. John Kane,* Sorted Legal Manuscripts, Box 2, KEMPE.

11. Christopher Hill, *Puritanism and Revolution: Studies in Interpretation of the English Revolution of the 17th Century* (New York, 1997), 301; Edmund S. Morgan, *American Slavery, American Freedom: The Ordeal of Colonial Virginia* (New York, 1975), 250–70; Kathleen M. Brown, *Good Wives, Nasty Wenches, and Anxious Patriarchs: Gender, Race, and Power in Colonial Virginia* (Chapel Hill, N.C., 1996), 159–70; Gideon Grindle's Deposition, 28 July 1766, *The King agt. John Kane,* Sorted Legal Manuscripts, Box 2, KEMPE.

12. See the Depositions of James Covey Jr., Ebenezer Weed, and Felix Holdridge, 23 November 1765, Unsorted Legal Manuscripts, Box 1; and David Akin's evidence for Prendergast's trial, n.d., Lawsuits, C-F, Box 4, both in KEMPE.

13. David Akin's evidence, n.d., Lawsuits, C-F, Box 4; Robert Hughson's deposition, 27 May 1766, Unsorted Lawsuits, Box 4, both in KEMPE; G. D. Scull, ed., *The Montresor Journals* (New York, 1882), 363–65; Kim, *Landlord and Tenant,* 389; Thomas Jones, *History of New York during the Revolutionary War,* ed. Edward Floyd DeLancey (1879; New York, 1968), 1:109; Daniel Horsmanden, *The New York Conspiracy,* ed. Thomas J. Davis (Boston, 1971); Thomas J. Davis, *A Rumor of Revolt: The "Great Negro Plot" in Colonial New York* (New York, 1985).

14. *The King agt. Edmund Green, Richard Chellers, Thomas Carle, Daniel Taylor and John Green,* tried on "Indictment for assault on Hannah Hobby by means whereof she miscarried," July Assizes, 1766; *The King agt. Edmund Green, Richard Chellers, Thomas Carle, Daniel Taylor and John Green,* for "breaking & Entring the House of John Gonnong," both in MSC. MSS., Dutchess County, "D," NYHS. The attack on Hannah Hobby indicates that middling and lower-class women worked in the fields during periods of intense labor such as harvests. For correlative indications of this, see Allan Kulikoff, *From British Peasants to Colonial American Farmers* (Chapel Hill, N.C., 2000), 244–45; Brown, *Good Wives,* 295–96; and Lucy Simler and Paul G. E. Clemens, "Rural Labor and the Farm Household in Chester County, Pennsylvania, 1750–1820," in *Work and Labor in Early America,* ed. Stephen Innes (Chapel Hill, N.C., 1988), 130–34.

15. Barbara Clark Smith, "Food Rioters and the American Revolution," *WMQ,* 3rd ser., 51 (1994): 3–38; Terri L. Snyder, *Brabbling Women: Disorderly Speech and the Law in Early Virginia* (Ithaca, N.Y., 2003); Alfred F. Young, "The Women of Boston: 'Persons of Consequence' in the Making of the American Revolution," in *Women and Politics in the Age of the Democratic Revolution,* ed. Harriet B. Applewhite and Darline G. Levy (Ann Arbor, Mich., 1990), 181–226; John Walter and Keith Wrightson, "Death and the Social Order in Early Modern England," *Past and Present* 71 (1976): 22–42; Patricia Higgins, "The Reactions of Women," in *Politics, Religion and the English Civil War,*

ed. Brian Manning (London, 1973), esp. 181–82; Cynthia A. Bouton, "Gendered Behavior in Subsistence Riots: The French Flour War, 1775," *Journal of Social History* 23 (1990): 735–54.

16. E. P. Thompson, "Rough Music," in *Customs in Common: Studies in Traditional Popular Culture* (New York, 1993), 499–505; Brown, *Good Wives,* chapters 1 and 7; David E. Underdown, "The Taming of the Scold: The Enforcement of Patriarchal Authority in Early Modern England," in *Order and Disorder in Early Modern England,* ed. Anthony Fletcher and John Stevenson (Cambridge, 1985), 116–36; Carole Shammas, "Anglo-American Household government in Comparative Perspective," *WMQ,* 3rd ser., 52 (1995): 104–50.

17. McConville, *These Daring Disturbers of the Public Peace,* 124–29; Simler and Clemens, "Rural Labor and The Farm Household," 106–43; David E. Narrett, *Inheritance and Family Life in Colonial New York City* (Ithaca, N.Y., 1992), 90–93; Cynthia Kierner, *Traders and Gentlefolk: The Livingstons of New York, 1675–1790* (Ithaca, N.Y., 1992), 20–21, 50–52.

18. David Akin's testimony, Lawsuits, C-F; Samuel Peters's deposition; Robert Hughson's deposition, 27 May 1766, all in Unsorted Lawsuits, Box 4, KEMPE; testimony of Peters and George Hughson in Mark and Handlin, "Land Cases in Colonial New York, 1765–1767; *The King v William Prendergast,*" 179–84.

19. Thompson, "Rough Music," in *Customs in Common,* 479–80; Natalie Davis, *Society and Culture in Early Modern France* (Stanford, Calif., 1975), 302–3, fn. 47; David Underdown, *Revel, Riot, and Rebellion: Popular Politics and Culture in England, 1603–1660* (New York, 1985), 100–103, 110–11; Robert Darnton, *The Great Cat Massacre and Other Episodes in French Cultural History* (New York, 1984), 96–97; Suzanne Desan, "Crowds, Community, and Ritual in the Work of E. P. Thompson and Natalie Davis," in *The New Cultural History,* ed. Lynn Hunt (Berkeley, 1989), 47–71; Fred Anderson, *A People's Army: Massachusetts Soldiers and Society in the Seven Years' War* (Chapel Hill, N.C., 1984), 124; Alfred F. Young, "English Plebian Culture and Eighteenth Century American Radicalism," in *Origins of Anglo-American Radicalism,* ed. Margaret Jacob and James Jacob (London, 1984), 184–212; Peter Linebaugh, "All the Atlantic Mountains Shook," in *Reviving the English Revolution: Reflections and Elaborations on the Work of Christopher Hill,* ed. Geoff Eley and William Hunt (London, 1988), 195–200; Cornelia Hughes Dayton, *Women Before the Bar: Gender, Law, and Society in Connecticut, 1639–1789* (Chapel Hill, N.C., 1995), 121–38.

20. Hezekiah Holdridge's deposition to John Bull of Westchester County, New York, 7 March 1758; unsigned letter from some of the men who attacked Holdridge addressed to William Kempe, 10 March 1758, both in Lawsuits, G-L, KEMPE.

21. Samuel Peters and George Hughson in Mark and Handlin, "Land Cases in Colonial New York, 1765–1767; *The King v William Prendergast,*" 180–87, quotes on 180, 183, 184, and 187, emphasis in original; Samuel Peters in *The King agt. Elisha Cole,* 13 June 1767, Sorted Legal Manuscripts, Box 2, KEMPE.

22. James H. Hutson, "An Investigation of the Inarticulate: Philadelphia's White Oaks," *WMQ,* 3rd ser., 28 (1971): 3–25; White-Oak, "Mr. Printer I am not a man of many words," Philadelphia, 1770, Early American Imprints, no. 11836.

23. Arthur Young, Esquire, "The account of the WHITEBOYS in Ireland," *The American Minerva,* 30 December 1793, emphasis in original; second quote from R. B. McDowell, *Ireland in the Age of Imperialism and Revolution, 1760–1801* (Oxford, 1979), 79. W. E. H. Lecky, *A History of Ireland in the Eighteenth Century* (Chicago, 1972), 115–31; Francis Joseph Bigger, *The Ulster Land War of 1770 (The Hearts of Steel)*

(Dublin, 1910), 14 and chapter 2; James S. Donnelly Jr., "The Whiteboy Movement, 1761–1765," *Irish Historical Studies* 21 (1978), 20–54.

24. Foote Papers, Chatauqua Historical Society; Anderson, *The Story of a Pioneer Family*, 1–18; Bonomi, *A Factious People*, 221–24.

25. Young, "English Plebian Culture," 194–95; Rhys Isaac, "Preachers and Patriots: Popular Culture and the Revolution in Virginia," in *The American Revolution: Explorations in the History of American Radicalism*, ed. Alfred F. Young (DeKalb, Ill., 1976), 125–58; Edmund S. Morgan, *The Gentle Puritan: A Life of Ezra Stiles, 1725–1795* (New Haven, 1962), 458–61.

26. Munro was identified by James Birdsell and Gideon Prindle in Mark and Handlin, "Land Cases in Colonial New York, 1765–1767; *The King v William Prendergast*," 190, 194. See also Henry Noble MacCracken, *Old Dutchess Forever! The Story of an American County* (New York, 1956), 274.

27. Gerrard Winstanley, "True Leveller's Standard Advanced," in his *The Law of Freedom, and Other Writings*, ed. Christopher Hill (Cambridge, 1983). See also Winstanley's "A New-Year's Gift for the Parliament and Army," ibid., 84; and Christopher Hill, *The World Turned Upside Down: Radical Ideas During the English Revolution* (New York, 1972), 45–48, 86–105.

28. Alfred F. Young, foreword to *The American Revolution,* ix; Nash, in Young, *The American Revolution,* 17; Dirk Hoerder, "Boston Leaders and Boston Crowds, 1765–1766," in ibid.

29. Justice Robert R. Livingston to Robert Livingston Jr., Woodstock, 1 May 1766, LP, roll 8. See also Robert Cambridge Livingston to Robert Livingston Jr., New York City, 29 May, LP, roll 8; Walter Livingston to Robert Livingston Jr., New York City, 29 December 1767, LP, roll 8; Scull, *Montresor Journals,* 25 April 1766, 28–29, and June 1766, 361–65; and "A Proclamation" issued by Governor Henry Moore for the arrest of Jacobus Gonsoles, Silas Washburn, James Secord, Elisha Cole, Isaac Perry, and Micab Vail, 20 June 1766, LP, roll 12.

30. *The Boston Gazette,* 14 July and 4 August 1766; *New-York Mercury,* 28 July 1766; Geographical, Historical Narrative, vol. 707, fols. 18–19, 32–33, noted in Mark, *Agrarian Conflicts,* 148–49.

31. Edward Countryman, *A People in Revolution: The American Revolution and Political Society in New York, 1760–1790* (New York, 1989), 68.

32. The justices were Daniel Horsmanden, John Watts, William Walton, Oliver DeLancey, Joseph Reade, William Smith Jr., Whitehead Hicks, and John Morin Scott. Robert R. Livingston sat in the audience. See Sabine, *Historical Memoirs,* 1:33–34; Scull, *Montresor Journals,* 19 August 1766, 384; and E. Marie Becker, "The 801 Westchester County Freeholders of 1763," *New-York Historical Society Quarterly* 35 (1951): 282–21.

33. See Kempe's remarks in Mark and Handlin, "Land Cases in Colonial New York, 1765–1767; *The King v William Prendergast*," 170–71; *The King agt. Elisha Cole,* 13 June 1766, both in Sorted Legal Manuscripts, Box 2, KEMPE; Governor Henry Moore to the Lords of Trade, New York City, 12 August 1766, *DRCNY* 7:849–50; Sabine, *Historical Memoirs,* 1:33.

34. *The Boston Gazette,* 15 September 1766.

35. *New-York Mercury,* 18 August 1766; *New-York Gazette,* 1 September 1766; *Boston Gazette,* 1, 8, and 15 September 1766; William Smith quoted in Staughton Lynd, *Anti-Federalism in Dutchess County, New York; A Study of Democracy and Class Conflict in the Revolutionary Era* (Chicago, 1962), 50.

36. *New-York Mercury,* 15 September 1766; Mark and Handlin, "Land Cases in Colonial New York, 1765–1767; *The King v William Prendergast,*" 168; Bonomi, *A Factious People,* 221–24; Anderson, *The Story of a Pioneer Family,* 1–8. The records do not reveal how or why Prendergast obtained a fee-simple hold on his land. He probably had his verbal agreement with the Philipses entered into a copy book and then obtained the land during the American Revolution, but this is speculative.

37. Mikhail Bakhtin, *Rabelais and His World,* trans. and ed. Hèléne Iswolsky (Bloomington, Ind., 1984), 81; Bill Buford, *Among the Thugs* (London, 1991), 205; Darnton, *The Great Cat Massacre,* 75–106.

38. Depositions of James Covey Jr., Ebenezer Weed, and Felix Holdrige, 23 November 1765, Unsorted Legal Manuscripts, Box 1; David Akin's Evidence for Prendergast's trial, n.d., Lawsuits, C-F, both in KEMPE; Samuel Peters, George Hughson, and Reuben Garlick quoted in Mark and Handlin, "Land Cases in Colonial New York, 1765–1767; *The King v William Prendergast,*" 180–85; Samuel Peters' Affidavit, 7 June 1766, Unsorted Lawsuits, P-U, Box 4; Robert Hughson's Deposition, 27 May 1766, Unsorted Lawsuits, Box 4, both in KEMPE; *The King agt. Edmund Green, Richard Chellers, Thomas Carle, Daniel Taylor and John Green,* in MSC. MSS., Dutchess County, "D," NYHS; "A Proclamation" issued by Governor Henry Moore, 20 June 1766, LP, roll 12.

39. Michel Foucault, *Power/Knowledge: Selected Interviews and Other Writings, 1972–1977,* trans. and ed. Colin Gordon (New York, 1980), chapter 1; Foucault, *Discipline and Punish: The Birth of the Prison,* trans. Alan Sheridan (New York, 1977), chapter 1; Rhys Isaac, "Evangelical Revolt: The Nature of the Baptists' Challenge to the Traditional Order in Virginia, 1765–1775," *WMQ,* 3rd ser., 31 (1974): 345–68; A. G. Roeber, "Authority, Law, and Custom: The Rituals of Court Day in Tidewater Virginia, 1720–1750," *WMQ,* 3rd ser., 37 (1980): 29–52; Steven Mullaney, *The Place of the Stage: License, Play and Power in Renaissance England* (Chicago, 1988), chapters 2 and 3. For quotes by Prendergast and Kent, see Mark and Handlin, "Land Cases in Colonial New York, 1765–1767; *The King v William Prendergast,*" 175, 191.

40. Handlin and Mark, "Nimham v. Morris, Robinson, and Philipse" is a reprint of "A geographic, historical Narrative or Summary of the present Controversy between Dan Nimham a native Indian; King or Sachem of the Wappinger Tribe of Indians so called in Behalf of himself and the whole Tribe aforesaid, on the one Part; and Messrs. Roger Morris, Beverly Robinson, and, Philip Philipse, all of the City and Province of New York, Heirs and legal Representatives of Col. Frederick Philipse late of said New York." The author remains unknown but indicated who said what and, in that way, provides a rough transcript of the proceedings. For Samuel Munro's plight, see Munro to John Tabor Kempe, New Goal in New York City, 5 May 1767, Unsorted Legal MSS., Box 1, KEMPE; MacCracken, *Old Dutchess Forever!* 284–85; and Frazier, *The Mohicans of Stockbridge,* 138–71.

41. Frazier, *The Mohicans of Stockbridge,* 154–59.

42. Peter Anjuvine, 217; David Ausin and Daniel Townsend, 218–19, 220; Samuel Castin, George Hughson, John Dupee, and Nehemiah Horton, 217–20, all quoted in Handlin and Mark, "Nimham v. Morris, Robinson, and Philipse."

43. John Morin Scott, 227; James Duane, 240, both quoted in Handlin and Mark, "Nimham v. Morris, Robinson, and Philipse."

44. Handlin and Mark, "Nimham v. Morris, Robinson, and Philipse," 205, 217–18.

45. John Morin Scott quoted in Handlin and Mark, "Nimham v. Morris, Robinson, and Philipse," 240.

46. Cadwallader Colden and Henry Moore quoted in Handlin and Mark, "Nimham v. Morris, Robinson, and Philipse," 205 and 242.

47. Nimham quoted in Handlin and Mark, "Nimham v. Morris, Robinson, and Philipse," 200.

4—LAND AND THE AMERICAN REVOLUTION

1. "The List of the Kings true subjects in reinbeck," 18 January 1776; "Letter to the King," Rhinebeck, 3 June 1776; Loyalty Oath, 1777, all in Travers Papers, Box 5, CCHS. The Association Oath had been copied into the July Loyalty Oath and did not include any names. I compared the list of the "Kings true subjects" with the list of Rhinebeck tenants in LP, roll 8. Edward Countryman, *A People in Revolution: The American Revolution and Political Society in New York, 1760–1790* (New York, 1989).

2. Staughton Lynd, "The Revolution and the Common Man: Farm Tenants and Artisans in New York Politics, 1777–1788" (PhD diss., Columbia University, 1962) and "Who Should Rule at Home? Dutchess County, New York, in the American Revolution," *WMQ*, 3rd ser., 18 (1961), 330–59; Philip Ranlet, *The New York Loyalists* (Knoxville, Tenn., 1986), 131.

3. Sung Bok Kim, "The Limits of Politicization in the American Revolution: The Experience of Westchester County, New York," *JAH* 80 (1993): 868–89; Jonathon Clark, "The Problem of Allegiance in Revolutionary Poughkeepsie," in *Saints and Revolutionaries: Essays on Early American History,* ed. David. D. Hall, John M. Murrin, and Thad W. Tate (New York, 1984), 285–317; Michael A. Bellesiles, *Revolutionary Outlaws: Ethan Allen and the Struggle for Independence on the Early American Frontier* (Charlottesville, Va., 1993).

4. Bernard Bailyn, *Ideological Origins of the American Revolution* (Cambridge, Mass., 1967); Gordon S. Wood, *The Radicalism of the American Revolution* (New York, 1992). Both authors posit that colonists absorbed republican rhetoric and that the colonists' developing ideology was the impetus for the American Revolution. These historians, however, rely on evidence produced primarily by people who were not representative of the rural people in New York, or of much of the colonial population.

5. Thomas S. Wermuth, *Rip Van Winkle's Neighbors: The Transformation of Rural Society in the Hudson River Valley, 1720–1850* (Albany, N.Y., 2001), 69–89; Clark, "The Problem of Allegiance in Revolutionary Poughkeepsie"; Joseph S. Tiedemann, "Patriots by Default: Queen's County, New York, and the British Army, 1776–1783," *WMQ*, 3rd ser., 43 (1986), 35–63.

6. See Governor Morris's comments in May 1775 in *The Papers of Charles Lee,* 4 vols., in *Collections of the New-York Historical Society* (1871–1874), 4:178; Thomas Jones, *History of New York During the Revolutionary War,* ed. Edward Floyd DeLancey, 2 vols. (1879; New York, 1968), 1:39–41; *Calendar of Historical Manuscripts, relating to the War of the Revolution,* 2 vols. (Albany, N.Y., 1868), 1:64; 158–59; *Journals of the Provincial Congress, Provincial Convention, Committee of Safety and Council of Safety of the State of New-York,* 2 vols. (Albany, N.Y., 1842), 1:1–8; and Kim, "The Limits of Politicization," 868–77.

7. See Coxsackie Association Oath, April 1775, AIHA; "The List of the Kings true subjects in reinbeck," 18 January 1776; "Letter to the King," Rhinebeck, 3 June 1776; and Loyalty Oath, 1777, all in Travers Papers, Box 5, CCHS. Bloomfield, Joseph, *Citizen Soldier: The Revolutionary War Journal of Joseph Bloomfield,* ed. Mark Edward Lender and James Kirby Martin (Newark, N.J., 1982), 54, 59; Countryman, *A People in Revolution,* 144–46; Kim, "The Limits of Politicization," 874–77, 881.

8. Frederick Philipse, ALC, 12, vol. 19; Beverly Robinson, ALC, 12, vol. 21; Kim, "The Limits of Politicization," 881.

9. Kim, "The Limits of Politicization," 883.

10. Timothy Dwight, *Travels in New England and New York,* ed. Barbara M. Solomon, 4 vols. (1821–1822; Cambridge, Mass., 1969), 3:345–46.

11. Countryman, *A People in Revolution,* 110–11, 118–20.

12. Philip Schuyler to the Continental Congress, Letterbook Copy, 7 January 1777, Albany, and 15 January 1777, Fishkill, Schuyler Papers, Reel 2, NYPL; "Minutes of the Committee of Safety of Livingston Manor," 7 February 1777, 338, and 11 March 1777, 340; John Wheelock to Governor Morris, 19 March 1777, Hanover, RRLP, roll 1; Robert R. Livingston to John Jay, 17 July 1775, quoted in Staughton Lynd, "The Tenant Rising at Livingston Manor, May 1777," *New-York Historical Society Quarterly* 48 (April 1964), 167–68; William H. W. Sabine, ed., *Historical Memoirs . . . of William Smith,* 2 vols. (New York, 1969–71) 2:127, 128. Abraham Yates's draft of the state constitution in Yates Papers, Box 4, NYPL; Pierre Van Cortlandt to the New York Delegates of the Continental Congress, Kingston, 17 July 1777, in Jacob Judd, comp. and ed., *Correspondence of the Van Cortlandt Family of Cortlandt Manor, 1748–1800,* 2 vols. (Tarrytown, N.Y., 1977), 2:213.

13. Walter Livingston quoted in Cynthia Kierner, "Landlord and Tenant in Colonial New York: The Case of Livingston Manor," *NYH,* 70 (1989), 145; Countryman, *A People in Revolution,* 167–69. See also James Sullivan, ed., *Minutes of the Albany Committee of Correspondence, 1775–1778,* 2 vols. (Albany, N.Y., 1923), 1:739; Sabine, *Historical Memoirs,* 2:130.

14. See the advertisement for Loyalist land in Pennsylvania, New Jersey, and Vermont in the *New York Packet,* 20 May, 1 July, and 2 September 1779. See also the "Petition of Simon Calkins and Others," 2 September 1779, quoted in Lynd, "Who Should Rule at Home?" 346.

15. Lynd, "The Revolution and the Common Man," 101–24; Countryman, *A People in Revolution,* 205–9.

16. Requests for rent from Robert G. Livingston, 20 October and 10 December 1778, 19 August and 2 September 1779, *New York Packet.* Thomas Tillotson to Robert R. Livingston, Fishkill, 13 December 1779; Robert R. Livingston to John Jay, Clermont, 4 March 1779; Egbert Benson to Robert R. Livingston, Poughkeepsie, 20 February and 20 March 1778, all in RRLP, roll 1; Countryman, *A People in Revolution,* 184–86, 206–9, 245–49.

17. Robert Benson to Henry Livingston Jr., Poughkeepsie, 3 August 1780; "The Clause of a Law which instructs the Commissioners from Leasing Lands"; leases offered by the Commissioners in March and April 1782, all in MSC. MSS., Dutchess County, "D," NYHS.

18. Harry B. Yoshpe, *The Disposition of Loyalist Estates* (New York, 1939), appendix 2, 123; Beatrice G. Reubens, "Pre-Emptive Rights in the Disposition of Confiscated Estates: Philipsburg Manor, New York," *WMQ,* 3rd ser., 22 (1965), 445–46; Alfred F. Young, *The Democratic Republicans of New York: The Origins, 1763–1797* (Chapel Hill, N.C., 1967), 62–66; Lynd, "The Revolution and the Common Man," 119–24; Countryman, *A People in Revolution,* 207–8, 214–15; Alan Taylor, *William Cooper's Town: Power and Persuasion on the Frontier of the Early American Republic* (New York, 1995), 6–7.

19. "The Comparative view of the Increases of B. Robinson's Rents from 1755 to 1777, ALC, 12, vol. 21. Leases offered by the Commissioners of Sequestration in March and April 1782, MSC. MSS., Dutchess County, "D," NYHS. For a

general description of the plan to sell confiscated Loyalist estates in 1780, see Ezra L' Hommediue to Robert R. Livingston, Kingston, 29 March 1780, RRLP, roll 1; and Lynd, "The Revolution and the Common Man," 119–24.

20. Robert Gilbert Livingston to Gilbert Livingston, Fishkill, 7 March 1781, RRLP, roll 1; tenant petitions to the New York State Legislature in 1781 cited in Lynd, "The Revolution and the Common Man," 122–24.

21. Reubens, "Pre-Emptive Rights," table 1, 448.

22. Compare Yoshpe, *The Disposition of Loyalist Estates*, table 2, 139–47; "The Rent Roll of Col. Frederick Philips's Estate, 1776–1784," *New York Genealogical and Biographical Record* 108 (1977): 74–78; and Reubens, "Pre-Emptive Rights," 447–48.

23. "The Following Publication, which Shews the Rancorous Disposition of the American Republicans," New York 1783, Early American Imprints, 1st Series, no. 17871, emphasis in the original.

24. Young, *Democratic Republicans*, 13–17; Countryman, *A People in Revolution*, 121–23.

25. Robert R. Livingston to John Jay, 17 July 1775, quoted in Lynd, "The Tenant Rising at Livingston Manor," 167–68. See also "The Minutes of the Committee of Safety of the Manor of Livingston," *The New York Genealogical and Biographical Record* 60 (1929), 239–43, 325–41.

26. Ronald Hoffman, "The 'Disaffected' in the Revolutionary South," in *The American Revolution: Explorations in the History of American Radicalism,* ed. Alfred F. Young (DeKalb, Ill., 1976), 275–316, quote on 285.

27. Thomas Gage to William Johnson, 10 March 1775, Boston, Gage Papers, Clements Library.

28. Ranlet, *The New York Loyalists,* 120–21; Daniel K. Richter, *The Ordeal of the Longhouse: The Peoples of the Iroquois League in the Era of European Colonization* (Chapel Hill, N.C., 1992); Countryman, *A People in Revolution,* 150.

29. Stockbridge Indians' response quoted in Patrick Frazier, *The Mohicans of Stockbridge* (Lincoln, Nebr., 1992), 197.

30. Foote Papers, Chatauqua County Historical Society, Chatauqua, N.Y.; A. W. Anderson, *The Story of a Pioneer Family* (Jamestown, N.Y., 1936), 1–18.

31. Determining ethnicity by surnames is at best problematic, but the names of the disaffected on the list indicate the mixed ethnicity of the tenant population on Livingston Manor. See the names in Victor Hugo Paltsits, ed., *Minutes of the Commissioners for Detecting and Defeating Conspiracies in the State of New York, Albany County Sessions, 1778–1781,* 3 vols. (Albany, N.Y., 1909), 1:142–43, 152, 239–40, 254, 275, 335, 338–40, 347, 394, 399, 403; and "The Minutes of the Committee of Safety of the Manor of Livingston," *The New York Genealogical and Biographical Record* 60 (1929), 239–43, 325–41.

32. Dirck Jansen to Abraham Yates Jr., District of the Manor of Livingston, 19 May 1776, Yates Papers, Box 4, NYPL. For the number of tenants on Livingston Manor during the Revolution, see the Assessment Rolls for Livingston Manor, 1779, Roll A-FM, 71, NYSL. For the number of people who appeared before the Livingston Manor Committee of Safety in 1776, see "The Minutes of the Committee of Safety of the Manor of Livingston," *The New York Genealogical and Biographical Record* 60 (1929), 239–43, 325–41. For Revolutionaries coercing loyalty, see "Letter to the King," Rhinebeck, 3 June 1776, Travers Papers, Box 5, CCHS. For the list of people brought before the Committee of Safety, and for the names of men who sat on it, see "The Minutes of the Committee of Safety of Livingston Manor," 326–40; *Calendar of Histori-*

cal Manuscripts, 2:191–235; and Paltsits, *Minutes of the Commissioners for Detecting and Defeating Conspiracies,* 1:142–43, 152, 237–38, 239–40, 254, 275, 334–37, 346–47, 394, 399, 403. For assessment rolls, see the rolls for Livingston Manor, 1779, NYSL; Countryman, *A People in Revolution,* 136–43; Richard D. Brown, *Revolutionary Politics in Massachusetts: The Boston Committee of Correspondence and the Towns, 1772–1774* (New York, 1976); and Richard Ryerson, *The Revolution Is Now Begun: The Radical Committees of Philadelphia, 1765–1776* (Philadelphia, 1978).

33. Jeffery Amherst had a low opinion of the poor service offered by colonists even when they did bother to fight. See Fred Anderson, *The Crucible of War: The Seven Years' War and the Fate of Empire in British North America, 1754–1766* (New York, 2000), 371–72.

34. Sabine, *Historical Memoirs,* 2:26; Countryman, *A People in Revolution,* 151–54; Kim, "The Limits of Politicization," 880–82; Clark, "The Problem of Allegiance in Revolutionary Poughkeepsie."

35. Although 102 people apparently were excused, only 96 names appear in the damaged and torn records. More may have applied or may have been excused, but not more than a few. Of the 96 names clear enough to read, 36 percent had Dutch or German surnames and 64 percent had English, Scottish, Irish, or Welsh surnames. The figures come from "A List of Persons in said District that were excused" from militia service, *Livingston Manor Committee of Safety Minutes,* 336–38, 27–28 December 1777.

36. The militia rolls and land bounty rights are in Berthold Fernow, ed., *New York in the Revolution* (Albany, N.Y., 1887), 2.

37. Kim, "The Limits of Politicization," 868–70.

38. "Account of a Skirmish at Taghkanick," May 1776, *Calendar of Historical Manuscripts,* 1:581; Ranlet, *The New York Loyalists,* 130–31.

39. Kim, "The Limits of Politicization," 868–89; J. Hector St. John de Crève-coeur, *Letters from an American Farmer* (New York, 1963), 198; Countryman, *A People in Revolution,* 116–23.

40. For the incidents involving Jury Wheeler, Jacob Miller, and Adam Kilmer, see "The Minutes of the Committee of Safety of Livingston Manor," 30 September, 1 October, and 7 October 1776, 325–26, 328–29; and Sabine, *Historical Memoirs,* 2:26.

41. "The Minutes of the Committee of Safety of Livingston Manor," 30 September, 1 October, and 7 October 1776, 325–26, 328–29. See also the ratings of the Kilmers, Pulvers, Butlers, and Lantmans in the Assessment Rolls for Livingston Manor, 1779, NYSL.

42. Kim, "The Limits of Politicization," 868–67; John Van Den Bergh quoted in Alice P. Kenney, "The Albany Dutch: Loyalists and Patriots," *New York History* 42 (1961), 340; Lynd, "The Tenant Rising at Livingston Manor," 169–70; Adam Shufelt quoted in the *Calendar of Historical Manuscripts,* 1:197, 22 May 1777.

43. Matthew Vischer quoted at Viele's trial, 24 May 1777, *Calendar of Historical Manuscripts,* 1:199; Aernout Viele's confession, 23 June 1777, and his petition, 24 June 1777, *Calendar of Historical Manuscripts,* 1:190–92.

44. A copy of the oath is in *Calendar of Historical Manuscripts,* 1:198–99; William Agnew, 27 May 1777, *Calendar of Historical Manuscripts,* 1:203; Ebenezer French's testimony against Jesse Bullis, 5 June 1777; investigation of Jacob Miller, 12 June 1777, both in the *Calendar of Historical Manuscripts,* 1:214–15, 220–25.

45. John Watts to the British Ministry, 30 October 1777, *Pennsylvania Evening Post,* reprinted from the *Morning Chronicle.*

46. Beverly Robinson's remarks about "frequent accounts" with Ethan Allen, letters dated 30 March 1780 and 2 February 1781, in William Slade, ed. *Vermont State Papers: Being a Collection of Records and Documents* (Middlebury, Conn., 1823), 142–44; Bellesiles, *Revolutionary Outlaws*, 96–97, 99–103, 110–11.

47. Quote in the *Proceedings of the New York General Assembly*, 5 February and 9 March 1774, *Vermont State Papers*, 37–38, 42–48; Ethan Allen to William Tryon, Esq., Bennington, 5 June 1774, *Vermont State Papers*, 24–25; "Copy of a Deposition of Oliver Church and Joseph Hancock," 22 March 1775, Box 6, KEMPE; "Riot and Bloodshed in Cumberland County," 23 March 1775, and the deposition of John Griffin, 27–28 March 1775, both in *DHNY*, 4:904–14.

48. Ethan Allen to John Hancock from the Dorset Meeting, May 1776, *Collections of the Vermont Historical Society*, 2 vols. (Montpelier, Vt., 1870–1871), 1:6–7; Countryman, *A People in Revolution*, 175–77.

49. Nicholas Rouwe's Deposition, 17 November 1781; Christian Cooper et. al. to Henry Clinton, 5 September 1781, Livingston Manor, both in Samuel Hake, ALC, 13, Bundle 114. The other signers of Cooper's letter apparently signed a separate sheet of paper.

50. Thomas Anderson's testimony given while sitting in Kingston Gaol, 24 June 1777; William Merfield's testimony against Arneout Viele, 24 June 1777, both in *Calendar of Historical Manuscripts*, 1:198, 193–94. Sabine, *Historical Memoirs*, 2:127–34; *Journals of the Provincial Congress*, 1:909–10, 2:247; Lynd, "The Tenant Rising at Livingston Manor," 171–75; Kierner, "Landlord and Tenant," 137–40.

51. Margaret Livingston to Reverend Westerlo, Clermont, 10 May 1777, Van Rensselaer Family Papers, Arnold Collection, AIHA; Sabine, *Historical Memoirs*, 2:132, 134; "Examination of Tories," *Calendar of Historical Manuscripts*, 1:193–94.

52. Sabine, *Historical Memoirs*, 2:132, 134; *Journals of the Provincial Congress*, 2:474; Countryman, *A People in Revolution*, 151–52; Kierner, "Landlord and Tenant," 139. Kierner contends that fewer tenants participated in the rioting, arguing that most of the tenants remained apathetic toward the Revolution. Disgruntled tenants may have been apathetic toward the Revolution and could still have rioted for land in 1777. Kierner, however, intimates that most of the rioters were Loyalists.

53. Kierner, "Landlord and Tenant," 141–43.

54. Kierner, "Landlords and Tenants," 141–43; Ranlet, *The New York Loyalists*, 131; Lynd, "The Revolution and the Common Man," 27; Lynd, "Who Should Rule at Home?" 330–59.

55. *Journals of the Provincial Congress*, 1:909–10, 912; Sabine, *Historical Memoirs*, 2:127–36; Paltsits, *Minutes of the Commissioners for Detecting and Defeating Conspiracies*, 1:254, 274–75; Lynd, "Tenant Rising at Livingston Manor," 174–76.

56. Sabine, *Historical Memoirs*, 2:128–34, quote on 134; Lynd, "The Tenant Rising at Livingston Manor," 174–75; Countryman, *A People in Revolution*, 151–52.

57. Benjamin Quarles, "The Revolutionary War as Black Declaration of Independence," in *Slavery and Freedom in the Age of the American Revolution*, ed. Ira Berlin and Ronald Hoffman (Urbana, Ill., 1986), 283–310, quote on 283; Gary B. Nash, "Forging Freedom: The Emancipation Experience in the Northern Seaport Cities, 1775–1820," in ibid., 2–48; Richard S. Dunn, "Black Society in the Chesapeake, 1776–1810, in ibid., 49–82; and Donald R. Hickey, "America's Response to the Slave Revolt in Haiti, 1791–1806," *JER* 2 (1982): 361–79.

58. See, for example, the material concerns of the Albany Committee of Correspondence, "A Letter to the Governor," 12 September 1778, *CHA*, 1:288.

59. Philip Schuyler quoted in Countryman, *A People in Revolution*, 287.

60. Lynd, "The Revolution and the Common Man," 27.

61. Governor Morris to Robert R. Livingston, Valley Forge, 10 March 1778; Trustees of Kingston to Robert R. Livingston, 13 March 1778, Kingston; Livingston to Trustees of Kingston, Kingston, 1 March 1778, all in RRLP, roll 1; Philip Schuyler to the General Committee at Tryon County, Coghanewaga, 17 March 1778, Schuyler Papers, NYSL.

62. Sabine, *Historical Memoirs*, 2:404; Sullivan, *Minutes of the Albany Committee of Correspondence*, 2:233–47, 331–32, 354–55, 388–89; Countryman, *A People in Revolution*, 151–52; John Barclay to the Albany Committee of Correspondence, Fort Edward, 22 July 1777, NYSL; Philip Schuyler to Governor George Clinton, Stillwater, 4 August 1777, Schuyler Papers, AIHA; E. P. Thompson, *Whigs and Hunters: The Origin of the Black Act* (New York, 1975); Roger B. Manning, *Hunters and Poachers: A Social and Cultural History of Unlawful Hunting in England, 1485–1640* (Oxford, 1993).

63. Peter R. Livingston to George Clinton, Manor Livingston, 12 June and 29 July 1778, *Public Papers of George Clinton, First Governor of New York* (New York, 1973), 3:452–53, 593–94.

64. "A Petition from the Northern Towns of Dutchess County and the Southern Manor Towns for Authority to Raise a Company of Rangers to Protect the Inhabitants from Robbers"; Clinton's response, August 1778, *Papers of George Clinton*, 3:675–76, 685–86; Countryman, *A People in Revolution*, 153.

65. "Indictment of William McRea for Treason," 19 May 1778, William H. Hill Papers, vol. 4, NYSL; Paltsits, *Minutes of the Commissioners for Detecting and Defeating Conspiracies*, 1:247–48.

66. Quote from the "New York Boundary Report" written by James Duane, John Morin Scott, and Egbert Benson, 1779, RRLP, roll 1; James Duane to Robert R. Livingston, n.p., 15 January 1780, RRLP, roll 1; Lynd, "The Revolution and the Common Man," 17–21; Young, *Democratic Republicans*, 17–22; Countryman, *A People in Revolution*, chapter 5.

67. Lynd, "The Revolution and the Common Man," 82; Schuyler quoted in Countryman, *A People in Revolution*, 287.

5—THE REVOLUTIONARY SETTLEMENT

1. "Abstract of the Rental of the Manor of Rensselaerswyck," 22 October 1797, Box 60; Rensselaerswyck Manor Ledger A, both in VRMP.

2. Daniel Dewey Barnard, *A Discourse on the Life, Services and Character of Stephen Van Rensselaer* (Albany, N.Y., 1839), 33–34; Reeve Huston, *Land and Freedom: Rural Society, Popular Protest, and Party Politics in Antebellum New York* (New York, 2000), chapter 1.

3. John Devoe to Abraham Ten Broeck, Heldebergh Patent, 13 August 1785; Ezekial Sayles to Ten Broeck, n.p., 15 November 1785; Ephraim Woodworth to Ten Broeck, Stillwater, 24 August 1785, all in Ten Broeck Family Papers, Box 1, AIHA; Stephen Van Rensselaer to Abraham Ten Broeck, n.p., 1 February 1786, Abraham Ten Broeck Papers, NYSL; "Notice to Tenants," 14 January 1795, Watervliet; "Proclamation to Tenants," n.d., Watervliet, both in Box 1, VRMP; "Names of Tenants who have called at the Office & Settled their accounts, 1797," Box 38, VRMP.

4. Eric Foner, *Politics and Ideology in the Age of the Civil War* (New York, 1980), chapter 4; Eric Foner, *Free Soil, Free Labor, Free Men: The Ideology of the Republican Party before the Civil War* (New York, 1970).

5. Three essential interpretations of this period use the framework of a revolutionary settlement as their central organizing theme. See John M. Murrin, "The Great Inversion, or Court versus Country: A Comparison of the Revolution Settlements in England (1688–1721) and America (1776–1816)," in *Three British Revolutions, 1641, 1688, 1776*, ed. J. G. A. Pocock (Princeton, N.J., 1980), 368–53; John L. Brooke, *The Heart of the Commonwealth: Society and Political Culture in Worcester County, Massachusetts, 1713–1816* (Cambridge, 1989); and Alan Taylor, *Liberty Men and Great Proprietors: The Revolutionary Settlement on the Maine Frontier, 1760–1820* (Chapel Hill, N.C., 1990).

6. Edward Countryman, *A People in Revolution: The American Revolution and Political Society in New York, 1760–1790* (New York, 1989), 243; Huston, *Land and Freedom,* chapter 1.

7. David M. Ellis, *Landlords and Farmers in the Hudson-Mohawk Region, 1790–1850* (Ithaca, N.Y., 1946), 42–43; Alfred F. Young, *The Democratic Republicans of New York: The Origins, 1763–1797* (Chapel Hill, N.C., 1967), 534–35.

8. Livingston Manor Rent Book, 1767–1787, NYHS; Sung Bok Kim, *Landlord and Tenant in Colonial New York: Manorial Society, 1664–1775* (Chapel Hill, N.C., 1978), 238; Huston, *Land and Freedom,* chapter 1.

9. I am basing these figures on leases signed by tenants between 1779 and 1797 in the "Lists of Tenants on Rensselaerswyck on the east side of Hudson's River," Box 86, VRMP; list of leases in Boxes 36 and 84; and Abraham Ten Broeck's Lease Ledger, Box 84, all in VRMP. John Devoe to Abraham Ten Broeck, Heldebergh Patent, 13 August 1785; Ephraim Woodworth to Ten Broeck, Stillwater, 24 August 1785, both in Ten Broeck Family Papers, Box 1, AIHA; Huston, *Land and Freedom,* 25–27.

10. J. H. French, *Gazetteer of the State of New York* (1860; repr., Baltimore, 1995), 155–57, 163–65, 243–44, 552–59; Robert J. Rayback, *Richard Atlas of New York State* (New York, 1965); Frederick W. Beers, *Atlas of the Hudson River Valley from New York City to Troy* (New York, 1891); Map of Rensselaerswyck, New York, Part of the Manor of Rensselaerswyck, 1798; Map of Livingston, Germantown, and Clermont, 1798, both in NYSL.

11. Huston, *Land and Freedom,* 27–28; the leases for Rensselaerswyck, NYSL.

12. Rent Ledger A, VRMP; Rent Ledger for the manor, LP, roll 8; Livingston Manor Rent Ledger, 1767–1784, NYHS.

13. "Abstract of the Rental of the Manor Rensselaerswyck, October 22nd 1797," Box 60, VRMP.

14. Rent Ledger A, VRMP.

15. Thomas S. Wermuth, *Rip Van Winkle's Neighbors: The Transformation of Rural Society in the Hudson River Valley, 1720–1850* (Albany, N.Y., 2001), 46–69.

16. Ellis, *Landlords and Farmers,* 42–43; Young, *Democratic Republicans,* 534–35; Alan Taylor, *William Cooper's Town: Power and Persuasion on the Frontier of the Early American Republic* (New York, 1995), 57–114; Huston, *Land and Freedom,* 14–18.

17. Allan Kulikoff, *The Agrarian Origins of American Capitalism* (Charlottesville, Va., 1992); Schuyler's plans for the canal, Schuyler Papers, roll 14, NYPL.

18. Countryman, *A People in Revolution,* 286.

19. Livingston to Alexander Hamilton, 13 June 1785, quoted in Countryman, *A People in Revolution,* 95–96, 196–98, 230–31, 245–47, 262–64, 269–71; Young, *Democratic Republicans,* 95–98.

20. Stephanie McCurry, *Masters of Small Words: Yeoman Households, Gender Relations, and the Political Culture of the Antebellum South Carolina Low Country* (New York, 1995); Edward E. Baptist, "The Migration of Planters to Antebellum Florida: Kinship and Power," *Journal of Southern History* 62 (1996), 527–54.

21. "The Petition of the subscribers Inhabitants of the part of the County of Columbia," 9 January 1789, which refers to the petition dated 24 February 1784; "The Petition of Simeon Roulee Robert Meckes and Truman Powell in behalf of themselves and their Associates," 25 January 1789, both in MSC. MSS., Columbia County, NYHS; "Notes and Depositions," *Beby & Others agt. Renselaer,* October 1762; John Tabor Kempe's brief for the case, both in Unsorted Legal Lawsuits, V-Z, KEMPE; "Deed of Surrender to the Crown of sundry parcels of Land formerly claimed by Colonel John Van Rensselaer as part of his Claverack Est." noted in Kim, *Landlord and Tenant,* 412, 357; William Smith Jr. to Philip Schuyler, New York City, 27 November 1772, Schuyler Papers, NYPL.

22. Philip Schuyler's Journal, 1787, Schuyler Papers, AAS.

23. Irving Mark, *Agrarian Conflicts in Colonial New York, 1711–1775* (1940; repr., Port Washington, N.Y., 1965), chapters 1 and 2; Philip J. Schwarz, "'To Conciliate the Jarring Interests': William Smith, Thomas Hutchinson, and the Massachusetts-New York Boundary, 1711–1773," *New-York Historical Society Quarterly* 59 (1975): 299–319; Kim, *Landlord and Tenant,* 87–127; Philip J. Schwarz, *The Jarring Interests: New York's Boundary Makers, 1664–1776* (Albany, N.Y., 1979), chapters 6 and 7; Cynthia Kierner, *Traders and Gentlefolk: The Livingstons of New York, 1675–1790* (Ithaca, N.Y., 1992), 46–86.

24. "The Petition of the subscribers [and] Inhabitants of the part of the County of Columbia and State of New York supposed to be included in within the Lines of a patent granted by the late Governor Tryon," 9 January 1989; "The Petition of Simeon Roulee, Robert Mecker & Truman Powell in behalf of themselves and their Associates," 25 January 1789, both in MSC. MSS., Columbia County, NYHS.

25. Stephen Van Rensselaer to Abraham Ten Broeck, n.p., 1 February 1786, Abraham Ten Broeck Papers, NYSL; "Notice to Tenants," 14 January 1795, Watervliet, Box 1; "Proclamation to Tenants," n.d., Watervliet, Box 1; "Names of Tenants who have called at the Office & Settled their accounts, 1797," Box 38, all in VRMP.

26. A manuscript of the broadside resides in Schuyler Papers, NYPL, 14 December 1790; *Address of General Philip Schuyler to the Tenants of Lands at Hillsdale, derived Through His Wife from her Father, John Van Rensselaer,* 12 November 1790, cited in Ellis, *Landlords and Farmers,* 34, fn. 65; Young, *Democratic Republicans,* 204.

27. Alexander Coventry's Diary, 25 October 1791, NYSL; minutes for *The People of the State of New York. agt. Thomas Southward, Jonathon Arnold, John West, Abel Hacket, Ebenezer Hatch, Robert Boze, John Boze, John Rodman, Joseph Fickner, and Jacob Virgil,* 2 December 1791; minutes for *The People v. Peter Showerman,* 8 February 1792, both in the Court of Oyer and Terminer Minutes, 1788–1831, CCCH; Ellis, *Landlords and Farmers,* 34–36; Taylor, *Liberty Men and Great Proprietors,* 181–207.

28. "A Letter," *Albany Gazette,* 31 October 1791, quoted in Young, *Democratic Republicans,* 204–5; Franklin Ellis, *History of Columbia County, New York* (Philadelphia, 1878), 62, 236; Ellis, *Landlords and Farmers,* 34–36; Alexander Coventry's Diary, 25 October 1791, NYSL; minutes for *The People of the State of New York. agt. Thomas Southward,* 2 December 1791; minutes for *The People v. Peter Showerman,* 8 February 1792, both in CCCH.

29. Robert F. Berkhofer Jr., *The White Man's Indian: Images of the American Indian from Columbus to the Present* (New York, 1978); Jill Lepore, *The Name of War: King Philip's War and the Origins of American Identity* (New York, 1998); Philip Deloria, *Playing Indian* (New Haven, 1998); Huston, *Land and Freedom,* 116–24;

30. Staughton Lynd, "Abraham Yates's History of the Movement for the United States Constitution," *WMQ,* 3rd ser., 20 (April 1963), 223–45.

31. Abraham Yates, "Speeches to Delegates, 1786," Yates Papers, NYPL; Lynd, "Abraham Yates's History of the Movement for The United States Constitution," 231.

32. Governor George Clinton, January 1792, in Charles Z. Lincoln, ed., *State of New York. Messages from the Governors* (Albany, N.Y., 1909), 2:319.

33. John Livingston to Walter Livingston, 16 February 1792, quoted in Young, *Democratic Republicans,* 206.

34. Names of the justices in the Court of Oyer and Terminer Minutes, 1788–1831, CCCH; Young, *Democratic Republicans,* 59, 205–6, table 6.

35. Trials of Southward, Arnold, and others in the Court of Oyer and Terminer Minutes, 1788–1831, CCCH; Ellis, *Landlords and Farmers,* 35–36.

36. Thomas Witbeck to Stephen Van Rensselaer, 4 August 1792, noted in William B. Finn, "Stephen Van Rensselaer: The Last Patroon" (PhD diss., Columbia University, 1950), 43–44.

37. *Journal of the Assembly of the State of New York,* 16th Session, entries dated 10 December 1792, 54; 26 December 1792, 83; 13 February 1793, 179; and 2 March 1793, 219–20, in Early American Imprints, 1st series, no. 25900.

38. Frederick Stefon, "The Wyoming Valley," in John B. Frantz and William Pencak, eds., *Beyond Philadelphia: The American Revolution in the Pennsylvania Hinterland* (University Park, Pa., 1998), 133–52; Brooke, *The Heart of the Commonwealth,* 204–13; Alan Taylor, "Agrarian Independence: Northern Land Rioters after the Revolution," in *Beyond the American Revolution: Explorations in the History of American Radicalism,* ed. Alfred F. Young (DeKalb, Ill., 1993), 222–37.

39. *The Massachusetts Gazette and Boston Weekly News-Letter,* 8 August 1771.

40. *Connecticut Courant,* 10 September 1787, quoted in Taylor, "Agrarian Independence," 235.

41. See Huston, *Land and Freedom,* 12; Taylor, "Agrarian Independence," 222–37; and Allan Kulikoff, *Agrarian Origins,* 127–51.

42. *Journal of the Assembly of the State of New York,* 16th Session, entries dated 10 December 1792, 54; 26 December 1792, 83; 13 February 1793, 179; and 2 March 1793, 219–20, in Early American Imprints, 1st series, no. 25900.

43. "Hillsdale Act," *Journal of the Assembly of the State of New York,* 16th session, 13 and 14 February 1793, 179 and 205, in Early American Imprints, no. 25900; Van Rensselaer Settlement, 1803, New York Laws, 27th Session, chapter 76, 215; Alexander Hamilton, *The Law Practice of Alexander Hamilton,* ed. Julius Goebel Jr. and Joseph H. Smith, 5 vols. (New York, 1964), 3:423–26.

44. The estate was divided among Robert Livingston Jr.'s five sons—Peter R. (1737–1794), Walter (1740–1797), Robert C. (1749–1794), John (1750–1822), and Henry (1753–1825). Chancellor Robert Livingston administered Clermont, the family's southern holdings. Kim, *Landlord and Tenant,* 418–19; Kierner, "Landlord and Tenant," 151.

45. "Plan for the Management of Lot Number 2 in the Manor of Livingston Belonging to the Representatives of Robert C. Livingston," Box 2, William Wilson Papers, Clements Library. I suspect that Wilson wrote this note in 1793 because of the placement of the document and because of the issues and people described in it.

46. *Journal of the Assembly of the State of New York,* 17th Session, March 1794, 135 and 157, in Early American Imprints, 1st Series, no. 27397. At much the same time, tenants in West Schoharie Valley petitioned the assembly for land currently claimed by James Duane, a prominent Patriot and then leader of the state government. Duane had amassed roughly thirty thousand acres of land southwest of

Schenectady on which approximately 250 tenant families lived. These tenants paid twenty-five bushels of wheat per one hundred acres after a five-year developmental period, and they asserted that they owned the land because they had lived and labored on it. Duane maintained that he owned the land on the basis of an eighty-year-old law that permitted him to claim the land by asserting his limited occupancy on it and his title to it. For his part, the landlord feared a trial in the new state courts both because he worried that the spirit of the Revolution might prompt judges to redistribute land to those who used it and because the "levelling incident to every republic exposes the landholder to much prejudice." See Ellis, *Landlords and Farmers*, 42–43; and James Duane quoted in Young, *Democratic Republicans*, 534–35.

47. "Petition of Petrus Pulver & Others Demanding Investigation into the Livingston's Title," 7 January 1795, *DHNY*, 3:834–41.

48. "Petition of Petrus Pulver & Others Demanding Investigation into the Livingston's Title," 7 January 1795, *DHNY*, 3:834–41; Florence Christoph, *Upstate New York in the 1760s: Tax Lists and Selected Militia Rolls of Old Albany County, 1760–1768* (Camden, Maine, 1992), 86–88; Assessment Rolls for Livingston Manor, 1779, NYSL; Henry Livingston's Correspondence with William Wilson, 10 July 1796, 22 July 1797, 27 September 1797, Wilson Papers, Boxes 2 and 3, Clements Library; "A Map of the Towns of Livingston, Germantown, and Clermont in the County of Columbia," 1798, *DHNY*, 3:491–92.

49. *Journal of the Assembly of the State of New York*, 18th Session, 1795, quote on 135, but see also 125–27 and 134–35, in Early American Imprints, 1st series, no. 29186; Foner, *Free Soil, Free Labor, Free Men*; Morton J. Horwitz, *The Transformation of American Law, 1780–1860* (Cambridge, Mass., 1977); Gary B. Nash, *Forging Freedom: The Formation of Philadelphia's Black Community, 1720–1840* (Cambridge, Mass., 1988); Christopher L. Tomlins, *Law, Labor, and Ideology in the Early American Republic* (Cambridge, 1993); Huston, *Land and Freedom*, 11–45, 195–217.

50. E. P. Thompson, *Whigs and Hunters: The Origin of the Black Act* (New York, 1975); Roger B. Manning, *Village Revolts: Social Protest and Popular Disturbances in England, 1509–1640* (Oxford, 1988); Roger B. Manning, *Hunters and Poachers: A Social and Cultural History of Unlawful Hunting in England, 1485–1640* (Oxford, 1993); Suzanne Desan, "Crowds, Community, and Ritual in the Work of E. P. Thompson and Natalie Davis," in *The New Cultural History*, ed. Lynn Hunt (Berkeley, Calif., 1989), 47–71.

51. I suspect that Abraham Yates was "A Citizen" because the argument, while popular among opponents of the landlords, closely parallels and then expands on his discussion in "Argument in an action at law being a history of the Manor of Rensselaerswyck and the rival claims of Albany and Schenectady," 1762, Yates Papers, NYPL.

52. Philip Schuyler and Thomas Tillotson both quoted in Staughton Lynd, "Abraham Yates's History of the Movement for the United States Constitution," *WMQ*, 3rd ser., 2 (April 1963), 225.

53. Yates, "History of the Movement for the United States Constitution," 244.

54. Thomas Witbeck, An Advertisement, *Albany Gazette*, 6 February 1795. The original announcement was dated 15 December 1794, and it reappeared in *Albany Gazette* on 20 March 1795; "Proclamation to Tenants," n.d.; "Notice to Tenants," 14 January 1795, both in Box 1, VRMP. Henry Livingston to William Livingston, Ancram House, 1795, Box 2; Robert R. Livingston to William Wilson, Clermont, 29 October 1796, Box 2; Henry Livingston to William Wilson, 17 March 1797, Box 3, all in Wilson Papers. John Livingston to Walter Livingston, 24 March 1795, RRLP, roll 6; Martin Bruegel, "Unrest: Manorial Society and the Market in the Hudson Valley, 1780–1850," *JAH* 82 (1996), 1393–424.

55. "A Citizen," *Albany Gazette,* quotes from 9 February, 6 March, and 20 March 1795. The other articles appeared in *Albany Gazette* on February 2 and 6, March 6 and 27, and April 3, 1795.

56. David S. Shields, *Civil Tongues and Polite Letters in British America* (Chapel Hill, N.C., 1997); David Waldstreicher, *In the Midst of Perpetual Fetes: The Making of American Nationalism, 1776–1820* (Chapel Hill, N.C., 1997); Simon P. Newman, *Parades and the Politics of the Street: Festive Culture in the Early American Republic* (Philadelphia, 1997); Mary P. Ryan, *Civic Wars: Democracy and Public Life in the American City during the Nineteenth Century* (Berkeley, Calif., 1997); William L. Miller, *Arguing About Slavery: The Great Battle in the United States Congress* (New York, 1996).

57. By 1792, Simeon Roulee had appeared as the primary author of at least three petitions to the state legislature and was joined by one hundred to two hundred people each time. Petrus Pulver joined 214 other people in 1795 in the latest petition as rural discontent simmered throughout the countryside. Lynd, "Abraham Yates's History of the Movement for The United States Constitution," 232.

58. Henry Livingston to William Wilson, Ancram House, 28 and 31 March 1797.

59. Henry Livingston to William Wilson, Ancram House, 12 April 1797, Ancram House; Henry Livingston to William Livingston, 27 and 28 July 1797, Ancram House; Henry Livingston to William Wilson, 27 September 1797; Peter Van Schaack to William Wilson, Kinderhook, 6 October 1797; John Parker to Chancellor Robert R. Livingston, Clermont, 6 August 1797, all in Box 3, Wilson Papers; Peter Van Schaack to William Wilson, Kinderhook, 4 November 1797, Box 4, Wilson Papers.

60. John Jay to the Senate, Albany, 22 February 1798, in Lincoln, *State of New York. Messages from the Governors,* 2:411–12; Young, *Democratic Republicans,* 535.

61. Henry Livingston to William Wilson, 13 May 1798, Udolpho, Box 4; Henry Livingston to William Wilson, 20 October 1798, Ancram, Box 5, both in Wilson Papers.

CONCLUSION

1. Cynthia Kierner, "Landlord and Tenant in Revolutionary New York: The Case of Livingston Manor," *NYH,* 70 (April 1989), 152, fn. 40; Thomas Summerhill, "The Farmer's Republic: Agrarian Protest and the Capitalist Transformation of Upstate New York, 1840–1890" (PhD diss., University of California, San Diego, 1993); Jonathon H. Earle, "The Undaunted Democracy: Jacksonian Antislavery and Free Soil, 1828–1848" (PhD diss., Princeton, 1996); Jamie L. Bronstein, *Land Reform and Working-Class Experience in Britain and the United States, 1800–1862* (Stanford, Calif., 1999); Reeve Huston, *Land and Freedom: Rural Society, Popular Protest, and Party Politics in Antebellum New York* (New York, 2000), 33–35.

2. Dixon Ryan Fox, *Yankees and Yorkers* (New York, 1940); Sung Bok Kim, *Landlord and Tenant in Colonial New York: Manorial Society, 1664–1775* (Chapel Hill, N.C., 1978).

3. Thomas Ainge Devyr, ed., *The Anti-Renter,* 13 September 1845.

SELECTED BIBLIOGRAPHY

PRIMARY SOURCES

Archival Sources

Albany County Clerk's Office, Albany, N.Y.
   Court of Common Pleas Books, 1763–1799
   Deeds and Wills, Book 6, 1720–1757
Albany Institute of History and Art, Albany, N.Y.
   Account Book "B" for John Van Rensselaer, 1 March 1783 to 6 August 1796
   Albany Committee of Public Safety Papers
   Albany Institute of History and Art Collection of Letters and Documents
      Relative to Albany in the Revolution
   Burghart Family Papers
   Coxsackie Association Oath, April 1775
   Henry Ten Eyck Papers, 1744–1795
   Morgan Lewis and Henry Bogart Papers, Manuscript Items Relative to the
      Revolutionary War in Albany, N.Y.
   Record Book of Leases for Bethlehem, Rensselaerwyck, 1771–1800
   Robert Livingston Letters, 1754–1789, Livingston, Bayard Burghart Papers
   Schuyler Family Papers
   Ten Broeck Family Papers
   Van Rensselaer Papers, Family, Mrs. Benjamin Wadworth Arnold Collections
   Van Rensselaer Papers, Vlie House
American Antiquarian Society, Worcester, Mass.
   Philip Schuyler's Journal
Center for Historic Urbanism, Architecture, and Preservation Planning
   Databases of the 1798 Federal Direct Tax Schedule for Kingston, Harley,
      Marbletown, and New Paltz, N.Y.
Clements Library, Ann Arbor, Mich.
   Henry Clinton Papers
   Thomas Gage Papers, 1721–1787
   William Wilson Papers
Columbia County Historical Society, Kinderhook, N.Y.
   Travers Papers
Columbia County Court House, Hudson N.Y.
   Court of Oyer and Terminer Minutes, 1788–1831
The David Library, Washington's Crossing, Pa.
   American Loyalist Claims, Great Britain, Public Record Audit Office, Micro-
      film Collection, volumes for New York

Franklin Delano Roosevelt Library, Hyde Park, N.Y.
    Livingston-Redmond Papers, 1630–1900, 13 Rolls of Microfilm
New-York Historical Society, New York, N.Y.
    Columbia County, Miscellaneous Manuscripts, "C"
    Dutchess County, Miscellaneous Manuscripts, "D"
    John Tabor Kempe Papers
    Livingston Manor Rent Ledger, 1767–1784
    Livingston Manuscripts, Uncatalogued
    Rensselaerwyck, Miscellaneous Manuscripts, "R"
    Robert R. Livingston Papers, 1707–1862, 52 Rolls of Microfilm
New York Public Library, New York, N.Y.
    Philip Schuyler Papers, Manuscripts and 15 Rolls of Microfilm
    Abraham Yates Papers, Manuscripts and 4 Rolls of Microfilm
New York State Library, Manuscripts and Special Collections, Albany, N.Y.
    Alexander Coventry's Diary, typescript, Coventry Papers
    Assessment Rolls for Counties, 1779, 1786, 1789, Microfilm Roll A-FM, N66, #71
    John N. Bleeker Papers
    Burgert Family Papers
    DeWitt Papers, Family and Business
    Fonda Papers
    Hampton Map of the Upper Patent of Philipsburgh, 1757, Miscellaneous, No.
        11068
    Gerrit Y. Lansing Papers
    "Laws of the Colony of New York," 9 March 1774, Revolutionary Broadsides
    Henry Livingston Papers
    John Livingston Papers
    "Notes on the Trial of the Defs. for the Several Murthers vizt. of Cornelius
        Ten Broeck, Thomas Whitney, and John Bull," *The King agt. Alex.
        MacArthur, Daniel MacArthur, Thomas Johnson, Levi Stockwell,* nd.
    Robert Sanders' Letterbook, Historic Cherry Hill Papers
    Schuyler Family Collections
    Spencertown Proprietors Books and Papers, 1755–1763
    Henry Stevens Collections, 4 Rolls of Microfilm
    Philip Van Rensselaer Papers, 1775–1895, Historic Cherry Hill Papers
    Van Rensselaer Family Papers
    Van Rensselaer Manor Papers
    Van Rensselaer Papers in the Townsend Collections
    Henry Van Schaack Papers
    Elkannah Watson Papers
Sleepy Hollow Restorations Library, White Plains, N.Y.
    Van Cortlandt Manor Papers
    Philipse Papers

Newspapers

    The Albany Gazette
    The American Minerva
    The Anti-Renter
    The Boston Gazette

New-York Gazette; or, Weekly Post-Boy
New-York Journal and Patriotic Register
New-York Mercury
New York Packet
Pennsylvania Evening Post
Pennsylvania Gazette

Published Works

Christoph, Florence. *Upstate New York in the 1760s: Tax Lists and Selected Militia Rolls of Old Albany County, 1760–1768.* Camden, Maine, 1992.

Collections of the Vermont Historical Society. 2 vols. Montpelier, Vt., 1870–1871.

Edes, Herbert, ed. "Memoir of Dr. Thomas Young, 1731–1777." *Publications of the Colonial Society of Massachusetts, Transactions* 11 (1906–1909): 2–54.

Fernow, Berthold, comp. *Calendar of Council Minutes, 1668–1783.* Harrison, New York, 1987.

"The Following Publication, which Shews the Rancorous Disposition of the American Republicans." New York, 1783, Early American Imprints, no. 17871.

Grant, Anne. *Memoirs of an American Lady: With Sketches of Manners and Scenery in America, as They Existed Previous to the Revolution.* 2 volumes. 1808. Reprint, New York, 1970.

Guillaumin, Emile. *The Life of a Simple Man.* Edited by Eugen Weber. Hanover, N.H., 1983.

Handlin, Oscar, and Irving Mark, eds. "Chief Daniel Nimham v. Roger Morris, Beverly Robinson, and Philip Philipse—An Indian Land Case in Colonial New York, 1765–1767." *Ethnohistory* 11 (1964): 193–246.

Hanson, J. Howard, ed. *The Minute Book of the Committee of Safety of Tryon County, the Old New York Frontier.* New York, 1905.

Horsmanden, Daniel. *The New York Conspiracy.* Edited by Thomas J. Davis. 1740. Reprint, Boston, 1971.

Johnston, Henry P., ed. *The Correspondence and Public Papers of John Jay.* 4 volumes. New York, 1970.

Journal of the Assembly of the State of New York. Early American Imprints, nos. 25900, 27397, 29186.

Journals of the Provincial Congress, Provincial Convention, Committee of Safety and Council of Safety of the State of New-York. 2 Vols. Albany, N.Y., 1842.

Judd, Jacob, comp. and ed., *Correspondence of the Van Cortlandt Family of Cortlandt Manor, 1748–1800.* 2 vols. Tarrytown, N.Y., 1977.

Klein, Milton, ed. *The Independent Reflector or, Weekly Essays on sundry Important Subjects More Particularly Adapted to the Province of New York.* Cambridge, Mass., 1963.

Lincoln, Charles Z., ed. *State of New York. Messages from the Governors.* Albany, N.Y., 1909.

Mark, Irving, and Oscar Handlin, eds. "Land Cases in Colonial New York, 1765–1767; *The King v William Prendergast.*" *New York University Law Quarterly Review* 9 (1940): 165–94.

McNear, Beverly, ed. "Mr. Livingston's Reasons Against a Land Tax." *Journal of Political Economy* 48 (1940): 63–90.

"Minutes of the Committee of Safety of the Manor of Livingston, Columbia County, New York." *The New York Genealogical and Biographical Record* 60 (1929): 239–43, 325–41.

Munsell, Joel, ed. *Annals of Albany.* 10 vols. Albany, N.Y., 1850–1859, 1869–1871.

——. *Collections on the History of Albany.* 4 vols. Albany, N.Y., 1876.

O'Callaghan, E. B., ed. *The Documentary History of the State of New-York.* 4 vols. Albany, N.Y., 1850.

——. *Documents Relative to the Colonial History of the State of New York.* 15 vols. Albany, N.Y., 1856–1883.

Paltsits, Victor Hugo, ed. *Minutes of the Commissioners for Detecting and Defeating Conspiracies in the State of New York, Albany County Sessions, 1778–1781.* 3 vols. Albany, N.Y., 1909.

Penrose, Maryly, ed. *Mohawk Valley in the Revolution: Committee of Safety Papers and Genealogical Compendium.* Franklin Park, N.J., 1978.

"The Philipsburgh Manor Rent Roll of 1760." *New York Genealogical and Biographical Record* 110 (1979): 102–4.

Prince, Carl E., ed. *The Papers of William Livingston.* 2 vols. Trenton, 1979–1980.

Public Papers of George Clinton, First Governor of New York. New York, 1973.

"Rent Roll of Col. Frederick Philipses Estate (Philipse Manor) 1776–1784." *New York Genealogical and Biographical Record* 108 (1977): 74–78.

Ricardo, David. *Principles of Political Economy and Taxation.* London, 1932.

Sabine, William H. W., ed. *Historical Memoirs . . . of William Smith.* 2 vols. New York, 1969–71.

Scott, Kenneth. "The Freeholders of the City and County of Albany, 1763." *National Genealogical Society Quarterly* 48 (1960).

Scull, G. D., ed. *The Montresor Journals.* New York, 1882.

Slade, William, ed. *Vermont State Papers: Being a Collection of Records and Documents.* Middlebury, Conn., 1823.

Smith, Richard. *A Tour of Four Great Rivers; the Hudson, Mohawk, Susquehanna and Delaware in 1769; Being the Journal of Richard Smith of Burlington, New Jersey.* Edited by Francis Halsey. New York, 1906.

Sullivan, James, ed. *Minutes of the Albany Committee of Correspondence, 1775–1778.* 2 vols. Albany, N.Y., 1923.

White-Oak. "Mr. Printer I am not a man of many words." Philadelphia, 1770, Early American Imprints, no. 11836.

Winstanley, Gerrard. *The Law of Freedom, and Other Writings.* Edited by Chistopher Hill. Cambridge, 1983.

Young, Thomas. *Some Reflections on the Disputes between New-York, New-Hampshire, and Col. John Henry Lydius of Albany.* New Haven, 1764.

SECONDARY SOURCES

Allen, Robert C. *Enclosure and the Yeoman: The Agricultural Development of the South Midlands, 1450–1850.* Oxford, 1992.

Anderson, A. W. *The Story of a Pioneer Family.* Jamestown, N.Y., 1936.

Anderson, Fred. *A People's Army: Massachusetts Soldiers and Society in the Seven Years' War.* Chapel Hill, N.C., 1984.

Andrews, K. M. *Trade, Plunder, and Settlement: Maritime Enterprise and the Genesis of the British Empire, 1480–1630.* Cambridge, 1984.

Appleby, Joyce. *Capitalism and a New Social Order: The Republican Vision of the 1790s.* New York, 1984.

Applewhite, Harriet B., and Darline G. Levy, eds. *Women and Politics in the Age of the Democratic Revolution.* Ann Arbor, Mich., 1990.

Baptist, Edward E. "The Migration of Planters to Antebellum Florida: Kinship and Power." *Journal of Southern History* 62 (1996): 527–54.

Bacon, Edgar Mayhew. *The Hudson River from Ocean to Source*. New York, 1902.

Bailyn, Bernard. *Ideological Origins of the American Revolution*. Cambridge, Mass., 1967.

———. *The Origins of American Politics*. New York, 1968.

Bakhtin, Mikhail. *Problems of Dostoyevsky's Poetics*. Translated and edited by Caryl Emerson. Minneapolis, 1993.

Barnard, Daniel Dewey. *A Discourse on the Life, Services and Character of Stephen Van Rensselaer*. Albany, N.Y., 1839.

Becker, Carl L. *The History of Political Parties in the Province of New York, 1760–1776*. Madison, Wis., 1960.

Becker, E. Marie. "The 801 Westchester County Freeholders of 1763." *New-York Historical Society Quarterly* 35 (1951): 283–321.

Beeman, Richard, Stephen Botein, and Edward C. Carter. *Beyond Confederation: Origins of the Constitution and American National Identity*. Chapel Hill, N.C., 1987.

———. "Deference, Republicanism, and the Emergence of Popular Politics in Eighteenth-Century America." *William and Mary Quarterly* 3rd ser., 48 (1992): 401–30.

Bekerman, Gerard. *Marx and Engels: A Conceptual Concordance*. Translated by Terrell Carver. Oxford, 1983.

Bellesiles, Michael A. *Revolutionary Outlaws: Ethan Allen and the Struggle for Independence on the Early American Frontier*. Charlottesville, Va., 1993.

Berkhofer, Robert F., Jr. *The White Man's Indian: Images of the American Indian from Columbus to the Present*. New York, 1978.

Berlin, Ira, and Ronald Hoffman, eds. *Slavery and Freedom in the Age of the American Revolution*. Urbana, Ill., 1986.

Bielinski, Stefan. *Abraham Yates, Jr., and the New Political Order in Revolutionary New York*. Albany, N.Y., 1975.

Bigger, Francis Joseph. *The Ulster Land War of 1770 (The Hearts of.Steel)*. Dublin, 1910.

Bliss, Willard F. "The Rise of Tenancy in Virginia." *Virginia Magazine of History and Biography* 108 (1950): 427–41.

Bonomi, Patricia. *A Factious People: Politics and Society in Colonial New York*. New York, 1971.

Bouton, Cynthia. "Gendered Behavior in Subsistence Riots: The French Flour War, 1775." *Journal of Social History* 23 (1990): 735–54.

Bouton, Terry. "A Road Closed: Rural Insurgency in Post-Independence Pennsylvania." *Journal of American History* 87 (2000): 855–87.

Bronstein, Jamie L. *Land Reform and Working-Class Experience in Britain and the United States, 1800–1862*. Stanford, Calif., 1999.

Brooke, John L. *The Heart of the Commonwealth: Society and Political Culture in Worcester County, Massachusetts, 1713–1861*. Cambridge, 1989.

———. "To the Quiet of the People: Revolutionary Settlements and Civil Unrest in Western Massachusetts, 1774–1789." *William and Mary Quarterly* 3rd ser., 49 (1989): 425–62.

Brown, Richard D. *Revolutionary Politics in Massachusetts: The Boston Committee of Correspondence and the Towns, 1772–1774*. New York, 1976.

Bruegel, Martin. "Unrest: Manorial Society and the Market in the Hudson Valley, 1780–1850." *Journal of American History* 82 (1996): 1393–1424.

Buford, Bill. *Among the Thugs.* London, 1991.

Butler, Joseph T. *The Family Collections at Van Cortlandt Manor.* Tarrytown, N.Y., 1967.

Chambers, J. D. "Enclosure and the Small Landowner." *Economic History Review* 10 (1940): 118–27.

Champagne, Roger. "Family Politics Versus Constitutional Principle: The New York Assembly Elections of 1768 and 1769." *William and Mary Quarterly,* 3rd ser., 20 (1963): 57–79.

Clark, Christopher. *The Roots of Rural Capitalism: Western Massachusetts, 1780–1860.* Ithaca, N.Y., 1990.

Clark, Jonathan. "The Problem of Allegiance in Revolutionary Poughkeepsie." In *Saints and Revolutionaries: Essays on Early American History,* edited by David D. Hall, John M. Murrin, and Thad W. Tate, 285–317. New York, 1984.

Clay, Christopher. "Lifeleaseholds in the Western Counties of England, 1650–1750." *Agricultural History Review* 29 (1981): 83–96.

Clemens, Paul G. E., and Lucy Simler, "Rural Labor and the Farm Household in Chester County, Pennsylvania, 1750–1820." In *Work and Labor in Early America,* edited by Stephen Innes. Chapel Hill, N.C., 1988.

Countryman, Edward. "Consolidating Power in Revolutionary America: The Case of New York, 1775–1783." *Journal of Interdisciplinary History* 6 (1976): 645–77.

———. "'Out of the Bounds of the Law': Northern Land Rioters in the Eighteenth Century." In *The American Revolution: Explorations in the History of American Radicalism,* edited by Alfred F. Young, 37–69. DeKalb, Ill., 1976.

———. *A People in Revolution: The American Revolution and Political Society in New York.* New York, 1989.

———. "The Uses of Capital in Revolutionary America: The Case of the New York Loyalist Merchants." *William and Mary Quarterly,* 3rd ser., 49 (1992): 3–28.

———. "'To Secure the Blessings of Liberty': Language, the Revolution, and American Capitalism." In *Beyond the American Revolution: Explorations in the History of American Radicalism,* edited by Alfred F. Young, 123–48. DeKalb, Ill., 1993.

Dangerfield, George. *Chancellor Robert R. Livingston of New York, 1746–1813.* New York, 1960.

Davis, Mike. *Ecology of Fear: Los Angeles and the Imagination of Disaster.* New York, 1998.

Davis, Natalie. *Society and Culture in Early Modern France.* Stanford, Calif., 1975.

Davis, Thomas J. *A Rumor of Revolt: The "Great Negro Plot" in Colonial New York.* New York, 1985.

Dayton, Cornelia Hughes. "Turning Points and the Relevance of Colonial Legal History." *William and Mary Quarterly,* 3rd ser., 50 (1993): 7–17.

Delafield, John Ross. "The Story of the Hermitage." *Dutchess County Historical Society's Yearbook* 24 (1939): 22–33.

Deloria, Philip. *Playing Indian.* New Haven, 1998.

Desmond, Alice Curtis. "Mary Philipse: Heiress." *New York History* 28 (1947): 21–36.

Dinkin, Robert J. *Voting in Provincial America: A Study of Elections in the Thirteen Colonies, 1689–1776.* Westport, Conn., 1977.

Division for Historic Preservation, Bureau of Historic Sites. *Schuyler Mansion: A Historic Structure Report.* Albany, N.Y., 1979.

Donnelly, James S. "The Whiteboy Movement, 1761–1765." *Irish Historical Studies* 21 (1978): 20–54.

Earle, Jonathon H. "The Undaunted Democracy: Jacksonian Antislavery and Freesoil, 1828–1848." PhD diss., Princeton, 1996.

East, Robert A., and Jacob Judd, eds. *The Loyalist Americans: A Focus on Greater New York.* Tarrytown, N.Y., 1975.

Edes, Henry Herbert. "Memoir of Dr. Thomas Young, 1731–1777." *Publications of the Colonial Society of Massachusetts, Transactions.* Boston, 1910.

Eley, Geoff, and William Hunt, eds. *Reviving the English Revolution: Reflections and Elaborations on the Work of Christopher Hill.* London, 1988.

Ellis, David M. *Landlords and Farmers in the Hudson-Mohawk Region, 1790–1850.* Ithaca, N.Y., 1946.

Ellis, Franklin. *History of Columbia County, New York.* Philadelphia, 1878.

Fink, William B. "Stephen Van Rensselaer: The Last Patroon." PhD diss., Columbia University, 1950.

Foner, Eric. *Free Soil, Free Labor, Free Men: The Ideology of the Republican Party before the Civil War.* New York, 1970.

———. *Politics and Ideology in the Age of the Civil War.* New York, 1980.

Foucault, Michel. *Power/Knowledge: Selected Interviews and Other Writings, 1972–1977.* Translated and edited by Colin Gordon. New York, 1980.

Fox, Dixon Ryan. *Yankees and Yorkers.* New York, 1940.

Frantz, John B., and William Pencak, eds. *Beyond Philadelphia: The American Revolution in the Pennsylvania Hinterland.* University Park, Pa., 1998.

French, J. H. *Gazetteer of the State of New York.* 1860. Reprint, Baltimore, 1995.

Gilje, Paul A. *The Road to Mobocracy: Popular Disorder in New York City, 1763–1834.* Chapel Hill, N.C., 1987.

———. *Rioting in America.* Bloomington, Ind., 1996.

Glassner, Barry. *The Culture of Fear: Why Americans Are Afraid of the Wrong Things.* New York, 1999.

Gordon, Joan. "Kinship and Class: The Livingstons of New York." PhD diss., Columbia University, 1959.

Gross, Robert A. *The Minutemen and Their World.* New York, 1976.

Gross, Robert A., ed. *In Debt to Shays: The Bicentennial of an Agrarian Rebellion,* Charlottesville, Va., 1993.

Guzzardo, John C. "Democracy Along the Mohawk: An Election Return, 1773." *New York History* 57 (1976): 30–52.

Hall, David D., John M. Murrin, and Thad W. Tate, eds. *Saints and Revolutionaries: Essays on Early American History.* New York, 1984.

Hall, Edward Hagaman. *Philipse Manor Hall at Yonkers, New York.* New York, 1912.

Hawke, David Freeman. "Dr. Thomas Young—Eternal Fisher in Troubled Waters, Notes for a Biography." *New-York Historical Society Quarterly* 54 (1970): 7–29.

Henretta, James A. "Families and Farms: Mentalité in Pre-Industrial America." *William and Mary Quarterly,* 3rd ser., 35 (1978): 3–32.

Herman, Bernard L. *The Stolen House.* Charlottesville, Va., 1992.

Higgins, Patricia. "The Reactions of Women." In *Politics, Religion, and The English Civil War,* edited by Brian Manning, 175–92. London, 1973.

Hill, Christopher. *God's Englishman: Oliver Cromwell and the English Revolution.* London, 1970.

———. *The World Turned Upside Down: Radical Ideas During the English Revolution.* New York, 1972.

———. "A Bourgeois Revolution?" In *Three British Revolutions: 1641, 1688, 1776,* edited by J. G. A. Pocock. Princeton, N.J., 1980.

———. *The Century of Revolution, 1603–1714.* New York, 1980.

Hoerder, Dirk. "Boston Leaders and Boston Crowds, 1765–1776." In *The American Revolution: Explorations in the History of American Radicalism,* edited by Alfred F. Young, 233–71. DeKalb, Ill., 1976.

———. *Crowd Action in Revolutionary Massachusetts, 1765–1780.* New York, 1977.

Holton, Woody. *Forced Founders: Indians, Debtors, Slaves, and the Making of the American Revolution in Virginia.* Chapel Hill, N.C., 1999.

Huntington, Samuel P. *Political Order in Changing Societies.* New Haven, 1968.

Huston, Reeve. *Land and Freedom: Rural Society, Popular Protest, and Party Politics in Antebellum New York.* New York, 2000.

Hutson, James H. "An Investigation of the Inarticulate: Philadelphia's White Oaks." *William and Mary Quarterly,* 3rd ser., 28 (1971): 3–25.

Innes, Stephen. *Labor in a New Land: Economy and Society in Seventeenth-Century Springfield.* Princeton, N.J., 1983.

Innes, Stephen, ed. *Work and Labor in Early America.* Chapel Hill, N.C., 1988.

Isaac, Rhys. *The Transformation of Virginia, 1740–1790.* Chapel Hill, N.C., 1982.

Jacob, Margaret, and James Jacob, eds. *Origins of Anglo-American Radicalism.* London, 1984.

Kars, Marjoleine. *Breaking Loose Together: The Regulator Rebellion in Pre-Revolutionary North Carolina.* Chapel Hill, N.C., 2002.

Kay, Marvin L. Michael. "The North Carolina Regulation, 1766–1776: A Class Conflict." In *The American Revolution: Explorations in the History of American Radicalism,* edited by Alfred F. Young, 71–123. DeKalb, Ill., 1976.

Kenney, Alice P. "The Albany Dutch: Loyalists and Patriots." *New York History* 42 (1961): 332–53.

Kerber, Linda K. *Women of the Republic: Intellect and Ideology in Revolutionary America.* Chapel Hill, N.C., 1980.

Kierner, Cynthia. "Landlord and Tenant in Revolutionary New York: The Case of Livingston Manor." *New York History* 70 (April 1989): 133–52.

———. *Traders and Gentlefolk: The Livingstons of New York, 1675–1790.* Ithaca, N.Y., 1992.

Kim, Sung Bok. "The Manor of Cortlandt and its Tenants, 1697–1783." PhD diss., Michigan State University, 1966.

———. *Landlord and Tenant in Colonial New York: Manorial Society, 1664–1775.* Chapel Hill, N.C., 1978.

———. "Impact of Class Relations and Warfare in the American Revolution: The New York Experience." *Journal of American History* 69 (1982): 326–46.

———. "The Limits of Politicization in the American Revolution: The Experience of Westchester County, New York." *Journal of American History* 80 (1993): 868–89.

Klein, Milton. "Prelude to Revolution: Jury Trials and Judicial Tenure." *William and Mary Quarterly,* 3rd ser., 27 (1960): 439–62.

———. *The Politics of Diversity: Essays in the History of Colonial New York.* Port Washington, N.Y.: National University Publications, 1974.

———. "From Community to Status: The Development of the Legal Profession in Colonial New York." *New York History* 60 (1979): 133–56.

Klein, Milton, ed. *The Independent Reflector; or, Weekly Essays on Sundry Important Subjects More Particularly Adapted to the Province of New-York.* Cambridge, 1963.

Kulikoff, Allan. *The Agrarian Origins of American Capitalism.* Charlottesville, Va., 1992.

———. *From British Peasants to Colonial American Farmers.* Chapel Hill, N.C., 2000.

Lamb, Martha J. "The Van Rensselaer Manor." *Magazine of American History* 11 (1884): 1–11.

Larson, Neil. *Ethnic and Economic Diversity Reflected in Columbia County Vernacular Architecture.* Kingston, N.Y., 1986.

Lemisch, Jesse. "Jack Tar in the Streets: Merchant Seamen in the Politics of Revolutionary America." *William and Mary Quarterly,* 3rd ser., 25 (1968): 371–407.

Lemon, James T. *The Best Poor Man's Country: A Geographical Study of Early Southeastern Pennsylvania.* Baltimore, 1972.

Lepore, Jill. *The Name of War: King Philip's War and the Origins of American Identity.* New York, 1998.

Linebaugh, Peter. "All the Atlantic Mountains Shook." In *Reviving the English Revolution: Reflections and Elaborations on the Work of Christopher Hill,* edited by Geoff Eley and William Hunt. London 1988.

Lynd, Staughton. "Who Should Rule at Home? Dutchess County, New York, in the American Revolution." *William and Mary Quarterly,* 3rd ser., 18 (1961): 330–59.

———. *Anti-Federalism in Dutchess County, New York; A Study of Democracy and Class Conflict in the Revolutionary Era.* Chicago, 1962.

———. "The Revolution and the Common Man: Farm Tenants and Artisans in New York Politics, 1777–1788." PhD diss., Columbia University, 1962.

———. "Abraham Yates's History of the Movement for the United States Constitution." *William and Mary Quarterly,* 3rd ser., 20 (1963): 223–45.

———. "The Tenant Rising at Livingston Manor, May 1777." *New-York Historical Society Quarterly* 48 (April 1964): 163–77.

———. *Class Conflict, Slavery and the United States Constitution; Ten Essays.* Indianapolis, Ind., 1967.

MacCracken, Henry Noble. *Old Dutchess Forever! The Story of an American County.* New York, 1956.

Maier, Pauline. "Popular Uprisings and Civil Authority in Eighteenth Century America." *William and Mary Quarterly,* 3rd ser., 27 (1970): 3–35.

———. "Reason and Revolution: The Radicalism of Dr. Thomas Young." *American Quarterly* 28 (1976): 229–49.

Mann, Bruce. "The Evolutionary Revolution in American Law: A Comment on J.R. Pole's 'Reflections.'" *William and Mary Quarterly,* 3rd ser., 50 (1993): 168–75.

Manning, Brian, ed. *Politics, Religion and the English Civil War.* London, 1973.

Manning, Roger B. *Village Revolts: Social Protest and Popular Disturbances in England, 1509–1640.* Oxford, 1988.

Mark, Irving. *Agrarian Conflicts in Colonial New York, 1711–1775.* 1940. Reprint, Port Washington, N.Y., 1965.

Mark, Irving, and Oscar Handlin, eds. "Land Cases in Colonial New York, 1765–1767; *The King v. William Prendergast.*" *New York University Law Quarterly Review* 9 (1942).

Matson, Cathy. "'Damned Scoundrels' and 'Libertisme of Trade': Freedom and Regulation in Colonial New York's Fur and Grain Trades." *William and Mary Quarterly,* 3rd ser., 51 (1994): 389–418.

Matthews, Richard K. *The Radical Politics of Thomas Jefferson: A Revisionist View.* Lawrence, Kans., 1984.

McConville, Brendan. *These Daring Disturbers of the Public Peace; The Struggle for Property and Power in Early New Jersey.* Ithaca, N.Y., 1999.

McCurry, Stephanie. *Masters of Small Worlds: Yeoman Households, Gender Relations, and the Political Culture of the Antebellum South Carolina Low Country.* New York, 1995.

McCusker, John J. *How Much is That in Real Money? A Historical Price Index for Use as a Deflator of Money Values in the Economy of the United States.* Worcester, Mass., 1992.

McCusker, John J., and Russell R. Menard. *The Economy of British America, 1607–1789.* Chapel Hill, N.C., 1991.

Mensch, Elizabeth V. "The Colonial Origins of Liberal Property Rights." *Buffalo Law Review* 31 (1982): 635–735.

Merrell, James Hart. *The Indians' New World: Catawbas and Their Neighbors from European Contact through the Era of Removal.* Chapel Hill, N.C., 1989.

Morgan, Edmund. *The Gentle Puritan: A Life of Ezra Stiles, 1727–1795.* New York, 1962.

———. *American Slavery, American Freedom: The Ordeal of Colonial Virginia.* New York, 1975.

Morgan, Edmund S., and Helen M. Morgan. *The Stamp Act Crisis: Prologue to Revolution.* Chapel Hill, N.C., 1953.

Nash, Gary B. *The Urban Crucible: Social Change, Political Consciousness, and the Origins of the American Revolution.* Cambridge, Mass., 1979.

Neeson, J. M. *Commoners: Common Right, Enclosure, and Social Change in England, 1700–1820.* Cambridge, 1993.

Newman, Paul Douglas. "Fries's Rebellion and American Political Culture, 1798–1800." *Pennsylvania Magazine of History and Biography* 119 (April 1995): 37–73.

Newman, Simon P. *Parades and the Politics of the Street: Festive Culture in the Early American Republic.* Philadelphia, 1997.

Norton, Mary Beth. *Liberty's Daughters: The Revolutionary Experience of American Women, 1750–1800.* Boston, 1980.

Pocock, J. G. A., ed. *Three British Revolutions: 1641, 1688, 1776.* Princeton, N.J., 1980.

Pole, J. R. "Reflections in American Law and the American Revolution." *William and Mary Quarterly,* 3rd ser., 50 (1993): 123–59.

Pruitt, Bettye Hobbs. "Self-Sufficiency and the Agricultural Economy of Eighteenth Century Massachusetts." *William and Mary Quarterly,* 3rd ser., 41 (1984): 333–64.

Pryde, George S. "Scottish Colonization in the Province of New York." *New York Historical Society Proceedings* 33 (1935): 138–57.

Purvis, Thomas L. "Origins and Patterns of Agrarian Unrest in New Jersey, 1735 to 1754." *William and Mary Quarterly,* 3rd ser., 39 (1982): 600–627.

Reubens, Beatrice G. "Pre-Emptive Rights in the Disposition of a Confiscated Estate." *William and Mary Quarterly,* 3rd ser., 22 (1965): 434–56.

Reynolds, Helen Wilkinson. *Dutch Houses in the Hudson Valley before 1776.* 1929. Reprint, New York, 1965.

Richter, Daniel K. *The Ordeal of the Longhouse: The Peoples of the Iroquois League in the Era of European Colonization.* Chapel Hill, N.C., 1992.

———. *Facing East from Indian Country: A Native History of Early America.* Boston, 2003.

Rosswurm, Steven. *Arms, Country, and Class: The Philadelphia Militia and "Lower Sort" during the American Revolution, 1775–1783.* New Brunswick, N.J., 1987.

Rothenberg, Winifred Barr. *From Market-Places to a Market Economy: The Transformation of Rural Massachusetts, 1750–1850.* Chicago, 1992.

St. George, Robert Blair, ed. *Material Life in America, 1600–1860.* Boston, 1988.

Schwarz, Philip J. "'To Conciliate the Jarring Interests'; William Smith, Thomas Hutchinson, and the Massachusetts–New York Boundary, 1771–1773." *New-York Historical Society Quarterly* 59 (1975): 299–319.

———. *The Jarring Interests: New York's Boundary Makers, 1664–1776.* Albany, New York, 1979.

Slaughter, Thomas P. *The Whiskey Rebellion: Frontier Epilogue to the American Revolution.* New York, 1986.

Smith, Barbara Clark. "Food Rioters and the American Revolution." *William and Mary Quarterly,* 3rd ser., 51 (1994): 3–38.

Smith, Billy G. "The Material Lives of Laboring Philadelphians, 1750 to 1800." *William and Mary Quarterly,* 3rd ser., 38 (1981): 163–202.

———. *The "Lower Sort": Philadelphia's Laboring People, 1750–1800.* Ithaca, N.Y., 1990.

Snyder, Terri L. *Brabbling Women: Disorderly Speech and the Law in Early Virginia.* Ithaca, N.Y., 2003.

Spooner, Walter W. *Historic Families of America Comprehending the Genealogical Records and Representative Biography of Selected Families of Early American Ancestry, Recognized Social Standing, and Special Distinction.* New York, 1907.

Summerhill, Thomas. "The Farmer's Republic: Agrarian Protest and the Capitalist Transformation of Upstate New York, 1840–1890." PhD diss., University of California, San Diego, 1993.

Taylor, Alan. "'A Kind of Warr': The Contest for Land on the New England Frontier, 1750–1820." *William and Mary Quarterly,* 3rd ser., 49 (1989): 3–29.

———. *Liberty Men and Great Proprietors: The Revolutionary Settlement on the Maine Frontier, 1760–1820.* Chapel Hill, N.C., 1990.

———. "Agrarian Independence: Northern Land rioters after the Revolution." In *Beyond the American Revolution: Explorations in the History of American Radicalism,* edited by Alfred F. Young, 221–45. DeKalb, Ill., 1993.

———. *William Cooper's Town: Power and Persuasion on the Frontier of the Early American Republic.* New York, 1995.

Thompson, E. P. *The Making of the English Working Class.* New York, 1966.

———. "The Moral Economy of the English Crowd in the Eighteenth Century." *Past and Present* 50 (1971): 76–136.

———. "Patrician Society, Plebeian Culture." *Journal of Social History* 7 (1974): 382–405.

———. *Customs in Common: Studies in Traditional Popular Culture.* New York, 1993.

Vickers, Daniel. "Competency and Competition: Economic Culture in Early America." *William and Mary Quarterly,* 3rd ser., 47 (1990): 3–29.

———. *Farmers and Fishermen: Two Centuries of Work in Essex County, Massachusetts, 1630–1850.* Chapel Hill, N.C., 1994.

Waldstreicher, David. *In the Midst of Perpetual Fetes: The Making of American Nationalism, 1776–1820.* Chapel Hill, N.C., 1997.

Wells, Robert V. "While Rip Napped: Social Change in Late Eighteenth-Century New York." *New York History* 71 (1990): 5–23.

Wermuth, Thomas S. *Rip Van Winkle's Neighbors: The Transformation of Rural Society in the Hudson River Valley, 1720–1850*. Albany, N.Y., 2001.

Wood, Gordon S. *The Creation of the American Republic*. New York, 1972.

———. *The Radicalism of the American Revolution*. New York, 1992.

Yoshpe, Harry B. *The Disposition of Loyalist Estates in the Southern District of the State of New York*. New York, 1939.

Young, Alfred, F. *The Democratic Republicans of New York: The Origins, 1763–1797*. Chapel Hill, N.C., 1967.

———. "George Robert Twelve Hewes (1742–1840): A Boston Shoemaker and the Memory of the American Revolution." *William and Mary Quarterly*, 3rd ser., 38 (1981): 561–623.

———. "English Plebeian Culture and Eighteenth Century American Radicalism." In *Origins of Anglo- American Radicalism,* edited by Margaret Jacob and James Jacob, 185–212. London, 1984.

———. "The Women of Boston: 'Persons of Consequence' in the Making of the American Revolution, 1765–1776." In *Women and Politics in the Age of the Democratic Revolution,* edited by Harriet B. Applewhite and Darline G. Levy, 181–226. Ann Arbor, Mich., 1990.

Young, Alfred F., ed. *The American Revolution: Explorations in the History of American Radicalism*. DeKalb, Ill., 1976.

———. *Beyond the American Revolution: Explorations in the History of American Radicalism*. DeKalb, Ill., 1993.

INDEX